PROFIT
IS NOT
THE CURE

PROFIT IS NOT THE CURE

A CITIZEN'S GUIDE TO SAVING MEDICARE

MAUDE BARLOW

M&S

National Library of Canada Cataloguing in Publication

Barlow, Maude
Profit is not the cure : a citizen's guide to medicare / Maude Barlow.

Includes index.
ISBN 0-7710-1085-0

1. Medical care – Canada. 2. Medical policy – Canada. 3. Public
health – Canada. I. Title.

RA412.5.C3B37 2002   362.1'0971   C2002-903922-3

We acknowledge the financial support of the Government of Canada
through the Book Publishing Industry Development Program for our publishing
activities. We further acknowledge the support of the Canada Council for
the Arts and the Ontario Arts Council for our publishing program.

Typeset in Sabon by Laura Brady
Printed and bound in Canada

This book is printed on acid-free paper that is 100% ancient forest friendly
(100% post-consumer recycled)

McClelland & Stewart Ltd.
The Canadian Publishers
481 University Avenue
Toronto, Ontario
M5G 2E9
www.mcclelland.com

1 2 3 4 5   06 05 04 03 02

Contents

"Our proudest achievement in the well-being of Canadians has been in asserting that illness is burden enough in itself. Financial ruin must not compound it. That is why medicare has been called a sacred trust and we must not allow that trust to be betrayed."

– JUSTICE EMMETT HALL

"Health Canada needs to remember they are here to look after the health of the country, and industry will look after industry. This isn't about money. It's about whether a government decides to organize its resources for the benefit of all the people of this country and not just the privileged few."

– SHIRLEY DOUGLAS

To the memory of Tommy Douglas,
the father of medicare

Introduction

We Canadians treasure our universal health care system. Polls consistently confirm that, no matter what turns the economy is taking or where the political winds are blowing, support for this core foundation of Canadian society never wavers. Yet we are currently experiencing the most sustained and deliberate assault on medicare in its nearly four decades of history. Unless ordinary Canadians from every part of the country rise up to defend it, our public health care system will not survive.

Throughout their deliberation, two major federal commissions, one led by former Saskatchewan premier Roy Romanow, and the other by Senator Michael Kirby, have been pressured by a powerful lobby to recommend a parallel private system to medicare. Ontario, Alberta, and British Columbia are in a race to establish private hospital services, delist currently covered services, and establish two-tier health care for their citizens. Federal Health Minister Anne McLellan, who refers to Canadians as "consumers" of health care, has declared that she is open to amending the Canada Health Act to allow for private hospitals and has signalled a new era of "co-operation" with the pro-privatization provinces in upcoming negotiations over the future of health care.

In fact, the Chrétien Liberals, having embraced all of the values of economic globalization, including nation-state competitiveness, privatization, and drastic funding cuts, and backed by the powerful right-wing newspaper chains and well-financed think-tanks, have signalled that they see medicare as a relic of another time. By enthusiastically espousing free trade agreements such as the North American Free Trade Agreement (NAFTA), the Free Trade Area of the Americas (FTAA), and the General Agreement on Trade in Services (GATS), the government has signalled the death of the Canada Health Act. The stakes are very high. These trade agreements have the potential to radically redefine our health care as a commercial service. Once any part of a service is privatized by any province, there is no turning the clock back. The fight to preserve medicare must include restricting the power of these institutions.

While governments plead that they can no longer afford to provide full coverage for Canadians, the truth is that money is not the issue – just the excuse. Before the deep funding cuts, Canada's public system was delivering better overall health care, more equitably, and at a substantially lower cost than private systems, such as that in the United States. The real issue is one of values. Even after the cuts, our system is vastly superior.

This is not to say that there are not serious problems with Canada's health care system today. Deep cuts and restructuring have left service providers scrambling to make up the short-fall. Crowded emergency rooms, long waiting lists, and nursing shortages plague Canadians in need of care. Several recent polls show that our faith in the system and our satisfaction with the quality of health care has strongly diminished in the last decade. These polls give great satisfaction to those who, for ideological reasons, want to privatize heath care in Canada.

Right from medicare's inception, there have been forces intent on undermining it. At first, it was a powerful medical establishment and private insurance companies who teamed up with right-wing governments to limit medicare's scope and to wait for the right climate to destroy it altogether. Those forces are renewed in vigour today. An international private service industry, anxious to get its hands on the estimated CAD$4 to $5 trillion global health care sector, is seeking out and finding friendly governments – including the Chrétien Liberals in Ottawa – in order to profit from this lucrative sector.

The Canadian people must become mobilized in order to stop this assault on our most treasured social program before it is too late. Working with national groups such as the Canadian Health Coalition, the Council of Canadians, and the Canadian Union of Public Employees, as well as provincial and local public health coalitions, we must make our governments hear our clear message – now.

Profit is not the cure for medicare. We can afford to maintain and even strengthen our health care system if we eliminate the current for-profit components that are causing some costs to spiral, such as patented drugs, fee-for-service, and overpaid administrators, and instead, turn to a primary care, community-based, fully public model run more equitably and more efficiently. Further, the right of Canadians is the right of every human being on the planet; Canada must recommit to its former position and work with other governments and the United Nations to see that universal, public health care is provided to the world.

This book grew out of a position paper I wrote for the Council of Canadians when we launched a national campaign to save medicare in January 2002 and was distributed widely at public town hall meetings we held across the country to coincide with the Romanow hearings. With two major commissions focusing the whole country on medicare, I felt it was essential that all Canadians, not just those who are "experts" on health care, should have an opportunity to put their opinions forward. In my travels, many Canadians have told me they feel helpless to save this program that they cherish. They are intimidated to argue the fine points of the economy or the history of medicare with people they see as authorities. My position is that every Canadian is an expert on medicare, and has a right to fight for its future.

The book is designed, therefore, to provide basic information on medicare and to promote an alternative to the privatization of health care that every Canadian can defend. It tells what life was like for Canadians before medicare and gives the history of the fierce struggle to secure our universal health care system in the first place. It compares our publicly funded system with the private models of other countries, particularly the United States, and shows that non-profit health care is much more equitable and less costly. It documents just what we spend on health care and the changing funding role of the various levels of government.

The book, however, also tells the story of a systematic undermining of medicare and how deep cuts and restructuring are creating serious problems and opening the door to privatization-friendly provincial governments. Combined with the corporate forces of economic globalization and the threats posed to public health services through new trade agreements, I argue that medicare is in deep trouble unless the Canadian people step in to defend it. This book offers a well-documented alternative that is also supported by health coalitions, nurses unions, and community groups across the country.

The council's campaign was designed to help our members and others become involved in the fight to save medicare and to let their views be known to the Romanow Commission. At our public meetings, which attracted hundreds of people in every community, we urged Canadians from all walks of life to make submissions, in person or written, to the commission and to join local health coalitions in their area. I had the opportunity to meet with many of the individuals and groups that made presentations and many of their voices are carried in these pages. While I have kept the book clear of footnotes and references to make it accessible, there is a reference section at the back that lists valuable sources, publications, and books to help in the fight to save medicare. There is also a listing of the national and regional organizations working together across the country to save medicare.

It is my sincere hope that this work contributes to the grassroots campaign to save and enhance our precious health care system. Our parents and grandparents fought, and in some cases died, so that all Canadians would have the right to good health care. In their name, and for the sake of those generations yet to be born, we must commit to save medicare. Its creation was the people's choice. It still is. It is not too late; medicare's fate is in our hands.

I

A People's Legacy

Medicare was born of a people's dream. Living next to the biggest superpower on earth, Canadians knew that they had to create ribbons of interdependence across the country if they were to survive as a separate nation-state on the northern half of the North American continent. This people rejected the American narrative of "survival of the fittest" and embraced a Canadian vision of "sharing for survival." As a fundamental right of citizenship, they decided that all Canadians, regardless of socio-economic background, ethnicity, or where they lived, had a right to comprehensive, accessible, portable, universal health care from cradle to grave.

The fight for medicare was a hard one. With the sole exception of Tommy Douglas's government in Saskatchewan, political leaders did not willingly give public health care to Canadians. Rather, citizens had to wrest it from reluctant politicians. The story of medicare is the story of a sustained struggle of a people. They fought for it with demonstrations, marches, and strikes. Churches demanded health care for the poor. Workers negotiated for it in collective bargaining. Women fought for its extension to families. It was earned as a right of citizenship by a people who had suffered greatly in its absence.

Beginnings

At the turn of the twentieth century, there was no such thing as social security in Canada, and no recognition of social or health rights. Class structures were rigid. Child labour was common. Churches, private charities, and minimal municipal assistance provided the only relief for the poor. The destitute, the ill, the insane, the homeless, and criminals were all sheltered together in poorhouses. Most health care was delivered at home by family members or neighbourhood midwives.

There were hospitals, but they varied wildly in quality. The wealthy could be checked into private hospitals like Toronto's Wellesley, which opened its doors in 1912 and provided top doctors and meals on fine imported china and silver. Most, however, were supported by churches and charities and were overcrowded, unsanitary health hazards where patients were more likely to pick up new diseases than get rid of existing ones. Surgical techniques were clumsy and patients were often felled by deadly infections they contracted in the hospital. With mortality rates of 85 to 95 per cent, reports the *Toronto Star*'s Peter Gorrie on February 3, 2002, most hospitals were places where poor people went to die.

Our current social system has its origins in two different ideologies. Upper Canada based welfare on the idea that the primary social and economic unit was the family, and responsibility for poverty was largely individual, rather than collective. Meanwhile, a more collective framework for social concern was developing in what is now Quebec, Atlantic Canada, and parts of the West. Almost everyone subscribed to the notion of a distinction between the "deserving poor" (the very young, very old, sick, or disabled) and the "undeserving poor" (the able-bodied unemployed).

However, within the different views of society, different

interpretations of these concepts were developing. The fusing of
Loyalist sentiment, agrarian collective values, traditions of feudal
hierarchy, and concern for the group (and later, social gospel
teachings) produced a counterforce to free-enterprise individualism across the country. This would form the basis for universal
social programs and anticipate future lines of contention.

Interrelationships were being formed everywhere during this
period between private charities, churches, municipalities, and
governments, as public monies were increasingly being sought
by those providing relief. Increases in the use of public money
in turn led to more government monitoring and regulation of
relief programs.

The First World War

A new Canada was beginning to emerge from the First World
War. It was clear that unfettered, unregulated capitalism was not
working for the majority. Anger at the old class structure – in
which a privileged few dominated government, not to mention
the economic and social lives of millions – exploded. The prop-
ertied classes had become richer from a war that had cost so
many working families their sons. The elites used their power to
suppress political dissent and resist workers' demands, fully
expecting to return to their pre-war status.

But Canadians had changed. Women had fought for and won
the vote. Western farm radicalism was growing. Grain growers
were forming co-operatives and establishing collective, prepaid
hospital services. Trade union membership was growing exponentially, from 20,000 in 1890 to almost 400,000 by 1920.
Medical protection for its members and their families was a top
priority of the labour movement. The first medical insurance
programs were won by mining and logging unions. During the
war, increased pressure was placed on the federal government to

provide health care and compensation in case of injury for the men on the front lines of the battlefield and the factory.

On the eve of the Great Depression, an ideology based on class analysis was fermenting in slums, in universities, on the factory floors, in mines and lumber camps, at rural revival meetings, in churches, and in kitchens. It would become the major influence on social policy development in the terrible years ahead, anticipating the concept of universal social and health rights. It would forever change the way Canadians live and work together. From the resulting convictions sprang courageous opposition to oppression in the form of labour marches, strikes, and other uprisings, most of which were brutally suppressed. This ideology would be further strengthened and defined in the twin crucibles of the Depression and the Second World War that lay ahead.

The Great Depression

Canadians were as hard hit by the Depression as any society in the world. At its height, two-thirds of prairie farmers and half the wage earners in the country were on relief. Employers terrorized their employees, paying wages as low as two cents an hour for work weeks as long as 100 hours. There was no sick leave, no paid holidays, and no insurance for unemployment or hospital care. More than 100,000 homeless men wandered the country, sleeping in alleys, riding the rails, or growing restless in the hundreds of relief camps (in which there were no medical services).

Federal transfers to the provinces grew dramatically in these years. Spending on social welfare as a percentage of government expenditures grew from 2.5 per cent in 1910 to almost 26 per cent in the mid-1930s. This fact became crucial to the debate over universality since, in the absence of any coherent national plan or notion of social and health rights, this money was often wasted. Relief was administered by the provinces and munici-palities, who were generally punitive in their approach to welfare and whose standards varied widely. Inspectors came unannounced into homes and denied aid to any families in pos-session of undeclared food, new clothes, or liquor.

Those seeking medical assistance were even worse off. Most municipalities had a one-year residency requirement – even for emergency health care. Health insurance was very expensive and, as policies were renewable annually, they were usually can-celled by the company if the insured patient developed any serious condition. There were no services for any kind of pre-ventative medicine; only the very ill or injured could apply to municipal authorities for admittance to local hospitals, and free care was doled out sparingly.

More commonly, families of the ill were left to scrape together enough money for admittance to a hospital, which charged for every procedure from blood tests to surgery. Patients whose bills exceeded the admitting fee were kept in the hospital until a family member came by to pay, and many a patient was unable to finish treatment that took more than one hospital visit.

Conditions for the staff were terrible then, as well. A nurse who served at the Empress Hospital in Alberta told Trudy Richardson of the United Nurses of Alberta that she and one other nurse worked opposite twelve-hour shifts, 365 days a year, with no sick time or vacation.

Life without Medicare

Before medicare, Canadians had to find the money for their care or go without. The poor had to delay treatment until they were severely ill. Many families had to use their savings, or sell the family farm when their children fell ill. Often, adults would go without health care in order to provide it for their children. As the Saskatchewan Federation of Labour recently told the Romanow Commission,

> Stories abound in this province of manual labourers forced to cope all their working lives with deteriorated joints or debilitating hernias, and small farmers who lived for years with unmedicated asthma or unsightly goitres, and pensioners with untreated cataracts or crippling arthritis . . . .
>
> And there are stories, too, about people with serious heart or kidney ailments discharged from hospital to go home to die, because pricey surgical procedures or long-term professional care was simply not a viable option for low-income people.

Dr. John Bury left his practice in England to start a new life in Saskatoon. He told the Romanow Commission that on his first day of practice, he wrote a prescription for penicillin to a patient who handed it back to him, explaining that he could not afford the drug. "This was an entirely new experience for me after being in practice for fifteen years. I had never experienced the intervention of cash between me and my patient before. I think I solved the problem by giving him a five-dollar bill."

In its Romanow brief, the Ontario division of Canadian Pensioners Concerned said,

Seniors remember what it was like before medicare, when we put off seeing the doctor as long as possible because our families could not afford to pay. Many of us bear scars from those days when we did not get appropriate and timely care. Families often experienced heavy debts from the costs of hospitalization for serious illnesses or accidents. In many cases, they were forced to sell their homes. Young people put off their extended education (sometimes indefinitely) to go to work to pay off family debts for health care.

In the moving collection of stories published in 1995 by the Ontario Coalition of Senior Citizens' Organizations, *Life Before Medicare: Canadian Experiences,* Canadian seniors share their memories of health care during these years. One remembers a young mother dying on the steps of a hospital in Grande Prairie while her husband was inside, begging them to admit her. Another senior describes his mother's struggle with cancer of the larynx. His father borrowed money from family members and neighbours to take her by train from Saskatoon to Toronto where she had her larynx removed, but he was unable to find enough money for further treatment when the cancer returned. He took her home to Saskatoon to die. Another young mother had to sell her two cows to pay the hospital bill for her dead baby before the hospital authorities would release the child's body.

A Manitoba senior recalls a neighbouring farm woman who was diagnosed with cancer. She knew that in order to get treatment in a hospital her family would have to sell the farm, so she decided to die at home. When her husband went out to work, she had him close all the windows so the neighbours wouldn't hear her screams of pain, and lock the doors from the outside to stop her from running to them for help. Her suffering lasted for two months, but she saved the family farm.

It is little wonder, given the dearth of government support, that during the 1930s, fully half of all Canadians did not receive any health care whatsoever. Nor that, when war broke out in 1939, almost half the young men called up for active service had to be rejected because of poor health. As Colleen Fuller documents in her comprehensive 1998 book, *Caring for Profit*, Canada ranked seventeenth among industrialized countries in infant mortality at that time, with rates of between thirty-eight and eighty deaths for every thousand live births, depending on the part of the country being looked at. Furthermore, because access to hospital care was limited, approximately three to five women died in childbirth for every thousand live births.

More than 9,800 Canadians died in 1940 alone from communicable diseases such as influenza, tuberculosis, diphtheria, measles, and whooping cough. Children and youth, reports Fuller, were found to be in alarmingly poor health. In 1941, for example, 70 per cent of Manitobans between thirteen and thirty years of age required some kind of medical attention. In each year between 1931 and 1941, an average of 15,000 Canadian children under one year of age died from preventable or controllable illnesses.

The Second World War

Then came the Second World War, and the same government that could not feed, house, clothe, employ, or provide medical care to the majority of Canadians suddenly had all the money it needed to send them into battle. Unemployment dropped to 0.3 per cent and trade union membership swelled to more than 700,000 by the war's end. The government's need to build a strong national war infrastructure coincided with its citizens' demands for a stable future. As the men of the relief camps, suddenly well paid and well fed, were sent to fight for their country, government was already being forced to plan for a post-war society, one that would include a modern social security system, the cornerstone of which would be universal health care.

Much of the pressure to build a welfare state came from the newly formed Co-operative Commonwealth Federation (CCF), a collection of farmers, academics, social reformers, urban socialists, labour unions, and social gospel adherents who had gathered in Regina in 1933 to launch a new social movement and political party that would have long-term ramifications for the country.

With its call to "conscript wealth as well as men," the CCF made rapid headway in several provinces, forming the government in Saskatchewan in 1944, and placing great pressure on the ruling Liberals under Mackenzie King at the federal level. In the election of 1945, with the CCF nipping at his heels, King campaigned on a theme of "building a new social order," and promised a whole new social infrastructure for Canadians, including public health care.

New Foundations

Several major studies set the stage for the government's post-war plan. The Rowell-Sirois Report on Dominion-Provincial Relations, published in 1940, established the principles of the modern Canadian state: federal authority over the economy and national welfare, including unemployment insurance and relief; provincial subsidies, with national standards attached, for education and social services; and regional equality and equalization.

The 1943 Report on Social Security for Canada, written by Dr. Leonard Marsh, proposed pooling protection for maternity, sickness, unemployment, and old age into one universal, comprehensive social insurance plan. It called for a policy of full employment, comprehensive health insurance for all Canadians, fully funded federal assistance programs for the unemployed, and universal children's allowances.

With two colleagues at McGill University in Montreal, Marsh had conducted a major analysis of class and health during the Depression. Based on their findings, he concluded that "if medical care is a contingency left to each individual to secure as best he can, it becomes a function of the distribution of wealth."

The Heagerty Report of the Advisory Committee on Health Insurance, also released in 1943, held that the provision of adequate medical care for all Canadians was essential to the maintenance and security of a democratic state. It called for a national, compulsory system of health insurance and a comprehensive system of public health. The whole population was to be eligible for medical, dental, pharmaceutical, hospital, and nursing services.

These reports did not spring up in a political void. They reflected the will of the Canadian people. As early as 1941, *Saturday Night* would declare: "Almost everyone agrees that health and unemployment insurance schemes, regulation of business, and a sharp limitation of profits are necessary to provide Canadians with real security." Canada must become a country fit for returning heroes, it added, and asked why anyone would want to go to war to preserve the kind of society that had existed before 1939.

The first real universal social program, introduced in 1945, was a family allowance for everyone with children under age seventeen. This was the first program without a means test, which forced those seeking social assistance to prove they were in need, a process that could involve home inspections, and the first indication that government was assuming some responsibility for the well-being of all Canadian families. The principle of universality, said Leonard Marsh, "enlists the direct support of the classes most likely to benefit at the same time as it avoids the evil of pauperization and undemocratic influence of state philanthropy." The income support afforded by the program was not merely symbolic. Family allowance in 1945 represented a substantial amount of family revenue: 20 per cent of the average income for a family with three children.

The second major universal social program, an old-age pension for those seventy years of age and older, was initiated in 1952. Many Canadian seniors were reluctant to apply for it; for them, pensions bore the stigma of means testing. It was only after Prime Minister Louis St. Laurent was photographed applying for his own benefits that many seniors gave in and accepted their pensions.

Powerful Foes

But on the health care front, powerful forces were aligned against the popular will. The British Columbia Manufacturers' Association, the B.C. Board of Trade, and the B.C. Chamber of Commerce had joined forces with the Canadian Life Insurance Officers' Association and the Canadian Medical Association (CMA) to defeat a popular public health insurance plan in British Columbia in 1936.

This coalition went on to work tirelessly inside the provinces to slow progress toward the acceptance of an agreement for universal health insurance drafted at the August 6, 1945, Dominion-Provincial Conference on the post-war reconstruction of Canada. While the four western provinces supported the federal government's strategy of steadily increasing federal grants for comprehensive provincial health insurance in exchange for provincial tax monies and the achievement of minimum standards, the remaining provinces, led by Ontario, balked. The talks broke down ten months later in a stalemate.

Meanwhile, as Colleen Fuller documents, an alliance was forming to unite the two types of insurance plans that had developed in Canada during the war years, although these had at first appeared to be at odds with one another. Physician-sponsored insurance was run on a non-profit basis, and was aimed at a different sector of society than was generally covered by the commercial insurance industry. Non-profit hospitals run by physicians did, in fact, enable many Canadians to obtain minimal health care for the first time. Commercial insurers, on the other hand, concentrated on the healthy employed, whose coverage was paid for by their employers. Their coverage, therefore, did not extend to families, the ill, or the elderly.

But, in spite of their differences, both types of plans were initiated to prevent governments from implementing what opponents called "socialized medicine." The CMA was so worried about popular support for a national compulsory plan that it brought all the provincially based, doctor-run plans under one national umbrella called the Trans-Canada Medical Plan. This new consortium joined the commercial insurers, now also under one banner, the Canadian Health Insurance Association, and the Canadian Hospital Association, also newly formed, to "prove" that Canadians were sufficiently insured and didn't need the government to introduce public medicare.

A People United

It is true that, by the mid-1950s, more than half of Canadians had some form of health insurance. But it was by no means equitably distributed. As Fuller documents, people with high incomes obtained the lion's share of health care services, even though the poor experienced ill health more often and for longer periods. Ironically, of course, this is in part because they could not access preventative medical treatment. Further, most insurance covered only part of the hospital bill. Blue Cross, for example, wouldn't pay for surgery, anaesthesia, drugs, lab work, or X-rays. This didn't mean that people weren't paying hefty premiums, however. The 1964 report of the Royal Commission on Health Services reported that insurers collected far more in premiums than they paid out in benefits.

The Canadian people were angry at such treatment and adamant that they were going to get their promised national program. By war's end, fully 80 per cent of the Canadian population supported a national health plan and this support only increased in the coming years.

Saskatchewan and British Columbia introduced universal hospital insurance in 1947 and 1949 respectively, and in 1957, in spite of fierce opposition from the insurance industry and the business community, the federal government passed the Hospital Insurance and Diagnostic Services Act, allocating funds to provinces that set up a universal hospital insurance program in accordance with national standards. By 1961, all ten provinces were eligible for the funds.

Meanwhile, Tommy Douglas's CCF government in Saskatchewan had entered into one of the most ferocious political fights in Canadian history. Saskatchewan had experimented with universal health care schemes for many years. The roots of this struggle lay deep in the prairie soil – in town halls and farm kitchens, the people of that province fought long and hard for a public health care system. There had been trials with salaried doctors in some communities as early as 1919, and some doctors went on relief during the Depression, unable and unwilling to charge their destitute patients.

Tommy Douglas was actually elected in 1944 on the promise of universal health coverage, "available to all without counting the ability of the individual to pay." Treatment for cancer, tuberculosis, and polio was provided free to all who needed it. A free

air ambulance service was set up to fly patients from remote set-
tlements to hospitals, and geriatric centres were built to provide
care for the chronically ill, free of charge. As early as 1945,
Douglas was prepared for a full public system, and was bitterly
disappointed that the federal government was unable or unwilling to deliver. (A federal health plan had been a Liberal promise
since 1919.)

During the 1950s, the battle in Saskatchewan heated up.
Douglas fought the Saskatchewan College of Physicians and
Surgeons, who went on strike; the Dental Association; the
Chambers of Commerce; private drug companies; and the right-
wing newspapers owned by the Sifton family. Douglas's feud
extended to the Canadian Medical Association, who helped
fund the opposition in Saskatchewan and who were working
with the American Medical Association, also waging a no-
holds-barred campaign against President John Kennedy's efforts
to introduce a prepaid scheme for the elderly in the U.S. in 1961.

The doctors' strike was fierce and it divided families and communities. At a March 6, 2002, Saskatoon town hall meeting
sponsored by the Council of Canadians, Saskatchewan senior
Betsy Bury remembers that a coalition of farmers, unions, academics, and others set up twenty-seven health co-operatives
across the province to service citizens during the strike. They
hired doctors from Britain and put them to work in the clinics
on salary. The Saskatoon Community Health Services Association hired two women doctors: Dr. Joan Whitney and Dr.
Margaret Mahood. For the three weeks of the strike, these
courageous doctors had to be escorted to their cars, remembers
Bury, because of daily death threats against them. Long after the
strike, the clinics thrived, as other services – such as prenatal
classes, diet clubs, anti-smoking programs, and outreach to
poor communities – were set up by social workers and nurses
who had joined the staff.

Former Saskatchewan premier Allan Blakeney, at the same town hall meeting, remembers that the doctors' strike was worldwide news. Reporters came from all over the world to Regina and fanned out to interview people in remote communities. The *New York Times* carried twenty-five stories on the strike and the *Times* in London carried twelve. The BBC, which aired thirty-eight reports on the story, named Tommy Douglas's fight with the doctors and other powerful forces its "news story of the decade."

But Tommy Douglas had the people on his side. He stood firm. Said Jack Scott in the *Vancouver Sun,* "This man Douglas is – well, a good deed in a naughty world. He's a breath of clean prairie air in a stifling climate of payola and chicanery and double-talk and pretence, global and local."

On July 1, 1962, the Government of Saskatchewan passed legislation that brought universal health coverage to every citizen of the province, regardless of income, ethnicity, or state of health. The people of Saskatchewan had spoken; now, a national plan was within sight.

The Hall Commission

In 1960, Prime Minister John Diefenbaker appointed Justice Emmett Hall to head up the Royal Commission on Health Services; four years and more than 400 submissions later, on June 19, 1964, the report was tabled. The commission had attracted an amazing amount of intense interest and debate. On one side was the vast majority of the public, the newly formed Canadian Labour Congress, churches, consumer groups, social workers, and others concerned with the common good; on the other was the same powerful alliance of business, insurance companies, and doctors who had been fighting the process for two decades.

Essentially, the former argued that health care should be a public service to which every Canadian, by right of citizenship, is entitled. Most were also seeking a publicly run system, like education, in which all medical personnel would be on government salary. The latter, on the other hand, advocated for public subsidies for the poor and the hard-to-insure so that they could buy into private plans for medical services.

As Colleen Fuller explains, in the great Canadian tradition, the royal commission opted for a compromise. It rejected a full public program and opted instead for a tax-supported public insurance model as the mechanism through which a self-regulated, privately administered health system would be financed, supplemented by federal grants where needed but "free of government control or domination." In other words, the commission favoured a public insurance system that paid for health services supplied mainly by the private sector.

Yet, in spite of the compromise position taken, the royal commission's report was a milestone in Canadian history in its explicit recognition of Canadian social values. In the introduction to the report, the commissioners said that the popular support for public health care came from Canadians' own history of community-based measures to counter epidemics in the earlier part of the century. They also praised the humanitarian concern of Canadians for their fellow citizens and the common understanding in Canadian society that "the well-being and happiness of society is simply the sum total of the well-being and happiness of its individual members."

The commissioners called for a universal and comprehensive health insurance system with uniform standards across the country, and laid out in no uncertain terms the responsibility of the federal government for the health and well-being of Canadians. They also stated that dental and optical services for children, expectant mothers, and welfare recipients should be included in the plan, as well as prescription drugs and home care.

Medicare at Last

On July 12, 1966, the Medical Care Insurance Act was passed in the House of Commons with only two dissenting votes. Federal-provincial wrangling, as well as divisions within the ruling Liberal party, would delay the implementation of the long-promised legislation for another two years. Although the act bowed to the medical establishment by allowing doctors to opt out of the program and extra-bill, and did not cover dental and optical services or drugs, it did finally establish a comprehensive, universal health care system for every Canadian.

Conditions for federal grants to the provinces for health care were clear: the provinces had to deliver non-profit, comprehensive, universal, accessible health care to their residents and ensure portability of benefits from one province to another. For the first time, a social minimum in health care for all Canadians was clearly defined and the federal government agreed to pay 50 per cent of all provincial health costs.

Most important was the notion that the major goal of medicare was the achievement of greater equity in health and access to health care. The government recognized, as expressed by the Hall Commission, "the fundamental principle that health is not a privilege but rather a basic right which should be open to all." Now every Canadian, regardless of ethnic origin, socio-economic status, age, sex, or region, had a right to quality health care.

There was a second goal. It was hoped that by creating equality of access to health care, medicare would reduce the poverty gap in the country and narrow class differences. No longer denied preventative care, it was argued, poorer Canadians would become healthier Canadians, and would be able to compete in the job market on an equal footing with their wealthier neighbours.

It had been a long struggle, for which many had paid a high price. We will never know the whole story of the thousands of ordinary people who fought to bring our country its greatest social program. Nor will we ever have a full tally of the suffering in the decades that preceded it. What we do know is that the vast majority of Canadians held steadfastly to a vision of a universal health care system, one to which every person was entitled access. With the passage of the 1966 Medical Care Insurance Act, Canadians finally had their cherished medicare.

2

Life with Medicare

To understand the context of today's struggle over medicare, it is important to take time to remember its history. Medicare was created in a time and context in which the assertion of democratic rights was very strong. To understand, we must also look back, to see how the dream of universal medicine became a reality.

Most Canadians have never known life without medicare. We expect to be able to see a doctor or go to a hospital whenever we need to. It is hard to imagine a society that would turn people in need of medical help away because they are unable to pay. But we need to understand that there are very different values in government and business today than there were when medicare was created. In Canada and around the world in the 1960s and 1970s, humanity was drawn by the possibility of eradicating world poverty and hunger. The United Nations had serious plans for bringing universal education and health care to the whole world. There was a vision that true social justice was possible, not just for Canadians, but for the whole world. It was in this climate that a generation crafted a new Canada: a nation of universal social rights and an international peacemaker.

The Leap Forward

Health care is not the only area that saw significant social reform. The main fabric of Canada's social safety net was completed in the rebellious times of the 1960s and early 1970s. The Vietnam War, the sexual revolution, the women's movement, the civil rights movement, the peace movement, the youth movement, and the war on poverty all formed the backdrop for far-reaching social reform. Advocacy groups – for tenants, the poor, seniors, consumers, aboriginal peoples, farmers, racial minorities – sprang up everywhere. The notion that equal treatment of all people, regardless of region, ethnicity, income, age, or gender, should be fundamental to social policy was taking deep root.

The Medical Care Insurance Act of 1966 was wrapped together with federal funding for hospitalization and post-secondary education into the Established Programs Financing Act, which guaranteed stable funding for these services and demanded accountability – ensuring that funds earmarked for health care went to health care.

The Canada Assistance Plan (CAP) consolidated all federal-provincial assistance programs into one comprehensive package and enshrined the right to social assistance for all Canadians in need. In order to be eligible for federal funds, the provinces would have to meet national standards by developing programs to help people in need achieve and retain independence; by meeting financial needs regardless of their cause; by improving standards of public welfare; and by granting certain benefits to the working poor. Provinces could not deny benefits on the basis of non-residency, and could not force recipients to work for social assistance benefits.

Similarly, the new Canada Pension Plan enshrined several key new rights: it lowered the qualifying age to sixty-five, it added a wage-related pension as a supplement to the universal pension, and it declared that Canadian seniors and the disabled should receive a government pension adequate to maintain a socially acceptable standard of living, rather than bare subsistence. For the first time, those who were widowed or had long-term disabilities were fully provided for.

The National Housing Act of 1964 provided loans to provincial housing corporations for public housing at reduced interest rates. A youth allowance extended family benefits to children up to the age of eighteen, and, in 1973, a new Family Allowance Act significantly increased funding to the existing program. The Department of Regional and Economic Expansion addressed underdevelopment in poorer provinces, and the new Unemployment Insurance Act of 1971 expanded benefits and access under the program, making it one of the most comprehensive in the world.

In adopting these far-reaching social programs, Canada had joined a number of progressive countries, such as Sweden, Norway, France, and Germany, that believed in a collective response to social problems, and distinguished itself from the individualistic track that had been chosen by the U.S. The overall goal of these programs, declared the Government of Canada in the preamble to the Canada Assistance Plan, was "the elimination of poverty among our people."

While many would fall short of the original dreams of their creators because of constant funding constraints and federal-provincial squabbles, these programs were seen by Canadians as synonymous with the progress of a modern nation-state. And they established important principles that have been key to our culture and our national identity ever since.

Principles of the Progressive Society

When these social programs were established in the 1960s, they reflected a consensus around a core set of values and principles. Although this consensus has broken down to some extent today, these principles still contain powerful universal truths that we should use to guide us in our deliberations on the future of health care.

Social Equality. Social programs should be universal. Limiting them to the poor transforms them from a right to a charity. Social security is not simply a means to relieve the conditions of the most unfortunate, nor even to establish a minimum standard of living below which no Canadian should have to fall. Social security is a right of citizenship, based on the fundamental notion that Canadians have equal social rights. One major goal of social programs is to narrow the gap between rich and poor.

National Standards. Effective social programs should be based on national standards, generating a sense of shared responsibility and community. National standards guarantee every Canadian in every part of the country access to social services as a right of citizenship. Universal standards give a sense of continuity and security to social funding, allowing people to plan ahead for their future. And they are a key tool of nation-building as they provide a national sense of purpose and community.

Public Delivery. National social programs require a strong public service. Private social, education, and health care service providers operating on a for-profit basis must find ways to cut costs in order to provide the required services and still show a profit. This is generally done by downgrading employees' pay and working conditions, and finding ways of recovering costs such as imposing user fees or reducing services. In the area of health care, it is not profitable, for example, to put resources into prevention; rather, the profits come from expensive surgeries, treatments, and medicines. A private social security system results in widening inequality, fewer choices, and less skilled and accessible care, and will always be more interested in expanding markets than in delivering quality care.

Canada's social and universal health care programs came into being only because generations of Canadians fought and, in some cases, died for them. We gained our rights through collective action and the formation of citizen and public advocacy groups. Governments reluctantly gave way to public demand in creating social security, and have often sought to undermine public will by whittling away at program funding. Canadians should not be grateful for medicare and other social programs; we secured them and they are our birthright.

International Commitments

Canada's growing commitment to social progress and universal health care at home was mirrored by a series of progressive commitments at the international level. As a founding nation of the United Nations, Canada agreed to promote human rights and to solve economic, social, and health "problems." Canada agreed, in signing the Constitution of the World Health Organization in 1946, to promote "the enjoyment of the highest attainable standard of health" as one of the "fundamental rights" of every human being. Health was defined by the WHO as "a state of complete physical, mental and social well-being and not merely the absence of disease or infirmity."

The 1948 Universal Declaration of Human Rights, which Canada signed, broke new ground on many fronts. It granted fundamental human rights of freedom, equality, life, liberty, and security to every person, without distinction according to race, colour, sex, language, religion, political opinion, national or social origin, property, birth, or other status. But the declaration went a lot further. It also included what could be called rights of citizenship: those services and social protections that every citizen has a right to demand of his or her government. Everyone, declared the United Nations, by right of citizenship, is entitled to a standard of living adequate for the health and well-being of the whole family, including food, clothing, housing, medical care, and the right to security in the event of unemployment, sickness, disability, and old age.

The International Covenant on Economic, Social and Cultural Rights came into effect in 1966. Canada adopted the Covenant in 1976; this committed the government to accept a moral and legal obligation to protect and promote the rights delineated in the declaration and contained the measures of implementation required to do so. The covenant bound its member nation-states to the active preservation of "the highest attainable standard of physical and mental health" of its citizens, including "the prevention, treatment and control of epidemic, endemic, occupational and other diseases," and "the creation of conditions which would assure to all medical service and medical attention in the event of sickness."

Canada was also a signatory to the declaration that came out of the World Health Organization Conference of 1978, whose fundamental goals were "health for all" and the delivery of primary health care all over the world.

These and other ensuing declarations and covenants gave individual citizens of the world the right to universal, publicly delivered health care, and committed the governments who signed them (including Canada's) to fulfil the promises they had made in so doing. Now, at home and internationally, Canada was firmly bound by law to provide its citizens with the best health care possible.

The Canada Health Act

By 1971, every province in Canada was a full participant in the national public health care program. To qualify for federal funds, provinces had agreed to administer a public, non-profit insurance program covering hospital and physician services. Every Canadian was now covered for basic hospital and medical care.

But in spite of steadily rising incomes, many doctors were still unhappy. They claimed that American doctors, free to bill patients under a private system, were making more money. Canadian doctors started extra-billing to increase their incomes above the levels possible through the public insurance system. At the same time, some provinces started charging user fees for hospital services. An unsympathetic Canadian public supported the Trudeau government's enactment of a law that would allow it to withhold funds from provinces that permit hospitals to charge user fees or allow physicians to extra-bill.

The 1984 Canada Health Act, described by the president of the Canadian Medical Association as "constitutional rape," was passed unanimously by the House of Commons. Basically, the act outlined what the provinces must do to receive money for health care from Ottawa. It forbade the sale of medically necessary services that are available through medicare and made it illegal for patients who could afford it to jump to the front of the line. It also outlawed extra-billing. During the first nine months after the passage of the new law, some $86 million in federal sanctions were invoked against provinces continuing to permit the collection of additional charges by physicians.

The new act also strengthened Ottawa's role in enforcing

national standards. It set out five conditions that the provinces must meet in order to receive transfer payments; the "principles" of medicare became the "conditions" of the Canada Health Act. According to the Canada Health Act: "The primary objective of the Canadian health care policy is to protect, promote and restore the physical and mental well-being of residents of Canada and to facilitate reasonable access to health services without financial or other barriers."

Principles of Medicare

The five conditions of the Canada Health Act are:

Universality. The health care insurance plan of a province must entitle all of the insured persons of the province to the health services provided for by the plan.

Accessibility. The health care insurance plan of a province must provide for insured health services on uniform terms and conditions and on a basis that does not impede or preclude, either directly or indirectly, whether by charges made to insured persons or otherwise, reasonable access to those services by insured persons. Equally important, those providing the services must receive "reasonable compensation."

Public Administration. The health care insurance plan of a province must be administered and operated on a non-profit basis by a public authority appointed or designated by the government of the province.

Comprehensiveness. The health care insurance plan of a province must insure all medically necessary health services provided by hospitals, medical practitioners, or dentists, and, where the law of the province so permits, similar or additional services rendered by other health care practitioners.

Portability. The health care insurance plan of a province must not impose any minimum period of residence in the province, or waiting period, in excess of three months before residents of the province are eligible for and entitled to insured health services. And it must provide for the payment of the cost of insured health services provided to insured persons while temporarily absent from the province.

The Canada Health Act was an important building block of Canada's health care system and gave the federal government stronger tools with which to enforce national standards across the country. It also fortified the legal framework within which the most cherished social program in Canada was delivered, and recognized the clear wishes of the Canadian people to maintain a universal, public, accessible, portable, and equitable health care system.

The System Delivers

Medicare works for Canadians. Health policy analyst and practitioner Dr. Michael Rachlis states that medicare has worked very well in terms of providing access, economic efficiency, a compassionate approach, and high-quality care. In fact, as soon as public hospital and health insurance programs were introduced, Canadians felt their effect. Within fifteen years of the institution of medicare in 1966, for example, the average life expectancy in Canada had risen four years.

Louise James worked at a large medical ward at Saint Michael's Hospital in Toronto in the early 1960s. In *Life Before Medicare*, she remembers turning away patients who could not afford admittance. "In those years, the elderly were not as healthy, nor did they live as long or as comfortably, in health, as they do today. After medicare, you could slowly see the rise in the number and lifespan of older people with a better health status." Second World War veteran M. A. Boyce adds, "If I had to have paid for all my medical care in these last years, I would not own my own house now, and I do not want to burden a nursing home as I get older."

Jaci White of the B.C. Government and Service Employees' Union echoed similar sentiments in her testimony before the Romanow Commission. "I am passionate in my desire to see the public medicare system protected. I couldn't begin to count the number of times I had to be rushed to hospital as a child because I couldn't breathe. I've been at death's door three times . . . . If my parents had to pay for those visits and hospitalizations, I likely wouldn't be here. As a cancer survivor and an asthmatic since childhood, I can't imagine what I would do if our medicare system ceased to exist, and either condition worsened."

In *Life Before Medicare,* senior Mildred Cleverley Holst of Delta, B.C., explains what medicare meant to her.

The major change, as I see it, is that medicare has made it possible for enormous advances in diagnosis and treatment. People no longer crave simple coverage for acute care, but expect a continuum of care: preventative, acute, specialized, rehabilitative, and long-term maintenance care, as well as chronic and home care. We expect inoculations to prevent illness, laboratory and ancillary services to diagnose, and appropriate medications and medical aids. The increased life expectancy of those with extremely severe disabilities and chronic illnesses, and the prolonging of life of the seriously and terminally ill, have been heroically achieved.

In the early 1990s, respected researchers Robin F. Badgley and Samuel Wolfe conducted a comprehensive survey of the literature on the impact of medicare during the first twenty-five years of its existence, called *Canadian Health Care and the State: A Century of Evolution.* While they found that intransigent class differences in Canada had undermined one of medicare's goals – that of reducing class and income differences – our universal public plan had nevertheless succeeded in its other, more important, goal: universal access to health care services.

Badgley and Wolfe found that medicare substantially "levelled out" long-standing regional disparities in the distribution of physicians and hospital beds, as well as in the availability of front-line services. It also greatly reduced regional variations in infant mortality and longevity. And medicare, they reported, had closed the class differences in access to medical services.

In their 2002 book, *First Do No Harm,* health care experts Terrence Sullivan and Patricia Baranek argue that, in particular, three fundamental aspects of medicare have proven beneficial to Canadians: it's an effective subsidy and transfer program, it is a simple program, and it creates a strong single purchaser.

First, through taxation, the public portion of health care is funded by a progressive transfer of money from the wealthier levels of our society to provide health services for all on the basis of need. This point is supported by a 2001 study published in *The Social Economics of Healthcare,* in which Terrence Sullivan and Cam Mustard looked at how the progressive pattern of taxation and health care benefits affected Manitobans in ten different income brackets. They found that those in the highest income brackets, on average, pay the most taxes and consume the fewest health care dollars (owing to their superior health). On the other hand, those in the poorest bracket, where there is the greatest disease burden, derive the greatest benefit in terms of the cash equivalent of health care services consumed.

Say the authors:

This transfer of benefits based on health is a distinguishing feature of the Canadian health care system . . . . Our health care system is one very important way in which Canada redistributes the burden of financing health care and health benefits to its citizens. And, in fact, there is very compelling recent research suggesting that the way we pool taxes to subsidize health services to poorer Canadians results in higher overall levels of health in Canada as compared to the United States.

Second, the mechanism of a single public payment keeps administrative and transaction costs to a minimum, eliminates overheads for sales and competition, and provides a national standard of public coverage for most medically necessary services.

Third, argue Sullivan and Baranek, medicare effectively controls costs because the bargaining power of a single payer determines how much care we will buy and what kinds of deals we can make. A strong single payer can cut better deals with workers, suppliers, and professionals. As a result of these three fundamentals, Canadians receive better, more equitably distributed care for less money.

Firmly Committed

As Roy Romanow found out recently when he crossed Canada, hearing from literally thousands of citizens, Canadians are passionate about medicare. Thomas Walkom of the *Toronto Star,* who crossed the country with the commission, reported on March 17, at the halfway point of the hearings, that the central message that Romanow heard was that "Canadians still desperately want medicare." Indeed, says Walkom, the most striking element of these hearings was what was *not* said. Almost no one came before the commission to recount the kind of horror story that so often makes headlines, and of those who did have tales of waiting lists, or doctor shortages, very few blamed medicare. In fact, it was just the opposite. The vast majority of those who appeared before the commission wanted an expansion of medicare and more funds committed to it.

Privatization proponents point to an April 2002 Gallup poll that they claim shows that Canadians are ready for two-tier health care. "Majority of Canadians Favour Two-Tiered Health Care," declares the poll's headline, which was promptly replayed in pro-privatization newspapers across the country. Said authors Dr. Thomas Hartley and Dr. Josephine Mazzuca, both of whom work for Gallup, "On the topic of a two-tiered health care system, a recently conducted national Gallup poll reveals that slightly over half of Canadians (51%) are in favour of the idea of a two-tiered health care system for the country."

Yet, an examination of the questions asked could lead to a very different conclusion. In the poll, Canadians were asked if they would support "the option of paying for any additional services they wanted" as long as there was still a "basic level of service funded by the government and available to all Canadians." By answering "yes" to this question, a respondent could feel assured that the five principles of the Canada Health Act were safe and that basic health care services were available, but that they could go outside the system for "additional" services. They could easily interpret "additional" services as non-essential care, as they have just been told that this choice is predicated on the existence of a full, publicly funded system.

Respondents were also asked if they would use the services of a private clinic if they got quicker services, specialized care, and trained, experienced staff. If asked this question, many Canadians would say yes. We all know that services have declined in many communities across the country as the result of deep cuts to health care. Agreeing that one would pay for services not now available through the public system is not the same as wanting a two-tiered system.

To get a fuller picture, one has to go to more comprehensive polls. Ekos Research tracks Canadian opinions on health care. In a series of polls taken in 1999 and 2000, Ekos found that 95 per cent of Canadians are committed to strong national standards and 93 per cent believe that the federal government should make the maintenance of our health care system its highest priority. A *Globe and Mail*/Environics poll conducted in November 2000 found that the five principles of the Canada Health Act have virtually universal support among Canadians. As well, in spite of concerns about the declining quality of care in Canada, 93 per cent of women and 83 per cent of men who were patients in the last year described themselves as very or somewhat satisfied with their care.

In a November 2001 *National Post* special entitled "The State of Health Care," polling company COMPAS Inc. reported not only that Canadians remain firmly committed to free, universal medicare, but that they reject private-sector solutions to the system's problems. Further, COMPAS Inc. president Conrad Winn stated that Canadian support for user fees, corporations running hospitals, and cost-cutting by closing hospital beds and reducing services is "plummeting." In fact, when asked whether they would support the introduction of a "Patient's Bill of Rights" that would guarantee all Canadians a certain level of medical and hospital services, 74 per cent of respondents said "yes."

Another Ekos poll for the Canadian Union of Public Employees, this one conducted in January 2001, found that 87 per cent of Canadians wanted medicare expanded to include a national drug program, and 90 per cent wanted it extended to include home care.

The Saskatchewan Federation of Labour captured the general feeling of the Canadians from all walks of life who came before or made submissions to the Romanow Commission with these words: "We regard medicare as nothing less than a treasure, and an unqualified blessing to working people and other Canadians. The arguments for retaining and strengthening it are convincing and compelling. Those who would weaken or erode our public health system are either misguided to the point of incoherence or they are unprincipled, self-serving plunderers."

3

A Tale of Two Systems

One way to highlight the strengths of Canada's health care system is to compare it to the health care system in the United States, which is largely private. Many Canadian proponents of privatization declare that they are also critical of health care in the U.S., and swear that this is not the system they are promoting for Canada. Why not look to other countries, such as New Zealand or Great Britain? they demand.

The answer to this question is very simple. Apart from the fact that there are also deep problems in other countries that have privatized part or all of their health care programs, the obvious response is that it is the United States, not New Zealand or Great Britain, with whom we share a border and with whom we are locked in a continental trade agreement that is swiftly integrating our two economies.

Canadian society is becoming more and more Americanized. We are scrambling to find ways to protect Canadian art and culture in the wake of trade challenges to Canadian content rules. Canadian business is heading south and head offices are moving to New York, Los Angeles, and Houston. We have given up our energy security in order to assure the United States a constant supply of oil and gas. Our social security net looks more and more like that of our neighbours to the south. We have

harmonized our unemployment insurance standards downward; unemployed Canadians are now just as insecure if they
lose their job as Americans are. And in the aftermath of
the September 11, 2002, terrorist attacks on New York and
Washington, Canada has adopted security and military measures largely dictated by Washington, even sending Canadian
troops into battle under American command.

Now, steadily, steadily, American health care companies are
moving into Canada, bringing their philosophies and practices
with them. Their insurance companies are buying up
Canadian insurance companies. Their home care companies
are supplying more private services every day. Their pharmaceutical companies dictate Canadian drug policy. And the
United States government has targeted Canada's public health
care system under new negotiations in services at the World
Trade Organization (see Chapter Eight). So, to truly understand what it will be like to live with a private health care
system in Canada, we must look to the American system,
because it is moving steadily north.

A Different Model

There is no question that the United States offers some of the
best medical care in the world. Because the country is so rich,
there are world-class medical schools and research facilities
where the wealthy of the U.S. and many other countries can be
treated by stellar physicians of every kind. Good services are
also available to those who are not very wealthy but who can
afford the kind of insurance that assures them of speedy care –
although one must also be healthy to be eligible for such insurance. But for the elderly, the poor, the unemployed, and even the
middle class, health care in the U.S. is another story.

Although the United States did institute the Medicare

program for the elderly and the disabled and the Medicaid program for the poor in the 1960s, universal health care has never been attempted in that country. When Hilary Clinton tried to introduce a national health program after her husband was first elected, she discovered just how deeply entrenched are the limits to new thinking on the matter in her country. In the U.S., health care is not considered a right of citizenship. Each person is responsible for his or her health care and the Medicare and Medicaid programs are seen as a form of charity. Indeed, massive and steady cuts to public health care in the U.S. since the 1960s have left increasing millions of Americans with no access to quality health care at all. The majority of Americans are dependent on their employers to provide prepaid health insurance through health maintenance organizations (HMOs).

While originally based on a non-profit model through which HMOs provided quality care for millions of employed Americans, in the 1990s, HMOs came increasingly under the control of large insurance corporations that now run them on a for-profit basis. Colleen Fuller calls this takeover of non-profit health care organizations by for-profit companies "the largest transfer of charitable assets in U.S. history."

The evolution of the HMO system has been driven by vertical and horizontal corporate mergers resulting in the formation of huge transnational health care corporations that dominate the Fortune 500. Large drug companies merged with the health insurance industry to swallow up hospitals, free-standing clinics, doctors' practices, nursing homes, outpatient clinics, and pharmacies. In 1993 alone, at the height of the mergers, the top ten HMOs saw profit increases ranging from 14 per cent to 270 per cent over the course of the year; and third-quarter profits in 1994 rose 732 per cent over the same quarter in 1993.

The annual profit of the corporate health care market in the United States now stands at almost U.S. $1 trillion. During the

1990s, the ranks of administrators swelled while the number of doctors did not, and the number of registered nurses plummeted. As a consequence, while health care spending was frozen, administrative costs soared.

Because they operate on a for-profit basis, HMOs "cherry-pick" by providing medical care to those with good health and a full-time job. Doctors are actually given bonuses for denying expensive care to patients, although this practice has come under fierce criticism. "Gag" rules preventing doctors from discussing the full range of medical options with their patients are set by the HMO, as are doctors' salaries. HMOs reward doctors who have large practices of healthy clients requiring few visits and little time. As one family physician in Puget Sound explains in Kenneth M. Ludmerer's book *Time to Heal*, "A doctor with lots of sympathy or possessing expertise in chronic illnesses like asthma pays a price: attracting sicker patients." And an unhappy HMO employer.

HMOs also depend on "efficiency" in order to make a profit and force doctors and nurses to maximize what they call "throughput." Essentially, patients have to be churned out in assembly-like fashion at ever-accelerating rates of speed. In the 1980s, most American physicians felt that thirty patients a day was all they could handle. By 2002, many HMO physicians were reporting that they see as many as seventy patients a day. American doctors now spend eight minutes on average with each patient, less than half as much time as a decade ago.

Even so, physicians' incomes have steadily decreased over the last decade in the United States, and doctors are understandably reporting more burnout, job dissatisfaction, and poor mental health. The HMO system effectively redistributes income from individual physicians to corporate executives and shareholders. According to the California Nurses Association Annual Report 2001, an average HMO executive's earnings is now close to

U.S.$10 million a year. Some do better than the average, of course. In 2001, William Donaldson of Aetna Inc. earned $12,650,393; Ronald Williams of Well Point Health Network Inc. earned $13,205,631; Wilson Taylor of Cigna Corporation earned $24,741,578; and William McGuire, CEO of United Heath Group Corp., earned a whopping $54,129,501.

With big profits comes fraud, which is now rampant. The General Accounting Office estimates that almost 10 per cent of all health care money spent in the United States is defrauded through overbilling and other abuses. Health care fraud costs Americans U.S.$100 billion annually. According to many inspectors with the FBI's Health Care Fraud Unit, established in 1992 as a separate unit within the Financial Crimes Section of the FBI's Criminal Investigation Division, health care fraud is the number-one white collar crime in America. The largest certified home care agency in Florida was recently caught in a huge fraud, in which U.S.$120 million in Medicare funds went to the company for non-existent patients or unneeded services. In another case, Fresenius Medical Care North America Inc., the world's largest provider of kidney dialysis products and services, agreed to pay the U.S. government U.S.$486 million for conspiracy and fraud, the largest civil fraud recovery in history. States Dr. Marcia Angell in the June 2000 issue of the *New England Journal of Medicine:* "The private managed-care market has been a miserable failure at delivering health care. It has creamed off even larger percentages of health care premiums in bloated administrative and marketing costs and profits; it has rewarded health plans that cherry-pick the healthy and avoid the sick; and it has resisted at every turn providing adequate services to those unfortunate enough to need them."

Americans agree. In a recent poll of attitudes toward a number of different industries, health insurance companies and HMOs were ranked second from the bottom in the public's view of how well they were serving consumers, surpassed in disfavour only by the tobacco industry.

Private Insurance

The results of relying on private health care insurance have frequently been devastating for ordinary Americans. People who change jobs find their chronic illnesses are no longer covered. And people who have recovered from a serious illness often find that they cannot get insurance because of their previous health record. According to the 2000 U.S. Census Bureau Report, forty-four million Americans are completely uninsured for health care, up one million in one year alone. Another thirty to fifty million have substandard care and more than 200 million do not have comprehensive coverage, i.e., coverage for items such as long-term care. More than 18,000 adults in the U.S. die every year because they have no insurance, according to a landmark study released in May 2002. In the report, *Care Without Coverage: Too Little, Too Late,* researchers at the Institute of Medicine add that at least ten million American children are at risk due to lack of insurance.

Families can also lose their life savings and homes paying their medical bills. The percentage of Americans' income spent on health care rose almost 200 per cent in the last quarter-century, according to Chuck Collins and Felice Yeskel, authors of *Economic Apartheid in America.* Some lose everything. Suzanne Gordon, author of *Life Support: Three Nurses on the Front Line,* and Steve Early, health care specialist with the Communications Workers of America, report that nearly half of the 600,000 bankruptcies declared each year in the United States stem from out-of pocket, un-reimbursed medical bills.

Small wonder that, when a patient is hospitalized, every service, medical supply, and consultation is itemized for later billing. Front-line nurses now cover their arms and hands with sticky bar codes and slap them on patients' "bill" charts to record each drug, treatment, or supply administered. If a patient has major surgery, the bill can be astronomical.

Dual citizen James Geiwitz, who lives in Victoria, B.C., had comparable recent surgery in both Canada and the U.S. He described his American experience at the Council of Canadians' town hall meeting in Victoria on March 11, 2002:

> When I got out of my American hospital, my troubles were just beginning, as two huge corporations (the hospital and the insurance company) argued about who owes whom how much. They don't communicate with each other – they argue through you. The hospital sends a bill, you send the bill to the insurance company. A month later, the insurance company sends you a cheque that you are to send on to the hospital. It is for an amount that bears no resemblance to the amount of the hospital bill, and lists charges in a nomenclature completely different from the hospital's. The hospital accepts the cheque and sends a new bill with a sizable balance . . . .
>
> You send it to the insurance company – the last you see of it, except for copies sent monthly from the hospital. The hospital sends new bills – operating room rental, physio-therapy, Tylenol at $20 a pill, janitorial services – and they disappear into the insurance abyss. Occasionally, the insurance company sends another cheque. It is impossible to correlate the payments with the bills. The hospital begins sending threatening letters that make no sense at all. The insurance company informs you that it is cancelling your coverage; you are a "bad risk" because you actually used the insurance. You sit at home, waiting for the police to come to arrest you . . . .

Well, perhaps I exaggerate a bit with that last statement, but this is pretty close to the way I felt. I really find the American health care system disgusting and inhuman. It creates millionaires over the dead bodies of its citizens. In Canada, I was treated as a patient, someone to comfort and heal, whereas in America, I was treated as a client, someone who might welsh on his bill.

Harriet Barnes of Ottawa describes a similar tale in a May 2002 letter to the editor of the *Ottawa Citizen*. Her daughter Colleen married an American and moved to a small community near New York City. In May 2001, Colleen's husband was involved in a car accident and almost died. He was airlifted to a trauma hospital by a helicopter company that sent Colleen a bill for U.S.$5,000 – which their HMO refused to pay because they had not authorized the airlift. Barely able to walk, and with tubes still sticking out of his body, Colleen's husband was sent home after only three weeks in hospital because the HMO refused to pay for a rehabilitation hospital. It also refused to pay for home care, so Colleen, now the sole provider, was forced to change his dressings and aspirate his badly damaged lungs although she has had no medical training whatever.

In a June 2001 report prepared for the Kaiser Family Foundation (as reported by the Canadian Federation of Nurses Unions), Georgetown University's Institute for Health Care Research and Policy found that private health insurance is very hard to come by for people without a good health record. The authors sent out applications for insurance on behalf of seven hypothetical families and individuals to sixty insurance companies. The policies that they sought, in an effort to remain in the "affordable" range, had a U.S.$500 deductible and a U.S.$20 copayment per physician visit.

The least expensive quote came in for "Alice," who was

described as twenty-four years old and suffering from hay fever. Her insurance quotes averaged U.S.$1,656 per year with the highest quote at U.S.$4,596. Despite her age, she was rejected by 8 per cent of the insurance companies. The "Crane family" was offered coverage by all sixty insurance companies, but nine of the offers excluded their son, "Colin," because of his asthma condition. "Denise," described as a seven-year breast cancer survivor, was denied any coverage at all 43 per cent of the time. A number of the companies that did offer her a policy excluded coverage for cancer of any type.

"Frank" was described as sixty-two, overweight, and a smoker with high blood pressure. He was rejected 55 per cent of the time, and the average price quoted by companies that were willing to insure him was almost U.S.$10,000 per year. "Greg" was described as HIV-positive. None of the sixty insurance companies would cover him.

Indoctrination

Inevitably, the profit imperative of the system affects the teaching hospitals and medical schools that must train young doctors for the system. In his 1999 book, *Time to Heal: American Medical Education from the Turn of the Century to the Era of Managed Care,* health care analyst Kenneth M. Ludmerer reports that, with the advent of managed care in the 1990s, the historic bond between medical education and practice in the United States has been broken. Having to return a profit to their HMOs, doctors can no longer spend the quality time with patients that they have been taught is necessary to good medicine. The time needed to allow learners to learn and teachers to teach has been taken away by the managed care system, which forces doctors to see the most patients in the least possible time. This, says Ludmerer, is having a terrible impact on teaching institutions, particularly academic health centres, which did not previously operate on a for-profit basis.

To stay afloat, academic health centres have had to court industry, and medical schools and teaching hospitals have established for-profit subsidiary corporations to run managed care practices. All have adopted a narrow, job-oriented approach designed to meet the specific needs of corporate health employers, rather than behaving like true teaching institutions. "How far would medical schools go in terms of becoming educational vassals of managed care organizations?" Ludmerer asks. Too far, is the answer. He states that managed care organizations demand that medical schools teach skills and attitudes that primarily serve the special needs of HMOs, such as submissiveness and docility.

Some want universities to teach young physicians to be advocates of the insurance payers, as well as their patients. Ludmerer tells the story of the University of California, Los Angeles, where some members of the faculty actually argue that it is their responsibility to indoctrinate students who might have misgivings about aspects of for-profit care. Says one official document of the university, "Medical educators not only need to find creative methods of introducing these content areas, such as managed care, into medical curricula, but should also anticipate the need for strategies to deal with negative attitudes held by students."

Left Behind

In 1998, more than 2,300 Massachusetts physicians signed a despairing memo printed in the *Journal of the American Medical Association*, in which they stated:

The time we are allowed to spend with the sick shrinks under the pressure to increase throughput, as though we were dealing with industrial commodities rather than afflicted human beings . . . . Physicians and nurses are being prodded by threats and bribes to abdicate allegiance to patients and to shun the sickest, who may be unprofitable. Some of us risk being fired or "delisted" for giving, or even discussing, expensive services, and many are offered bonuses for minimizing care.

Not surprisingly, services in the United States' impoverished public system have deteriorated in the last decade as well. Thousands of registered nurses have been laid off, replaced by unqualified health care "aides," and millions of beds have been closed. To deliver cheaper care, administrators are cutting nurse-to-patient ratios, substituting qualified professionals with untrained workers (called "generic workers"), and shifting to a part-time workforce. Nurses are doubling up on their workload. Sheets go unchanged, tests are less frequent, and housekeeping standards are falling.

Suzanne Gordon and Steve Early report that with 126,000 vacant nursing positions reported nationwide in the United States, many hospital emergency rooms, operating theatres, intensive care units, and other hospital wards face temporary or permanent shutdowns due to understaffing. One recent study found that two out of ten major emergency rooms were closed on any given day in greater Boston.

In March 2002, the U.S. Department of Health and Human Services found that nine out of ten U.S. nursing homes lack adequate staff. The result, reports the HHS, is that elderly patients suffer from preventable bedsores, pneumonia, malnutrition, and dehydration. In September 2001, the *American Journal of Public Health* reported on another study of private, for-profit nursing home chains: "Investor-owned nursing homes provide worse care and less nursing care than non-profits . . . . Rates of severe deficiencies at investor-owned facilities were 40.5 per cent higher that at non-profit homes."

Even employed people with insurance policies are at risk when employers cut costs and shift them to employees who now must pay for medicines, doctors, and hospital visits. Americans are dependent on their employers for coverage. Ninety per cent of private insurance policies in the United States are taken out by employers. And that coverage is getting more expensive. In April 2001, it was estimated that annual premiums for employer-sponsored plans were more than $2,500 for single coverage and more than $7,000 for a family. The employees now pay between 50 and 70 per cent of these costs. The remaining costs borne by employers cost them nearly $100 billion in 2001, a jump of 11 per cent in one year. William Mercer Ltd., a major North American benefit plan manager and pension actuary, predicts that insurance costs will rise another 13 per cent in 2002.

As Suzanne Gordon and Steve Early explain, employers – not employees – decide which health care plan is offered. There is little range: 91 per cent of all companies with fewer than ten employees and 47 per cent of large firms offer only a single choice. Millions of Americans report that they are reluctant to change jobs for fear of losing medical benefits.

Lives at Risk

In a 1999 article in the *Journal of the American Medical Association,* called "Quality of Care in Investor-Owned vs. Not-for-Profit HMOs," two professors of medicine at the Harvard Medical School, Steffie Woolhandler and David Himmelstein, estimated that there would be an extra 5,925 breast cancer deaths annually in the United States if the remaining 25 per cent of HMOs that still operate on a non-profit basis were to become for-profit. Woolhandler and Himmelstein also report that for-profit hospitals spend 11 per cent less on clinical care, particularly nursing care, than other hospitals.

Several other recent studies show that for-profit hospitals have higher death rates than not-for-profits. The biggest was a major review and meta-analysis of studies comparing mortality rates between private for-profit and not-for-profit hospitals in the U.S., done by McMaster University in Hamilton and published in the *Canadian Medical Association Journal* in May 2002. The study found that death rates in for-profit hospitals are significantly higher than in not-for-profit hospitals. The review, which surveyed 38 million adult patients in 26,000 U.S. hospitals, directly linked these death rates to the corners that for-profit hospitals must cut in order to achieve a profit margin for investors, as well as to pay high salaries for administrators. "To ease cost pressures," stated Dr. P. J. Devereaux, a cardiologist at McMaster and the lead researcher for the study, "administrators tend to hire less highly skilled personnel, including doctors, nurses and pharmacists . . . . The U.S. statistics clearly show that when the need for profits drives hospital decision-making, more patients die."

The study demonstrated that those receiving care in a for-profit hospital had a 2 per cent higher risk of dying in hospital or within thirty days of being discharged than those receiving care in a not-for-profit. If Canada were to switch to for-profit hospitals, Devereaux noted, more than 2,000 Canadians would die every year. Moreover, the report warned, it is the very same large U.S. hospital chains examined in the study that would be purchasing hospitals in Canada if this country were to move to a for-profit system.

Horror stories abound. In December 2000, one Cambridge,

Massachusetts, woman who had just undergone major heart surgery suffered post-operative complications. The ambulance took her to a Cambridge hospital only to find that its emergency facilities were "under diversion." Rerouted twice, the patient died.

A series by Steve Twedt, entitled "A Question of Skill," which ran in the Pittsburgh *Post Gazette* in February 1996, provides more examples. In 1993, a generic worker at a Rhode Island hospital mistakenly filled a syringe with potassium chloride instead of saline and used it to clean out an intravenous line. The mistake killed an eleven-month-old girl. In 1994, a generic aide was left alone at a major Boston hospital to feed a plate of food to an elderly burn patient in the intensive care unit. A nurse was called when the patient started to choke from the food stuffed into her mouth. The aide had fed the patient as instructed, but had failed to notice that she wasn't swallowing. The patient died. At a hospital in Allegheny, an unlicensed aide fed an eighty-one-year-old patient food through a tracheotomy tube, flooding his lungs with the liquid.

Small wonder that medical malpractice rates are soaring. As reported by Steve Sebelius in the Las Vegas *Review-Journal* on March 5, 2002, state legislators and senators told a public hearing in Las Vegas, Nevada, that the state's doctors are in crisis. A survey showed most doctors facing rising insurance rates, some as high as $250,000. They were having to lay off staff and cut services just to stay afloat. A majority had been sued, some three times or more. One doctor told the assembled politicians that most of them were now practising "defensive medicine."

A May 2001 Associated Press investigation published in the *Chicago Tribune* found that poorly trained or overwhelmed nurses are responsible for thousands of deaths and injuries each year in U.S. hospitals. Since 1995, at least 1,720 hospital

patients have died and 9,548 others have been injured because
of mistakes made across the country. The report followed an
earlier study from 1999 by the Institute of Medicine estimating
that medical mistakes kill anywhere from 44,000 to 98,000
patients every year. In fact, medical errors now constitute the
third leading cause of death in the U.S., after deaths from heart
disease and cancer.

The *Tribune*'s investigation also found that many hospitals
have increasingly turned to part-time and generic personnel
from temp agencies, and that many of the patients who died
were under the care of unlicensed, unregulated nurses' aides.
Under cost-saving programs in at least two Chicago hospitals,
housekeeping staff assigned to clean rooms were pressed into
duty as aides to dispense medicine. Mandatory overtime and
sixteen-hour shifts were also cited as major problems. Said one
nurse quoted in the study: "Every day I pray, 'God protect me.
Let me make it out of there with my patients alive.'"

The Forgotten

Perhaps the group most left behind in America's experimenta-
tion with for-profit health care are those former residents of psychiatric wards who were "returned" to their communities after
their wards and institutions were closed down in the 1960s and
1970s. Some returned to families poorly equipped to cope with
them; others turned to the streets. A huge number, however,
became residents of a whole new system: "adult homes" run by
private operators on a for-profit basis. In April 2002, the *New
York Times* published a scathing three-part series reporting on a
year-long investigation it conducted into the adult home
program in New York City. What Clifford J. Levy found, and
published, has proven to be a major headache for city, state, and
federal health authorities.

The homes have become "another universe," says the *Times,* one in which the mentally ill are preyed upon by ruthless opportunists. On one side are the homes' operators, who are paid a small daily fee per resident taken from their monthly social security disability cheques. The operators top up this income by charging rent to the residents (the *Times* calls it "theft") and by charging fees to for-profit health care providers who in turn have access to a huge, docile "clientele." Residents are brought before a swarm of outside providers for treatment that they often don't need and for which they – and the state – are charged. The operators even charge residents for the vans that take them to unscheduled medical visits.

Nearly all the residents can legally sign consent forms and don't dare refuse. Workers at the homes told the *Times* that if residents refuse treatment, they are threatened with hospitalization and that their "spending money" – their own money, which the operators confiscate and give back to them sparingly for good behaviour – will be withheld. While residents are regularly denied proper psychiatric and medical care, they are paraded before allergists, vocational therapists, dermatologists, and podiatrists, among others. At least once a month, without their consent, they are lined up to see a podiatrist to have their toenails clipped at $50 to $75 per clipping. The podiatrist at one home has a licence plate that reads "FOOTBIZ."

In one of the more shocking examples, the *Times* told about vans pulling up at the Leben Home for Adults in Elmhurst, Queens, collecting at least thirty residents, and taking them to an eye surgeon, who performed cataract operations and laser surgery on them. Not one of the residents had complained of eye problems and none were told ahead of time where they were going or that they were about to undergo surgery.

"They didn't warn me or anything," said Robert Fazio, sixty-one, who cannot bathe or dress himself. "They just took me and then he put a laser beam in my eye." Gail Barnabas, fifty-three, who suffers from severe depression, told the *Times* about her experience: "He said it was cataracts, and if he corrected it, it would be beautiful. We were all brought into the van on the same day. We were there from the morning until 4 p.m. and just made it back for supper. Everybody had it. The whole van was filled." Kurt Trentmann, fifty-five, reported that his cataract surgery impaired his vision and that he had reported this to his home's operator. Two years later, he was still waiting for an answer. Robert Dowling, fifty-nine, who speaks in half sentences, was given four eye operations in four months and has no memory of any of them. His brother told the *Times* that he had no eye problems whatsoever.

Meanwhile, all this money wasn't going to improve the living conditions of the residents. Here are some excerpts of the *Times*' investigation:

- Anna Erika, Staten Island: "Resident with dementia wore urine-stained clothes for three days. Another had lesions draining onto clothes that went unchanged for two days. Another hid in room for days without eating or bathing. When pills went missing, workers borrowed from other residents' prescriptions. Workers flushed pills down toilet instead of distributing them."

- Brooklyn Manor, Brooklyn: "Resident had old and new blood stains on face and body, and was filthy. Staff did not respond to emergency calls from rooms. One resident lost 54 pounds in one year; home did not determine why. Records were inaccurate, incomplete or nonexistent. Kitchen and many rooms infested with flies. Residents made to work as janitors."

- Garden of Eden, Bensonhurst: "Operator routinely threatened residents with eviction, verbally harassed them and demanded compliance with unlawful rules, creating abusive environment. Resident vomited for two days, no one called doctor or family, or monitored her. Meals meagre and unappetizing."

- Leben, Elmhurst: "Rooms so decrepit that 60 residents evacuated. Security guards distributed pills. Incontinent resident wandered home with wet pants. No activities in home, numerous fire hazards. Many residents 'ill-groomed and malodorous.' Workers psychologically abusive to residents. One resident burned in fight, another shot."
- Parkview, the Bronx: "Anorexic resident allowed to deteriorate so much that she weighed only 76 pounds and then died. Of 15 case management evaluations sampled, none completed. Workers did not know basic first aid."
- Ocean House, Far Rockaway: "Rooms infested with cockroaches. Residents sleeping on soiled sheets. Kitchen floor rotted. Widespread hazardous conditions due to dilapidated home, ongoing renovations. Operator and son accused of embezzling millions of dollars from home and Medicaid. Serious deficiencies in medication handling and residents' hygiene."

The *Times* reported that Ocean House reaped at least $185,000 in rent annually from five for-profit health care providers, including $120,000 from a hospital that was "paying" for space it never occupied and $36,000 from a home care company that paid for a waiting area and parking spaces at Ocean House that it never used. The newspaper indicated that this suggests a kickback scheme.

Two Systems

A comparison of the Canadian and U.S. health care systems shows that Canada's more egalitarian model saves lives. According to the Statistics Canada Web site, Canada ranks second in the world in terms of life expectancy; the United States ranks twenty-fifth. Canada's infant mortality rate is 5.6 per thousand live births; in the U.S., the rate is 7.8. Maternal mortality in Canada stands at 7 out of 100,000; in the U.S., that number is 14.

The World Health Organization (WHO) has an index that measures how efficiently health systems translate expenditures into health, taking into account such factors as patient choice and the equity of health care distribution. Canada ranks thirtieth on the 2000 index; the United States ranks seventy-second. On another WHO index, from 1998, measuring the effectiveness of health care services, including confidentiality and the quality of basic amenities, Canada ranks seventh and the U.S. ranks fifteenth.

The irony of the U.S. health care system is that, in spite of extraordinary measures to cut costs (in order to increase profits), the United States spends more per person on health care than any other country in the world. According to two reports, the Canadian Institute for Health Information 2001 preliminary provincial and territorial government health expenditure estimates and the Centres for Medicare and Medicaid Services National Health Expenditures Aggregate and Per Capita Amounts 1980–2000, the U.S. spends U.S.$4,637 (approximately CAD$7,000) a year per person on health care, and millions go without care, while Canada spends CAD$3,298 and insures every citizen. Canada's administrative costs are about ten cents on the dollar; administrative costs in the U.S. are more than double that, close to twenty-four cents on the dollar. This difference can be attributed to the administrative efficiencies of a publicly funded system.

In 1971, Canadian health care costs were 7.4 per cent of the GDP, compared to 7.6 per cent in the United States. Since then, Americans' health care expenditures have almost doubled, to more than 14 per cent, while Canadians' have remained relatively stable, rising to just over 9 per cent.

The costs borne by employers also differ greatly between the two countries. Health insurance premiums paid by American employers amount to 8.2 per cent of gross pay, as reported by the *Globe and Mail*'s Virginia Galt on February 12, 2002. Detroit-based General Motors alone provides health care for 1.25 million workers. New York investment firm Morgan Stanley Dean Witter & Co. says this equates to close to U.S.$4 million in health care benefits – or $3,000 per employee annually. Put another way, health insurance adds U.S.$931.70 to the cost of every GM vehicle produced in the United States every year. And as noted earlier, employers are paying average annual increases of 12 per cent in their health insurance premiums every year.

Health insurance premiums paid by Canadian employers, on the other hand, amount to only 1 per cent of gross pay. This gives Canadian business a huge advantage. A recent study by Stewart MacKay of New York–based KPMG's Vancouver office found that Canada is the least costly place to do business out of nine industrialized countries. After comparing wage and benefit costs, taxes, transportation, and utility costs in North America, Europe, and Japan, KPMG reported that Canada has a 14.5 per cent cost advantage over the United States. The company cited Canada's health benefits as the single biggest factor in this difference. A 1998 Industry Canada study also cited Canada's health benefits as translating into a 9.8 per cent labour cost advantage over U.S. manufacturers: $4.03 versus CAD$9.82. In fact, the World Competitiveness Report has identified Canada's universal health care system as a major competitive advantage. Canada's health care system has been shown to save the auto industry, for example, between $1,200 and $1,500 for every car assembled here, as reported in the *Globe and Mail* on November 30, 1999.

Says Theodore Marmor of the Yale School of Management: "For all the criticism of Canada's Medicare program, I for one, would be delighted to have its manageable problems in place of those in the United States."

In a February 21, 2002, presentation to the Senate Committee chaired by Michael Kirby, Dr. Arnold Relman, professor emeritus of medicine at the Harvard Medical School and emeritus editor-in-chief of the *New England Journal of Medicine,* summed up two decades of his research on the American health care system with these words:

> My conclusion from all of this study is that most of the current problems of the U.S. system – and they are numerous – result from the growing encroachment of private for-profit ownership and competitive markets on a sector of our economy that properly belongs in the public domain. No health care system in the industrialized world is as heavily commercialized as ours, and none is as expensive, inefficient, and inequitable – or as unpopular. Indeed, just about the only parts of U.S. society happy with out current market-driven health care system are the owners and investors in the for-profit industries now living off the system.

In his presentation, Relman agreed with those who tout the United States as being a world leader in medical science and technology and said that, yes, its major medical centres may provide some of the best and most sophisticated care available anywhere. But taken as a whole, which, he said, is the important measurement, the American health care system is failing badly.

Relman told the senators that the administrative costs of running Medicare and Medicaid – still largely operated by governments and serving about 25 per cent of the American public – are less than 3 per cent, whereas the corporate and administrative costs of the private insurers are between 15 and 30 per cent. Private health care companies also outsource many other services they use to control costs by restricting the use of expensive resources. As a result, only 50 to 60 per cent of the premium dollar ends up with those actually providing the care.

When asked by one of the senators whether he would eliminate all for-profit facilities and health care businesses if he could, Relman answered, "Yes. As a scientist, I am evidence-driven. And no one has ever shown in fair, accurate comparisons, that for-profit makes for greater efficiency or better quality, and certainly never shown that it serves the public interest any more. Never."

Relman also had a warning for Canadians considering a similar system:

We in the U.S. are belatedly learning this lesson and soon may be ready to try other options that will depend more on public action. Many of us south of the border have always believed that you Canadians had the right idea in deciding that the financing of health care is primarily a public responsibility. We still think you are right and that we ought to emulate you, rather than vice versa. I am surprised and disappointed in your Committee's Interim Report, which seems to favour policy options dependent on private market involvement in Canadian health care. Before making your final recommendations, I hope you will look more closely at the U.S. experience – which ought to convince most evidence-driven observers that markets can't solve public problems like health care, and can in fact make them worse.

American citizen Sandra Malasky of Penacook, New Hampshire, wrote a passionate letter to Roy Romanow expressing similar sentiments:

The Canadian health care system, flawed as it may be, is still a beacon of justice and common sense on this continent. The medical system in the U.S. dazzles regularly with its technological change and seemingly endless range of choices. But more people than the entire population of Canada have no access to even the most basic services. Now that's a broken system. I applaud your efforts to study and debate, but for God's sake, keep the social contract that has made you a great society.

4

The Internal Assault

In spite of the ongoing popularity of our public health system with the Canadian people, the forces opposed to medicare have never stopped trying to undermine it. They regrouped after they failed to block the creation of medicare in 1966 and have been active ever since. Medicare's opponents consist of a number of right-wing provincial governments, conservative think-tanks, corporate-controlled newspapers, business lobby groups, transnational health care corporations, giant drug companies, American HMOs wanting to move into Canada, the American government who backs them, and federal Liberal politicians who either don't understand how their government's policies are threatening medicare or who understand all too well.

Today, the anti-medicare viewpoint is very popular in elite circles who have adopted the values and policies of economic globalization. But this attitude had a harder time of it in the anti-big-business decade that followed the creation of medicare.

Heady Days

The Pearson Liberals were pushed sharply left during the 1960s as a consequence of forming several minority governments with a new and aggressive NDP holding the balance of power, and a politically active populace thinking twice about who they support. As a result, the Liberals unleashed not only the social programs described in Chapter Two, but also a whole host of laws and initiatives that would come to define the Canadian state: bilingualism, a new labour code, the doubling of external aid, collective bargaining for the public service, the Royal Commission on the Status of Women, and the "war on poverty." In fact, the social assistance reforms created in those years were so broad that, by 1965, federal welfare expenditures exceeded the nation's defence bill for the first time.

David Lewis and his "corporate welfare bums" campaign kept the pressure up on the minority government of the Trudeau Liberals in the early 1970s. By the mid-1970s, high employment, decent wages, and social security had given working Canadians substantially increased economic and political clout. They saw their social programs as rights and were empowered, freed from any sense of shame, in claiming services.

At this time, Canadians overwhelmingly believed that Canada was not sufficiently independent of American foreign policy, and were deeply worried about economic survival. Driven by strong public concerns about the increased amount of foreign control over Canadian industry and natural resources, the government created the Foreign Investment Review Agency, the National Energy Program, the Canada Development Corporation, and Petro-Canada. As a result, foreign ownership declined from 35 per cent of the Canadian economy in the mid-1960s to about 20 per cent in the early 1990s, when it started to rocket upwards again. (Canadians now control a smaller portion of our productive wealth than any other industrialized country on earth.)

Counterforce

All this sat very badly with Canadian big business (much of it foreign-owned). After all, the Canadian welfare state was originally created with only the reluctant support of the private sector. During the 1930s, capitalism had been on trial, its failures there for everyone to see. Communism and socialism were on the rise around the world; real modifications were going to have to be made if capitalism was to survive. Thus, business leaders of the day reluctantly helped Mackenzie King create the foundations of the welfare state and committed themselves to accept unions and rising wages.

Now, in the early 1970s, the same progressive forces were dominating the public discourse again. Further, as Tony Clarke documented in his 1997 book, *Silent Coup,* opinion polls in North America showed support for business at an all-time low as a result of the behaviour of the giant oil companies during the 1973 energy crisis. As millions of Americans and Canadians braced themselves for a quadrupling of oil prices by the OPEC countries, and North America slipped into recession, the big companies continued to post record profits. The unpopularity of the oil companies spread to big business in general.

Business in other sectors was also facing a faltering economy and a squeeze on profits during this time, which it attributed to ongoing demands for wage increases and social protections, and an insufficiently co-operative government. The public sector had become too intrusive, big business decided – both as a regulator of economic activity (to ensure that the economy operated for the public good), and as a producer encroaching on their turf. There was, they believed, an "excess of democracy," characterized by the growing political influence of groups that challenged corporate interests.

This time, the big-business community decided to fight back.

To counter the erosion of its power, business leaders set in motion a multifaceted effort to make their agenda the agenda of government, and to influence the political culture of society. The anti-medicare forces hitched a ride on this bandwagon and never looked back.

National Citizens' Coalition

In 1967, the business community supported Colin Brown, a millionaire insurance agent with a deep antipathy to unions and medicare, when he formed the National Citizens' Coalition (NCC) to wage a "ceaseless war" against government. The NCC spends hundreds of thousands of dollars on negative advertising at every election targeting candidates who support social welfare, and it has consistently fought legislation designed to curb corporate influence on the political process. The NCC once predicted that Canadians would die as a result of the adoption of medicare, and it has consistently called for the privatization of medical insurance and hospitals. It advocates the position that corporations and charities ought to take over the social functions now performed by government, and believes that government's role ought to be limited to national defence, protection of private property, and law enforcement.

NCC bylaws forbid policy meetings of its general membership; instead, its political decisions are made by the real "coalition," a small cadre of directors and corporate and foundation backers that runs the organization like a private lobbying firm. The group's advisory board, past and present, reads like a who's who of the Canadian establishment. Through the NCC, wealthy individuals and corporations can promote their political goals with total anonymity; even investors are not allowed to know whether companies they invest in contribute to the NCC, and businesses are allowed to claim donations as business expenses.

Stephen Harper, leader of the Alliance party, is a former CEO of the NCC and has no doubt carried its views into the Parliament of Canada with him.

The Fraser Institute

In 1975, the Vancouver-based Fraser Institute was created. The brainchild of MacMillan Bloedel, handsomely funded by large Canadian banks and resource corporations, this institute has become a powerful presence in Canada, even regularly providing "statistics" and "studies" to the mainstream media and to university and college professors as federal government cutbacks have dried up government sources of information. It has been maintaining a presence on Canadian university campuses for more than twenty years.

The Fraser Institute considers Canada's social security system both immoral and an inefficient use of taxpayers' money. It advocates a mix of private and public charity for the "deserving poor," i.e., the unfortunate, not the irresponsible. And it argues that the extent of poverty in Canada has been exaggerated by "special interest groups" in order to justify public "overspending." In a 1992 publication, it stated that poverty is not a major problem in Canada and recommended a new definition of poverty to apply only to those families who lack the "cost of basic necessities for absolute physical survival." President Michael Walker adds, "In some cases, poverty is simply a reflection of the fact that the sufferers were dealt an unlucky physical or intellectual allocation from the roulette wheel of genetic inheritance."

The Fraser Institute has also worked tirelessly against medicare since its creation, advocating a system in which public medical insurance would cover only catastrophic illness.

The C. D. Howe Institute

The C. D. Howe Institute is the oldest and most influential of Canada's corporate-funded policy think-tanks. Its several hundred members and sponsors include many prominent players in corporate Canada, including Alcan, Barrick Gold, General Motors, Merck Frosst, Molson, Shell Canada, and most of the major banks. There is substantial overlap between the C. D. Howe Institute and the membership of the Business Council on National Issues (see "The BCNI/CCCE" below), and most its large corporate sponsors also financially support the federal Liberal party and provincial right-wing governments. During the 1960s and early 1970s, the C. D. Howe Institute promoted the mainstream Canadian values of full employment and strong social programs, even as it spoke out for business interests as well.

However, in the late 1970s, the institute shifted its official policy position, moving dramatically to the right. It supported the Canada–U.S. Free Trade Agreement, the GST, deficit reduction, and a major overhaul of Canada's social programs. It was an early advocate of privatization in health care and, in 1994, published a study, *Social Canada in the Millennium*, that called for the elimination of federal cash transfers for health care to the provinces and advocated more provincial power over health care. Said economist Tom Courchene, the study's author, "Canadians now have to filter our long-standing values of fairness, sharing and equity through the new realities of fiscal restraint, globalization and the information revolution."

The C. D. Howe study was largely adopted by the Chrétien government in its so-called "Green Paper," *Improving Social Security in Canada*, which came out only weeks later and formed the basis for the infamous budget of 1995 – in which social spending in Canada was cut to the bone.

In May 2002, the C. D. Howe Institute weighed into the debate again with a new paper, *Funding Public Provision of Private Health: The Case for a Copayment Contribution through the Tax System.* In it, the authors suggest that Canadians who use more health care services should pay higher taxes. The proposed new tax would be linked directly to how much users cost the medicare system each year. "The higher the burden an individual imposes on the system, the higher would be his or her contribution," says the report. Christine Burdett of Friends of Medicare in Alberta stated that this proposal would amount to a tax on the sick and force the poor to put off seeking treatment.

The BCNI/CCCE

In 1976, Canada's business elite formed the influential Business Council on National Issues (BCNI), which recently changed its name to the Canadian Council of Chief Executives (CCCE). It is made up of the 160 biggest corporations in Canada and was first led by former Trudeau adviser Thomas d'Aquino, who remains its CEO today. Modelled on the powerful right-wing American corporate lobby group, the Business Roundtable, the BCNI/CCCE set out to create a more hospitable public climate for big-business concerns. According to them, government's role had to change; instead of acting as a protector of society against the excesses of the market, government would become the protector of a favourable climate for business. The values of community and co-operation would be replaced with the values of individualism and competitiveness. In other words, the values long associated with Canada would be replaced by American values.

Based on the twin gospels of deregulation and privatization, the BCNI/CCCE set out its wish list: a freeze on social spending and a return to targeted, not universal, social assistance; restrictions on government borrowing; reduced unemployment premiums; lower corporate taxes; the deregulation of energy; a war on the deficit; privatization of public services; and the removal of foreign investment reviews. It focused on key issues through task forces that paralleled government departments, becoming a virtual shadow cabinet.

The BCNI/CCCE knew that it needed to enlist the support of powerful media and recruit its own economists. BCNI/CCCE members put themselves on the editorial boards of newspapers they increasingly control, as well as on the boards of governors of the major universities, where they promote the corporate control of research; private-sector funding of courses, programs, "chairs," and capital costs; and the raising of tuition fees.

The BCNI/CCCE was the original and major catalyst for free trade and a big backer of Conservative leader Brian Mulroney. Mulroney became prime minister in 1984 and, shortly thereafter, started free trade negotiations with the United States. In his 1998 book, *Wrestling with the Elephant: The Inside Story of the Canada-U.S. Trade Wars,* Gordon Ritchie, who was the deputy chief negotiator to the Canada-U.S. Free Trade Agreement, boasted openly about the fact that BCNI/CCCE members (who spent millions in public advertising to sell free trade during the 1988 election) acted as co-negotiators with the government to secure the deal.

"In a radical departure from past practice," writes Ritchie, "I assigned two [Trade Negotiations Office] staffers to each of [the Sectoral Advisory Groups on International Trade] . . . . Over the opposition of traditionalists, I shared our intelligence with these [business] advisors, who were naturally sworn to confidentiality . . . . Their contribution was absolutely indispensable and changed forever the way the government managed trade policy." Once established, this relationship between the trade bureaucracy in Ottawa and the country's business elite has never been broken. If anything, in the January 2002 cabinet shuffle, which named right-winger John Manley as deputy prime minister and put him in charge of North American integration, the relationship was strengthened.

The BCNI/CCCE was also instrumental in promoting the GST and the "war" on the deficit, and has been crucial to the fight to dismantle Canada's social programs and medicare. Its official position on social policy is "to do more with less, target those in need and create incentives that encourage individual self-reliance." In other words, reject universality. CCCE members are the power behind the hundreds of corporate lobby groups who pay middlemen to act on their behalf to lobby governments in their interests. Through deepening informal ties with politicians and making huge financial contributions to politicians they favour, corporations of the CCCE have come to wield enormous power in Ottawa and the provinces. They are the most important sector in Canadian society in the eyes of government, and have become the driving force behind all public policy decisions today.

In its submission to the Romanow Commission, the BCNI/CCCE stated that Canada's health care system should be taken out of the hands of the politicians and bureaucrats and turned over to provincial Crown corporations that would be run by "experienced businesspeople." A Crown corporation "run like a business" with "performance bonuses and incentives for innovation" would "eliminate political considerations" and bring "corporate discipline" to health care, including "private-sector innovation." The Canadian Chamber of Commerce echoed this ideological position when it appeared before the Romanow Commission. The chamber called for the "greater use of voluntary, private sector delivery of health care services . . . and private sector investment" as well as the injection of more competition among suppliers of health care services. These powerful corporate lobby groups, sensing that Canada's public health care system is in trouble, are using the occasion to seek its demise.

Hearts and Minds

But it is never enough to become influential with those in power. To really have lasting influence, it is necessary to change the hearts and minds of ordinary people and to shape the political culture of a society. As Michael Walker of the Fraser Institute says, "If you really want to change the world, you have to change the ideology of the world."

To accomplish this, a powerful set of myths was introduced into Canadian society – toxic myths about the failure of the public systems of education and health, the laziness of the poor, and the suffocating drain of a "bloated" public service. These toxic myths, repeated continually in the corporate-dominated mainstream media, are part of a campaign to reduce Canadians' expectations for their own well-being and that of their families, at work and in retirement.

In this ideology, government is the problem by definition, as is any notion of entitlement. Families must take responsibility for themselves and stop relying on government. Children are the sole responsibility of their parents; so, too, is child poverty. Public services are merely products that the private sector could deliver better. Citizens are consumers who should have the "choice" to buy the best health care and education "products" they can afford. Families, not governments or communities, are the defining unit of society. (Margaret Thatcher often famously said that there is no such thing as society, only individuals and families looking out for themselves.) The role of educators is to help sort winners from losers in order to help stream young people into the appropriate slots in the new class structure of the global economy.

Social programs have failed, we are told. They have robbed

Canadians of our initiative and created a crippling legacy of debt. This particularly pernicious myth persists despite a groundbreaking 1994 Statistics Canada study by government economists Hiratio Mimoto and Peter Cross that found that government spending, and specifically social spending, held steady between 1975 and 1991, the years in which the Canadian debt spiralled. In fact, the authors found that the growth of the debt was due entirely to the compounding of interest on the original debt: by 1991, interest payments on the debt were costing Canadian taxpayers more than the combined spending on transfers for education, health, welfare, and unemployment insurance together. According to Mimoto and Cross, "Social program spending has not increased relative to Gross Domestic Product (GDP) over the last 16 years."

Perhaps no one has verbalized the toxic myths of Canadian "inferiority" better than Conrad Black, who abandoned his powerful Canadian newspaper chain (which he used effectively to promote his views) in 2001 to take his place in the British House of Lords. In a *Financial Post* article on February 6, 1991, Black stated that, because of its welfare state, Canada is "uncompetitive, slothful, self-righteous, spiteful, an envious nanny-state, hovering on the verge of dissolution and bankruptcy." Its people, a "society of over-compensated self pitiers," suffer from the "great Canadian sloth, the spirit of smug entitlement."

In an article in the *Financial Post* on May 17, 1989, Black took special aim at universality, which he called "plundering" and "bribery." "Canada extended the safety net to encompass not simply the genuinely unfortunate," he wrote, "but rather anyone who is second-rate. We would rather take care of the second-rate people than reward the first-rate for their initiative." While his views are more extreme than most, an increasingly corporate-dominated print media in Canada has voiced largely the same editorial position for a number of years.

CanWest Global Communications Corp., owned by Winnipeg's Asper family (who are prominent Liberals), now owns the *National Post*, fourteen major metropolitan newspapers, 126 smaller papers, and Global Television. In most markets in which the company operates, it is the only game in town. The company has backed privatized health care in national editorials. "Profit needn't be a dirty word," wrote Murdoch Davis, vice-president (editorial) and editor-in-chief of CanWest's Southam News, in a national Southam editorial on December 10, 2001. A number of CanWest's local papers, such as the *Ottawa Citizen,* have taken an aggressive pro-privatization position in their editorial pages as well. And the *Globe and Mail* has joined the privatization chorus. In spite of polls that indicate the opposite, the *Globe* felt able to declare that, "People do not care who owns the hospital or clinic that treats them, as long as they receive timely, high-quality care" in a January 22, 2002, editorial.

Retreat

The trouble with these toxic myths, of course, is that they work. While most wealthy Canadians have long been willing to support government withdrawal from universal social programs in return for tax breaks, only in the last decade have many middle-class Canadians reluctantly joined the call for tax cuts. The trick is to allow public services to become so underfunded and rundown that they no longer serve their constituency; citizens then demand their tax money back in order to "buy" services no longer provided by the state. As governments began to withdraw funding from Canada's social programs, Canadians began to doubt the viability of their universal social security system, even though they still support it in principle.

From the mid-1980s to the early 1990s, the Conservative government of Brian Mulroney savaged Canadian social programs, eliminating universal child benefits, "clawing back" family allowance and old-age pension payments, and restructuring the unemployment insurance program so that it was entirely funded by employer and employee contributions. The Chrétien Liberals followed suit. Finance Minister Paul Martin's 1995 budget cut an unprecedented 40 per cent out of federal cash transfer payments to the provinces for health care, social assistance, and post-secondary education.

Most important, the 1995 budget killed the Canada Assistance Plan (CAP), which had provided a universal standard for Canadians in need and had funded social services and post-secondary education. By losing the shared cost aspect of welfare, citizens of provinces that reduced their debts on the backs of the poor lost their safety net of last resort.

The repeal of the CAP also negatively affected a wide range of services that directly or indirectly affect the health of the Canadian people: community assistance for people with disabilities; homemaker and Meals on Wheels services for the elderly; home care services for people newly discharged from hospitals, and many other assistance programs. With the death of the CAP, the distinction between "deserving" and "undeserving" poor was fully reintroduced to Canadian society. Freed from national standards for social assistance, provinces were able to slash welfare budgets and impose stringent conditions on welfare recipients.

The results of all these changes have been devastating for many Canadians. Funding for social programs is at its lowest level since 1950. Billions have been taken from public pensions. Cuts of about $7 billion a year to the unemployed have left only one-third of unemployed workers eligible for Employment Insurance benefits, compared to 85 per cent in 1989. The cuts to social programs and to the unemployed have been so deep that on July 15, 1999, the *Ottawa Citizen* reported that

Standard & Poor's, the New York–based ratings institute, argued that the myth of a "kinder Canada" must be put to rest. In 1999, for the first time, it states, Canada spent less on its elderly and unemployed than the United States did. Further cuts by most provincial governments have left many citizens without a social safety net.

Not surprisingly, while corporate profits and CEO earnings soared during the 1990s, the real incomes of most Canadians eroded to less than they were in 1980, according to Statistics Canada. During the 1990s, the number of millionaires tripled and corporate salaries grew at a rate of about 15 per cent a year, while workers' wages rose just 2 per cent – less than the rate of inflation.

Tragically, child poverty exploded during this decade as well. According to the 1999 Annual Report of Campaign 2000, a coalition of Canadian groups that includes the Canadian Council for Social Development and the National Council of Welfare, since 1989 (the year Parliament unanimously voted to eradicate child poverty by the year 2000), the number of poor children has grown by 60 per cent; the number of children in families with incomes of less than $20,000 has grown by 65 per cent; the number of children in families needing social assistance has grown by 51 per cent; and the number of children living in rental housing for which the rent takes an unsustainably large proportion of family income has grown by 91 per cent.

Next Target: Medicare

It can come as little surprise that in this environment, medicare has become the next social program to be targeted for destruction. Because of medicare's enduring popularity with Canadians, however, few people with political ambitions will openly tell Canadians the truth about what is happening to our universal health care system. In fact, with the exception of Alberta's Ralph Klein, no politician who has dared to run on a campaign to privatize health care has been elected. Even Klein has had to sell his privatization schemes as just a way of improving medicare by shortening the waiting lists for medical services for ordinary working Albertans.

Yet the undermining of medicare began almost as soon as it became the law, and has escalated in recent years. In 1977, the Trudeau government, worried about the lack of upper limits to increases in health care costs, passed the Established Programs Financing Act (EPF). The new arrangement ended the fixed fifty-fifty cost-sharing formula to fund health care and made it clear that the federal government would not share costs with the provinces in new areas of spending, such as home care and drug benefits. It also gave notice that the federal government would not continue to cost-share hospital expenses after 1980.

The EPF replaced the fifty-fifty formula with a block funding arrangement that included a complicated system of transfer payments, grants, and tax points. In exchange for dollars, the federal government allowed the provinces to raise more taxes. Over time, the provinces wanted more and more tax point credits because these tax revenues did not have to be spent on health care. As a result, the federal government lost a fair amount of power over provincial health care spending. The block funding arrangement also allowed a steady reduction in federal cash transfers that started out modestly, but became huge over time, intensified by successive, massive cuts to health care spending.

By the time Brian Mulroney's Conservatives took power in 1984, the federal share of health care spending was down to 33 per cent, from 42 per cent in the mid-1970s. When the Chrétien Liberals took power in 1993, the proportion had been further reduced to 23.5 per cent. By 1998–99, it hit an appalling low of 10.2 per cent. This can come as no surprise, since between them, the Mulroney and Chrétien governments had cut $36 billion from federal transfer payments for health care. The new formula, together with the huge cuts to health care funding, weakened the ability of the federal government to enforce national standards in health policy.

Not coincidently, these cuts and the changes to the fifty-fifty formula began around the same time that the big business community launched the BCNI and its assault on social security. And the assault intensified as the influence of corporate Canada became more prominent in Ottawa's halls of power.

As University of Regina political scientist John Conway explains in an op-ed piece that ran in the Regina *Leader-Post* on February 17, 1999, the business lobby sees a strong central government as a real threat to the expanding political hegemony that business now enjoys. The devolution of social programs and the curbs on the federal government's ability to enforce national standards, as a result of the reduction of its financial participation in social programs, are key to a number of long-term corporate objectives.

"The business lobby," Conway says, "wants to continue downsizing social programs and the public sector, remove government as a central actor in the social and economic life of Canadians, and open up the social spending basket, especially the huge baskets in education and health, to the private sector. National standards and enforcement make this difficult." The provinces are more amenable to two-tiered health care systems, he adds – a second tier funded publicly and characterized by underfunding and low quality, and a first tier funded jointly by governments and consumers.

Living with Cuts

As predicted when these terrible cuts were enacted, they have had a powerful and negative impact on the public. A March 2002 study by Statistics Canada revealed that there has been a sharp increase in the number of Canadians who report problems getting health care in recent years. About one in eight Canadians reported difficulties getting health care between 2001 and 2002, up sharply from a similar study in the mid-1990s, when only one in twenty-four reported such problems. The study stated that both sexes and all age groups reported significant increases in unmet medical needs, although the greatest increase in dissatisfaction was among people aged thirty-five to sixty-four. The most pressing problems sited were long waiting lists and the unavailability of needed services.

These concerns were reflected in a February 2002 Ipsos-Reid poll, which found that eight in ten Canadians now say that their provincial health care systems are "in crisis." While they remain confident that they would get care if they had a serious problem, only half as many Canadians now feel that the quality of their health care is "excellent" or "very good" as did just a decade ago.

In a series of community forums across Ontario in 2001, the Ontario Federation of Labour and the Ontario Health Coalition heard the sad realities of the cuts on workers and their families. The Service Employees International Union, reporting on these hearings in its submission to the Romanow Commission, identified the biggest concerns: lengthy waits for cancer treatment; patients getting discharged "quicker and sicker"; emergency departments in chaos and ambulance workers searching for a hospital to which to take patients in crisis; seniors, young people, and others on limited incomes unable to afford their prescription drugs; serious staffing shortages in all health occupations; severe lack of services and supports for psychiatric survivors; and inadequate home care and long-term care services.

Dr. Gordon Guyatt, a medical professor at McMaster University, told the *Ottawa Citizen*'s Norman Greenaway on March 14, 2002, that these findings show that Canada's health care system is suffering from the "predictable result" of the major cuts to health care in Paul Martin's 1995 budget. He argued that the trend can only be reversed with the restitution of all the funds that were taken out of the system.

The CHST

The EPF was just the first of several key structural changes that undermined Ottawa's role in enforcing the provisions of the Canada Health Act. In his 1995 budget, Finance Minister Paul Martin introduced the Canada Health and Social Transfer (CHST), which combined transfers to the provinces for health, education, and social assistance into a single, smaller block grant and chopped the funds by a whopping 40 per cent over the next two years. Not only would there be less money for these services, but the provinces were given the right to determine where the money would be used; it was no longer tied directly to particular programs.

By withdrawing its direct financial commitment, the federal government surrendered its capacity to maintain national standards in all three areas. This was most obvious in the area of social assistance. By killing the Canada Assistance Plan (CAP), the federal government left the welfare field altogether. Although there never were legislated standards in the area of post-secondary education, federal transfers that were directly tied to this sector had given a role to the federal government. Now, this was gone. In the area of health care, of course, the Canada Health Act was still technically the law. But the act was always and only enforced by the shared-cost funding formula; now, with dwindling enforcement capacity, the federal government was suddenly much less able to defend medicare.

"Bluntly put," said the National Council of Welfare in a press release at the time, "the Canada Health and Social Transfer is the worst social policy initiative undertaken by the federal government in more than a generation."

Social Union

Not surprisingly, over the next several years, the provinces and territories grew increasingly impatient with this situation. Here were the Chrétien Liberals talking about their love of universal health and boasting about (and running elections on) their defence of medicare, all the while hollowing out the federal role in this area to pre-1950 levels. They were challenging the provinces' proposals of user fees and privatization schemes as if they were still delivering 50 per cent of the funding for medicare, when they were providing only 10 per cent. Several provinces were clamouring to take over full responsibility for health care and determine for themselves the level of privatization their citizens wanted.

And all were looking for ways to accommodate Quebec's desire for more autonomy in the delivery of its social and health services while riding on its decentralization coattails. So in February 1999, the federal government and the provincial premiers signed a framework agreement for an accord that has since shifted the balance of powers between the federal and provincial governments in the delivery of social security.

This so-called Social Union established several key principles: 1) the right of provinces to opt out of federal social programs with full financial compensation as long as the province pursues a program with "similar objectives;" 2) an end to the enforcement of national standards for social programs by Ottawa, to be replaced by a vague provincial consensus on standards with no meaningful enforcement mechanism; 3) strict limits on Ottawa's use of federal spending power for the creation of future social programs such as home care and daycare, requiring provincial consultation and consent for any new social programs; and 4) the transfer of almost the entire administration of social programs, including those heavily funded by Ottawa, to the provinces.

The only concession Ottawa could claim was that the provinces agreed in principle to the five pillars of the Canada Health Act. In exchange, the provinces were promised all of the above, plus the partial restoration of funding, particularly in the area of health care.

At first blush, these funds, which were announced in the 1999 and 2000 budgets, appeared to be substantial: total federal cash transfers through the CHST will increase from $12.5 billion in 1998 to $21 billion by 2005–06, and the health care portion of that total will go from $5.3 billion to more than $13 billion.

However, an analysis of these figures done by the Economics Division of the Library of Parliament shows that cash transfers in 2005–06, with the infusion of this new money taken into account, will not reach even the levels they were a decade ago. This is because the increase does not consider inflation or population growth. As well, some of the increase is a one-time supplement, and none of it is cumulative; rather, it is added to the newly set base of $15.5 billion (up modestly from the former base of $12.5 billion). As the Canadian Labour Congress explains in *Health Care Spending in Canada* (October 3, 2001), this is akin to giving workers yearly bonuses instead of wage increases on the wage grid. When this deal is up, a future government can go back to the base amount, leaving the provinces worse off than ever.

Furthermore, provincial public health costs will grow faster than the federal contributions, even with the infusion of new money. The additional cash transfers for health care will raise the federal share of health care spending from its current level of 13.8 per cent to 19.2 per cent in 2002–03. But the federal share will start to fall again the next year; by the fiscal year 2007–08, the share will be down to 16 per cent of health care spending. Unless clear steps are taken to reverse this trend, with the institution of the Social Union, and the continued decline of the federal government's financial participation, the role of the federal government in medicare will continue to erode.

Public Funds, Private Profit

The most dangerous aspect of the Social Union is that the provinces are now allowed to decide whether money earmarked for health care will be put into public or private services. This was the quid pro quo for their agreement to maintain the principles of the Canada Health Act. As long as they continue to guarantee their citizens access to hospitals and doctors, the provinces are now free to use federal transfer payments to contract out to private service deliverers.

A prime example is the $1 billion federal medical equipment fund that was established on September 11, 2000, as part of the Social Union agreement to allow the provinces to buy much-needed MRIs and other diagnostic machines. The Canadian Medical Association conducted a study, called *Prescription for Sustainability,* of how the money actually got spent by the provinces. The report, released in July 2002, found that almost half the fund – $468.8 million – has yet to be accounted for. Some of the money, says the association, may not even have gone to hospitals or been spent on any type of health care.

According to articles by Lisa Priest in the *Globe and Mail* (April 4 and June 10, 2002) and April Lindgren in the *Ottawa Citizen* (April 8 and June 16, 2002), New Brunswick bought paper shredders, shelving, fax machines, ice cube dispensers, cleaning machines, floor scrubbers, and a dishwasher with some of its $24.5 million share of the fund. Newfoundland bought bulk food transfer carts, a laundry truck, and a steamer cooker. The Alberta Mental Health Board bought woodworking saws, sewing machines, a projection screen, a radio, and camera equipment. Saskatchewan bought ice machines, while British Columbia purchased a washing machine, two hot water tanks, and bedside tables with its share of the funds.

Much of what did get spent on health care from the fund went to private companies. As reported by the *Globe and Mail* and the *Ottawa Citizen,* Ontario used more than $60 million of its share of the fund for grants to privately owned radiology clinics including major players listed on the stock market, and to purchase bathtubs, beds, and mattresses in for-profit long-term care facilities. DC DiagnostiCare Inc., a publicly traded, for-profit diagnostic corporation based out of Edmonton, received more than $9 million of the funds to buy forty-seven ultrasound machines, fifteen mammography units, and three X-ray machines.

Many in the health care community were angry. "God, this is awful. It's outrageous," said Normand Laberge, chief executive officer of the Canadian Association of Radiologists. "It's not what we would have expected with this fund . . . . Profit and medicare don't go together." Laberge said the use of these funds, intended for not-for-profit service providers, is a form of "money laundering." Henry Haddad, president of the Canadian Medical Association, agreed. "I think that money was intended to go to radiology sections, departments, which were housed according to what we feel are the standards. That money was not intended for for-profit radiology clinics."

To add insult to injury, DC DiagnostiCare Inc., which has been sold to another for-profit company called Canadian Medical Laboratories Ltd., has recently sold several of its 113 clinics in Ontario because they were not turning a profit. After receiving both local and federal subsidies, the company is closing its unprofitable clinics, leaving these communities without services. Local doctors and politicians, stung by these closures, say they are proof that profits and health care don't mix.

Ontario also gave $1.9 million from the public federal funds to private long-term providers owned by CPL Long-Term Care Real Estate Investment Trust, which trades on the Toronto Stock Exchange and earned more than $9 million in 2001; $1.7 million to twenty-four long-term care homes operated by Extendicare (Canada), a publicly traded company and one of the largest operators of long-term care in North America that made a profit of almost $7 million in 2001; more than $550,000 to eight centres operated by Leisureworld Inc., a privately held company; and $591,000 to Merivale Medical Imaging Inc. of Ottawa. Alanna Racine, manager of the Merivale clinic, couldn't believe her good fortune. As she told April Lindgren of the *Ottawa Citizen*, "We just lucked out that the government had this program. Normally, we just pay for everything," adding that the equipment they bought with the money they would have purchased in any case.

When challenged about the use of a federal, publicly financed fund being given to for-profit companies, the federal government said its hands were tied. "It's up to the provinces to spend the money as they wish," said Finance Ministry spokesman Jean-Michel Catta. "It's a block transfer and it's for their own priorities and their own needs. The provinces have to justify it to their populations." Gord Haugh, a spokesman for Ontario Health Minister Tony Clement, concurred. He said that federal government now had "no restrictions" on how the money is spent by the provinces.

Not good enough, say health care professionals in the public sector desperate for that money. "Do we have enough money to meet our needs? Certainly not," declared Richard Wilson, vice-president of finance at the Ottawa Hospital. "Could we have used the money they gave to private enterprises? Certainly!"

Another Broken Promise

When they signed the Social Union framework on February 4, 1999, the federal and provincial governments promised a full review of the contentious provisions within three years. The final paragraph of the document states: "By the end of the third year of the framework agreement, governments will jointly undertake a full review of the agreement and its implementation and make appropriate adjustments to the framework as required. This review will ensure sufficient opportunity for input and feedback from Canadians and all interested parties, including social policy experts, private-sector and voluntary organizations."

But well past the deadline, the promised review is nowhere in sight and citizens concerned about structural changes wrought by both the CHST and the Social Union have nowhere to take their message. In a paper she prepared in November 2001 for the Institute for Research on Public Policy, called *Citizen Engagement and the Social Union Framework: Fake or Genuine Masterpiece*, Susan Phillips, a professor of public administration at Carleton University, argues that the governments "failed miserably" to deliver on their promise of citizen involvement. Not only was there no review of the Social Union, she points out, there was no process for citizen feedback, as promised.

Phillips is highly critical of the Chrétien government's approach to consultation, basically reporting that it is superficial at best, non-existent most of the time. She writes, "To the extent that effective citizen engagement requires new mechanisms or institutions, or the reform of existing ones, the process is hampered by the Chrétien government's firm resistance to institutional change."

These structural changes to the delivery of Canada's health care were a serious blow to medicare's future. Yet very few Canadians even know that they took place. They are serious because, between them, the CHST and the Social Union did far more than transfer responsibilities for health care from one level of government to another; rather, they opened the way to a fundamental realignment of power from governments to markets and from the public sector to the private sector. Now, private-sector-friendly provincial politicians are free to spend federal public funding on their corporate friends. As waiting lists get longer, and services harder to come by, these companies are waiting in the wings to set up a parallel, competitive system to medicare.

5

Medicare in Retreat

The downloading of health care and social security to the provinces represents a new stage in Confederation. It has opened the door to widespread privatization, the introduction of user fees, and the steady move to a two-tiered parallel system. It has also caused a restructuring in the delivery of health care, one that has seen a diminished role for registered nurses and other front-line health care workers and a bloating of the upper levels of administration in hospitals.

Before examining the current privatization trend in Canada's health care system, it is important to distinguish between for-profit and not-for-profit private services. Most of Canada's doctors, clinics, and hospitals are currently not-for-profit private providers. Canada's mix of private delivery and public funding for health care can be traced back to the compromise made when medicare was first implemented in 1966. The original intent of medicare's drafters was a fully public system, one that would have been run like public education, with doctors and other professionals on staff.

But, as discussed in an earlier chapter, fierce opposition to this model caused its authors to compromise on medicare. Canada ended up with a hybrid system. Medicare is, in effect, a tax-based, public insurance system that pays for health services supplied mainly by the private sector.

As the Canadian Health Coalition reminds us, more than 95 per cent of hospitals in Canada operate as private, non-profit entities, and are run by community boards, volunteer organizations, municipalities, or regional health authorities. Hospitals are funded by governments to provide publicly insured hospital care. (This care currently does not include the full spectrum of outpatient rehabilitation, counselling, nursing, home care, dental care, or long-term care – a real problem resulting from the original medicare compromise.) Most doctors and specialists run private, not-for-profit practices and negotiate fee-for-service payments with provincial governments through their professional associations.

This is very different from the American system, which is based on a for-profit private model; not only does the HMO have to make enough profit to pay its staff and cover operational costs, it has to report to a board of directors and investors, and must, therefore, build in at least a 15 per cent profit annually. It is the move to this for-profit model in Canada that is threatening medicare and the five principles of the Canada Health Act, and around which a national citizens' movement is mobilizing.

Privatizing Medicare

For-profit private health services are steadily growing in Canada and account for an expanding slice of the health care pie. In the mid-1970s, according to the Canadian Labour Congress study *Health Care Spending in Canada* (October 2001), the combined public provincial and federal share of total health care spending was more than 75 per cent. A quarter-century later, it stood at only 70 per cent and the private sector represented almost

30 per cent of the total national health care budget. In Quebec, public funding is down to just 69.1 per cent of total spending; in Ontario, it has dropped to 66.9 per cent. The private sector now accounts for a bigger slice of the health care pie than the federal government does.

Although the December 2001 annual report of the Canadian Institute for Health Information showed that the private sector share as a percentage of the whole was falling slightly (due to the 1999–2000 federal infusion of public dollars into health care), and likely stands at 27.4 in 2002, the private sector is continuing to grow in Canada. Private spending on health care increased dramatically in the decade from 1988 to 1998; overall, in those years, private health care spending grew from $12.7 billion in 1988 to $25 billion in 1998 – an increase of 96 per cent.

The high proportion of private health spending in Canada is one of the reasons why the World Health Organization ranked Canada's health system in thirtieth place and not higher internationally in its 2000 World Health Report, behind France, Italy, Spain, Norway, Greece, the United Kingdom, and even Morocco. According to the report, 17 per cent of Canada's health care costs are paid out-of-pocket by patients at the point of service delivery, and private insurers pay another 11 per cent of the bills. In comparison, patients' out-of-pocket expenses account for only 3 per cent of the total bill in the United Kingdom.

The Faces of Privatization

For-profit private services are proliferating in Canada. Ideologically driven governments such as those in Ontario, British Columbia, and Alberta have used the funding crisis to prove that the public system doesn't work, and that the "more efficient" private sector can do the job better. One contract at a time, most provinces have steadily introduced the private delivery of at least some health care services, and some are now openly courting a fully private, for-profit hospital system.

Essentially, for-profit privatization takes three forms: private insurance, such as in the United States where private insurance companies compete with one another and have the right to turn a client down; private delivery, which would open up competition among health care professionals; and user fees, where patients pay for services out of their own pockets. The latter is often forced on people when governments delist services that were previously covered by public insurance.

These three could work in combination. A purely private system would have all three. Most privatization proponents in Canada swear they are not interested in the private insurance program. They say that Canada should keep our "single payer" system but allow competition among service providers. Some say all competitive services would be publicly funded; others are promoting user fees for these services to "top up" the public system. Many want a "parallel" system – a public system with "core" services for everyone and a "competitive" service for those who can afford to go to the front of the line and pay for better services.

The for-profit private sector currently operates in a variety of ways in Canada's health care system. As fewer services are listed on public plans, costs are shifted to employer-sponsored plans where premiums have been rising by 18 to 20 per cent per year, according to Colleen Fuller. Individuals and families, particularly those employed by small and medium-sized businesses, are being forced to shoulder more and more of the cost of medical care. According to the Canadian Labour Congress study, *Health Care Spending in Canada,* between 1990 and 2000, average spending on health-related care such as dental care, health insurance premiums, drugs, and delisted services grew by 31.3

per cent per person (compared to public expenditures on health care that grew by under half that per person in the same years).

These numbers represent real people caught in real crises. In December 2001, the *Prince Albert Daily Herald* ran a story by Betty Ann Adam, entitled "Cab ride saves heart attack victim's life," about an elderly man in Saskatoon having a heart attack who called a taxi rather than an ambulance because he could not afford the $250 ambulance fee. Fortunately, the taxi driver was a kind man who got the patient to the emergency department of the local hospital, helped him get inside, and didn't charge him for the cab ride.

In addition, public funding cuts are leading hospitals to narrow the scope of their "core business;" outpatient services are being privatized, and hospitals are contracting with the corporate sector to provide a broad range of "non-core" services such as lab work, MRI and CT testing, dietary services, and housekeeping. Private clinics, such as Canada Diagnostic Centres, now offer "virtual colonoscopy" services in Calgary for $1,000 and CAT screening in Vancouver for $1,200.

According to the *National Post*'s Tom Arnold (July 5, 2002), private clinics are establishing a tighter grasp on the health care market. Just three years ago, they captured 1 per cent of the MRI market; in 2002, they control more than 10 per cent. Tony Clarke and Darren Puscas of the Polaris Institute in Ottawa report that the for-profit health industry is growing in Canada. In their July 2002 report, *Waiting in the Wings: How For-Profit Health Corporations Are Planning to Cash-In on the Privatization of Medicare in Canada*, they give several examples. Toronto-based MDS, specializing in the marketing of medical goods and services, sells its services to 17,000 physicians and institutions through 380 locations in Canada. MDS now controls 55 per cent of the distribution of medical supplies in Canada and has cornered 30 per cent of the Canadian laboratory market.

More than 40 per cent comes from the public purse. MDS has a partnership with the world's largest for-profit hospital chain, Columbia/HCA, to install their auto lab system in Columbia's U.S. hospitals. MDS vice-president Robert Brecken says that the U.S. contacts are important. "Working with the United States provides us with the experience and knowledge of new directions we can carry into Canada."

A number of provinces are constructing private hospitals that will be built and operated by the private sector from public funds, and from whom government will then contract services. According to the Ontario Council of Hospital Unions brief to the Romanow Commission, financing is only available for private hospital construction if the right to build, own, and operate the facility is transferred to the financiers, who make 25 per cent profits on average each year for contracts running from thirty to sixty-six years. This money comes directly from the hospitals' operating budgets.

As well, as demand for home care and long-term care facilities grows, private companies are entering the market in force. According to Margaret MacAdam (in "Homecare: It's Time for a New Model," *Healthcare Papers,* Fall 2000), there are at least 663 private home care agencies now operating in Canada. Ninety-three per cent of them receive some public funding and at least half receive all their funding from the public purse. Extendicare, based in Markham, Ontario, one of the world's biggest for-profit nursing chains, also receives large public grants. As Tony Clarke and Darren Puscas report, Extendicare is building eight new centres in Ontario, where government is heavily subsidizing the project. Extendicare centres will now get $10.35 per day, per resident for 900 beds, totalling $700 million over twenty years from Ontario taxpayers. The company, which was slapped with the largest abuse and neglect verdict in Florida's history (worth U.S.$20 million, with an appeal that was settled for an undisclosed amount) over an Alzheimer's patient who died of a gangrenous bedsore, gave $37,000 to the Ontario Tories in political donations between 1995 and 1999. In September 2000, Extendicare divested its Florida holdings.

Medical Savings Accounts

Alberta is exploring Medical Savings Accounts, an idea that formed the basis for an experimental bill signed into law in 1996 by then President Bill Clinton and much favoured by current President George W. Bush. MSAs are also strongly advocated by the Fraser Institute and have been looked upon favourably by the Kirby Committee.

MSAs are based on the theory of "the tragedy of the commons" – the notion popular in business schools around the world that anything "free" or in the public realm is bound to be wasted. Because health care in Canada is public, goes the theory, it is probably being abused. Under a MSA system, governments would give individuals and families a set amount of money to spend on their own health care needs. A common amount being discussed is $1,800 per Canadian – $1,000 for minor medical needs and $800 to buy high-deductible catastrophic insurance policies.

The obvious conundrum with MSAs, reported health analyst Dale Holmberg of Moose Jaw, Saskatchewan at the Regina Council of Canadians' town hall meeting on March 4, 2002, is what to do with the money if it is not used for real health care needs. If it is allowed to be accumulated, healthy people will reap big rewards. If it must be returned if not used in a certain time, people will go "health shopping" rather than return it to the system – ensuring a boutique private-sector health market. The greatest danger, however, is that many people on fixed incomes – seniors, students, single parents, and others – will put off medical treatment and use the money for food, housing, or tuition.

As well, MSAs would benefit the insurance industry primarily because of the need for catastrophic insurance, thus giving the insurance companies a great deal of control over the system. Depending on private companies to provide for catastrophic illnesses would open Canada to the same insurance abuses, including cherry-picking for healthy clients, that now exist in the United States. Because less-healthy individuals would no longer be pooled with healthy individuals, insurance companies would dump many high-risk patients. MSAs would, in fact, propel any province into a full-blown private system. People would have to turn to private insurance companies; they would be paying user fees to service deliverers of their choice; and by "shopping" for services, they would be promoting competition among service providers.

Advocates say that MSAs are a big success story in Singapore, which implemented an MSA program in 1984. However, as S. E. D. Shortt of the Queen's University Centre for Health Services and Policy Research reports in "Privateers Hide Creed of Greed" (Francis Russell, *Winnipeg Free Press.* January 25, 2002), since then, per capita health care costs have risen faster, and the government has had to introduce supply-side restrictions because the demand-side was not dampened sufficiently by MSAs. The Singapore government had to restrict technology, put price caps on services, restrict the number of available beds, and tighten controls on physicians. A similar experiment in China was unable to control costs – the Chinese government had to limit diagnostic procedures, medications, and remuneration to health care providers.

As Holmberg points out, sides have formed on this issue in the United States. On one side are consumers' groups, teachers' federations, nurses' unions, churches, public health associations, disability groups, seniors, anti-poverty organizations, farmers, mental health associations, and many others. On the other side is the Archer MSA Coalition, a group named after former Texas Republican congressman Bill Archer, comprised of anti-tax coalitions, business groups, insurance companies, and right-wing think-tanks such as the Cato Institute.

Malik Hasan, M.D. and CEO of Foundation Health Systems in the U.S., is quoted in the *New England Journal of Medicine* in 1997 as saying: "We would make out like bandits, but as a physician, I have very serious concerns that we would be fragmenting the insurance pool . . . . We are going into MSAs because these things are going to be a gold mine . . . let there be no doubt. They are a scam and we will get our share of the scam."

These battle lines clearly show the ideological nature of this proposal. Medical Savings Accounts are not the benign tools they are being made out to be by proponents like Alberta's Ralph Klein. They are an immediate back door to a full, for-profit health care system in Canada.

Private Care Fallout

For-profit privatization in Canada will kill medicare. A publicly funded system will be doggedly undermined by the profit motive. Says the Service Employees International Union, Canada, in its Romanow submission:

> Mixing public and private financing in the same system creates a two-tiered system where the top tier provides allegedly superior service, preferential treatment and queue-jumping privileges for those who can afford them. Mixing public and private funding also provides a direct subsidy to private health corporations. For example, the Ontario government allows private facilities to receive public financing through the tax system *and* charge user fees at the same time. This is just one of the many ways that

corporations like Medical Data Services get a guaranteed share of the lucrative market.

The irony is that, while privatization proponents claim that their ideas will make health care delivery less expensive and more efficient, there is simply no proof that this is so. In fact, the proof lies almost exclusively in the other direction. The Canadian Union of Public Employees has studied privatization in the workforce extensively and was able to state unequivocally that it doesn't work. As the union argued in its submission to the Romanow Commission, "Research done by our union and other organizations strongly shows that privatization and con-tracting out of services is more costly and compromises accountability. Our union also conducted many studies showing that private, for-profit companies providing housekeeping, food services, laboratory and home care services are more expensive, less accountable and of lower quality than similar services pro-vided publicly."

There are many examples. For instance, the Alberta Consumers' Association studied the system for cataract eye surgery in the province. In its study, *Canada's Canary in the Mine Shaft: The Consumer Experience with Cataract Surgery and Private Clinics in Alberta, 2000,* it found that costs were highest and waiting lists longest in regions dominated by private health clinics. In Calgary, where 100 per cent of all cataract surgery is done in private clinics, patients had an average waiting period of sixteen to twenty-four weeks, even though Calgary has the most eye surgeons in the province. These patients could expect to pay an additional $250 to $750 fee. In contrast, patients only had an average waiting period of five to seven weeks in Edmonton, where 80 per cent of cataract surgery is performed in public facilities. And in Lethbridge, where all cataract surgery is done in public hospitals, waiting lists averaged four to seven weeks and patients received up-graded lenses for free.

An extensive survey of its members from 1997 to 1999 by the Manitoba Nurses' Union, the *Manitoba Nurses' Union Report on Long Term Care* (2001), found that nurses rated public long-term care facilities over private long-term care facilities in many areas, including provisions of services such as medications, bathing, feeding, treatments, and toileting, and in psychological support to patients and the supervision of staff.

In another Manitoba study, researchers examined medical records of more than 15,000 nursing home residents. They were looking for factors that increased a resident's chance of being sent to hospital, focusing on eight common medical conditions. Some of the factors were predictable – age, sex, and health conditions all affected hospitalization rates. What was most disturbing was that residents in for-profit nursing homes had significantly higher hospitalization rates than those in not-for-profit homes for four major conditions: dehydration, pneumonia, falls, and fractures.

This experience was confirmed by a Manitoba nurse who identified herself only as "S. Mason" in her testimony before the Romanow Commission:

> Until 1993, I always worked in the public health care system. Since then I have worked for a private company in a long-term care facility. I have come to believe that, in the private system, profit is number one. We never have enough staff – many of them leave to go to higher paying facilities. We are always told that there is not enough money to pay wages equivalent to these other facilities, yet the company always shows good profits. I understand they want to keep the shareholders happy so they will keep investing. There lies the problem; health care should NEVER be dependent

on profit. I firmly believe that health care, from birth through to death, should be publicly administered.

If medicare is privatized, said the Canadian Federation of Nurses Unions in its Romanow submission, the cost won't be reduced for governments, who will have to offer health insurance to their own workers. And business will come knocking on the taxpayers' doors looking for tax subsidies for the new health insurance costs they will incur. The providers of private health care will want tax breaks, too. Privatization is a losing proposition for all but the big insurance companies, private service providers, and drug companies.

It is not the public, non-profit part of the system that is driving costs up. When health care is treated as a public service, it can be delivered very well at low cost. When it is a business, it must realize a profit for someone in the system. Investors expect profits in the range of at least 15 per cent annually. The more the health care system is run as a business, the more it will be squeezed for profit all the way down the line. Ironically, to make money in health care, the private sector must promote opportunities for health care services; hence, it is more profitable to put the emphasis on illness rather than prevention.

Other Countries

Study after study in other countries show that market forces in health care cause costs to rise and efficiencies to fall. For-profit hospitals and clinics cost more to operate, charge higher prices, spend far more on administration, and often provide poorer services than non-profit institutions. Private operators must pay for expensive marketing campaigns and invest time in investor relations. And private clinics make waiting lists longer. Channelling funds to the private sector makes the wait for the vast majority, who can't afford private care, much longer. Private delivery, even if the insurance is maintained as a publicly funded service, bleeds the public system of some of its best professionals.

As the Canadian Labour Congress said in its submission to the Romanow Commission:

> It's no surprise that evidence from other countries shows that where delivery systems are a mixture of public and private, pressure is not taken off the public system. Rather, the large body of research evidence shows that waiting times for treatment increase and quality of service falls in the public system. As this occurs, more care takes place in the more expensive for-profit sector, raising health costs overall. It only stands to reason that if high-quality care with minimal waiting times for service was the norm in the public tier of care, almost no one would agree to pay privately for care . . . .
>
> To create demand for a private tier of care, the public system must be deficient. In order for that demand to be created, physicians must be able to practice in both the public and private systems and charge patients whatever they want to in addition to the reimbursement levels from the public plan. This provides a strong incentive to provide minimal care in the public system, thereby creating the waiting lists and public dissatisfaction that serve as the basis for creating a market for private care.

Sweden is often held up to Canadians as another, more positive model of privatization, because health care user fees have been introduced there successfully – or so the argument goes. But as Dale Holmberg points out, the Swedish example is not a particularly good one for privatization's proponents. For one thing, the Swedish fees are minimal. Canadians pay almost double the amount of user fees. More importantly, the Swedes start from a more level playing field. Sweden has a much lower rate of poverty than Canada and income inequality is nowhere near as great as it is in Canada. And in Sweden, unlike Canada, 100 per cent of the population is covered by public drug plans for more than 70 per cent of their drug needs.

Even so, user fees are a problem in Sweden. In November 2001, Roy Romanow visited Sweden to examine that country's experience with user fees. He told the *Ottawa Citizen*'s Mark Kennedy in an interview published on May 15, 2002, that Swedish patients are charged about CAD$35 when they visit a hospital and about half that when they use a primary care facility. While these modest patient fees don't raise much money (only about 4 per cent in total revenues) for the country's health care system, there is evidence, reported Romanow, that they prevent a large number of patients from seeking medical care. He said that one study, not yet complete, found that 20 per cent of Swedes did not visit their doctor even once in the previous year because of financial restraint.

New Zealand, another country that pro-privatization proponents like to use as a model, implemented a market-led health model with user fees in the late 1980s. Quality of care and access deteriorated so badly that health care became a major issue in recent elections. The Quebec Health Coalition reports that privatization boosters predicted up to a 30 per cent reduction in New Zealand's health care costs with privatization. In fact, there was a 30 per cent increase in costs as well as a substantial increase in waiting time for treatment. Health care spending as a share of the country's GDP rose while access to services decreased and out-of-pocket costs increased.

Privatization meant that New Zealanders were charged for visiting their family doctor. One recent study found that 20 per cent of respondents said they had a medical problem but did not visit a doctor due to cost. Fourteen per cent declined to have a needed test, treatment, or follow-up visit due to cost. And the country introduced hospital charges at the height of its honeymoon with privatization in the 1980s, but had to abandon the practice as impractical and unfair. As a result of these and other problems, New Zealand is now working to abolish the market-based health care system and return to a public health service.

Australia took another route, contracting out the management of its public hospitals to private, for-profit companies. As the Canadian Labour Congress stated in its submission to the Romanow Commission, reports by auditors general in two states confirmed soaring costs. One contract expected to save the public purse $15 million ended up costing an additional $93 million over the term of the contract – further, the company will own the hospital at the end of the term. In the second year of a twenty-year contract to manage hospitals, a health corporation launched a $10 million lawsuit against the state of Victoria, claiming that there was insufficient funding in their contract to provide services.

Waiting lists in the public sector have grown as doctors have been lured away from the public hospitals to the more lucrative private ones. One Australian auditor general has said that the money being pumped into the private sector is enough to eliminate the waiting lists in the public sector. With the privatization of their health care system, 40 per cent of Australians found themselves with no public insurance whatsoever and thus were relegated, when sick, to second-rate teaching hospitals.

About 80 per cent of patients in France, where doctors charge around CAD$40 per visit, take out supplementary insurance to pay for the charges. Until 2000, the other 20 per cent were left to fend for themselves and one in four reported that they were putting off health care because of the cost. The government, under public pressure, now provides free supplementary insurance for those on low incomes. The French, like the Americans, pay for health care through employment schemes; it costs an employer, on average, about CAD$120 a week for each employee, compared to Great Britain, where employers pay about CAD$10 a week through the national insurance program.

In Germany, where people on higher incomes have a choice between the public insurance offered by sickness funds and private insurance, two-thirds choose the public option because it is considered to be cheaper and less risky. No private scheme covers all the treatments one might need in a lifetime, and which the public system offers. Both Germany and France are tightening up regulations to cover private insurance companies, and are moving from employer-sponsored insurance toward a greater use of general taxation, such as Canada's system.

Ireland has a mix of public and private health care, and its health costs consume only 6 per cent of its GDP. As a result, Ireland is another country that pro-privatization proponents advance as a model for Canada. However, a recent report out of the University College Dublin School of Business reveals glaring inequalities in the Irish medical system. Patients in the public system face lengthy waiting lines while patients in the private system are seen in a few days. The author of the study, Ray Kinsella, states that "the public/private acute hospital system is inequitable, regressive and skewed against those who are most disadvantaged."

The study shows that access to private insurance is related to economic circumstances. About 60 per cent of people with a university education have private insurance, compared to only 37 per cent of those with high school education. About 68 per cent of people in professional categories have private insurance, compared to about 40 per cent of skilled labour and 18 per cent of unskilled manual labour workers.

The situation in Northern Ireland is particularly bad. According to the Canadian Labour Congress, more than 50,000 people are on the waiting list for hospital beds and the list is growing. The Royal Victoria Hospital was forced to cancel heart operations due to a shortage of intensive care beds. Watchdog agencies raise concerns about the number of emergency patients requiring beds who can't get them. Health professional organizations confirm the deterioration on access to services and their quality.

The British Turnaround

Under Margaret Thatcher, Great Britain introduced a parallel, competitive private system to that country's traditional system. The government continued to fund health care, albeit with greatly reduced resources, but allowed the private sector to bid for the provision of services. Competitive tendering and hospital outsourcing allowed private companies to profit from public monies devoted to the provision of health care. Patients with money could now go to the front of the line in a public hospital if they "topped up" doctors' salaries with additional funds, or go to superior private hospitals in England and abroad using their public funding allotment in addition to private funds.

Thatcher also dramatically cut funding to the public sector, and chronic underfunding plagued future governments. Between 1972 and 1998, a cumulative CAD$450 billion less was invested in health care in Great Britain compared to the European Union average. Britain only spends about 7.7 per cent of its GDP on health care, including the parallel private system introduced under Thatcher. Dr. David Wright of McMaster University stated in a *Globe and Mail* op-ed piece on December 12, 2000, that the drive to keep health care costs down has led to registered nurses' salaries so abysmally poor that recruitment and retention in the profession constitute a crisis.

Canadian health care worker Willemien Schurer told of her experience as a professional and a patient with Great Britain's system in a letter (June 26, 2002) to the *Globe and Mail*. Schurer recently gave birth in London in a public National Health Service hospital. (The private system would have cost £6000.) "The NHS hospitals are filthy," she wrote, "(think pre-Florence Nightingale), waiting times are intolerable and the staff is generally inexperienced and underpaid. Meanwhile, the private hospitals have experienced staff and hotel-like standards of cleanliness and service."

This experiment has proved very unpopular with the British people, who are deeply committed to their universal system, the National Health Service, first introduced in 1948. In 1997, Frank Dobson, then health secretary for the Labour Party government, said: "We must undo the damage the market has created – the never-ending paper chase of invoices, the flawed measures of efficiency, which concentrate on numbers of patients being treated rather than their outcome."

In a remarkable March 20, 2002, speech to the Social Market Foundation in London, U.K. chancellor Gordon Brown admitted that underfunding had put his country's health care in jeopardy. In his speech, he rejected user fees ("put starkly, user charges would mean the sick pay for being sick"), rejected private insurance ("it fails both the equity and efficiency tests"), and called for a recommitment to the original principles of the National Health Service:

> There could be no clearer statement of the principle of equity: the NHS was built around the cornerstone of universal access to health services, regardless of ability to pay. And at its core is the recognition of health care as a fundamental human right, not a consumer commodity . . . .

While private insurance covers some of the people some of the time, the evidence is that what people want is a health care system that covers all of the people all of the time. So people want the NHS at its best to combine the universality of access with universality of provision – and thus offer the best insurance policy in the world, without the ifs and buts of small print of private insurance policies but with, as far as possible, everything and everyone covered . . . .

And far from it being valid for the needs of the 1940s but not for now, a tax funded system is Britain's better way forward for coping with the challenges facing health care . . . . Reformed and renewed, it can be the most efficient and equitable guarantee of health care for millions, provide the better choices and service they need and become, for the British people, the best insurance policy in the world; the best for each of us and the best for all of us.

A month after this speech, the government of Tony Blair announced in the annual budget its plan to increase health care spending a whopping 7.4 per cent after inflation in each of the next five years, more than double the rate of other spending. Over these five years, Britain plans to have 15,000 more nurses, home care workers, and nurses, 30,000 more therapists and lab technicians, 10,000 new hospital beds, and 750 community health centres. Britain will eventually be spending close to 11 per cent of its GDP on health care as a result of this commitment; in an April 28, 2002, *Toronto Star* article, Michelle Landsberg reports that an amazing 72 per cent of voters, including a majority of Conservatives, support the health tax increase.

However, the Blair government has not totally abandoned the private model. A 1990 law called the NHS and Community Care Act established hospitals as independent business units in the public sector and required them to pay for their use of capital

through trusts that must make a surplus, after paying their operating costs and making a charge for depreciation, equal to 6 per
cent of the value of their land. Under the Private Finance
Initiative (PFI), all new hospitals are designed, financed, built,
and operated by a private-sector consortium. In return, the
National Health Service pays an annual fee to cover both the
capital cost, including the cost of borrowing, and maintenance
of the hospital and any non-clinical services provided over the
25- to 35-year lifespan of the contract.

A study entitled "Private Finance and 'Value for Money' in
NHS Hospitals: A Policy in Search of a Rationale?" published in
the May 18, 2002, edition of the *British Medical Journal* by
several leading British doctors and medical academics, led by
Professor Allyson Pollock of the University of Manchester,
showed that PFI has burdened the National Health Service with
a heavy debt that has diverted funds from clinical budgets,
forced the sale of assets, and resulted in dramatic cuts to bed
capacity and front-line staff.

Yet, the Blair government adopted this Tory initiative when
it came to power, in spite of many members of the Labour
Party who were critical of the policy. There are eighteen PFI
hospitals currently under construction in England. According
to the study, these new privately financed hospitals will have at
least 26 per cent fewer beds, 30 per cent fewer clerical staff,
and 38 per cent fewer porters, cleaners, and kitchen, laundry,
and maintenance staff than public hospitals. Says British jour-
nalist George Monbiot, "The result of the decline in beds and
staff will inevitably precipitate hospitals to reduce the number
of prolonged and expensive treatments they offer. Those who
can afford it will buy insurance and be treated privately. Those
who cannot will wait and wait for services which may never
materialize."

Devalued Workers

Another direct and negative consequence of the restructuring of our health care system is the devaluation of the role of registered nurses and other front-line health care practitioners. To reduce their own costs in the wake of government cuts, hospitals, clinics, and home care providers have frozen wages, laid off health care workers, replaced qualified registered nurses with unqualified personnel, shifted full-time workers to part-time, and contracted out core functions such as laundry, dietary, and cleaning services. Hospitals are dirtier and food standards have fallen.

For health care workers, conditions have steadily deteriorated under the combined effects of inadequate staffing levels, widening wage gaps, overwork, the intensification of work, shifting management strategies, and the undervaluing and underutilization of skills. These factors have all made recruitment and retention of health care workers in the Canadian system increasingly difficult.

A January 2002 study entitled *The Health Care Workplace in Crisis,* by the Ottawa-based Canadian Policy Research Network (and partially funded by Health Canada), found that the health care sector is one of the unhealthiest to work in because of widespread stress and uncertainty. Researcher Grant Schellenberg found that the people responsible for keeping the rest of the population healthy suffer from more burnout, fatigue, and stress-related ailments than people in almost any other sector. Working conditions have deteriorated to such an extent that the sector will face massive labour shortages in the near future. "For the past decade," states the report, "the call has been to ask these people to do more with less." There will come a time when they will be unable to continue, it adds.

Such conditions are taking a toll on hospital standards.

Ottawa Citizen reporter Sharon Kirkey catalogued the new dangers in Canada's hospitals in a special report (March 3 and 4, 2001). Hospitals have become a breeding ground for deadly bacteria, she found, including drug-resistant superbugs. More than 8,000 Canadians are expected to die each year from hospital-based infections, and the cost of treating patients for infections acquired in hospitals reached an estimated $1 billion in 2001. According to the Community and Hospital Infection Control Association of Canada, about 200,000 patients will suffer from infected surgical wounds, blood infections, and antibiotic-resistant organisms after they are admitted to hospital in 2002.

Medical analysts say the cause is clearly related to shortages and funding cuts. The sickest patients, more at risk of spreading infection, are put in close quarters to other patients in overcrowded hospitals. Beleaguered staff have less time for basic hygiene practices, such as hand-washing and keeping patients clean. Compounding the problem is the shift towards shorter hospital stays. A British auditor general study found that 50 to 70 per cent of surgical wound infections appear after the patient is sent home.

Demoralized Nurses

Perhaps no group has been harder hit with the restructuring than front-line nurses. According to the Canadian Federation of Nurses Unions, there are currently about 232,000 registered nurses in Canada. They represent the largest single occupational group in the health workforce and provide 75 per cent of the hands-on professional care in the system today. However, instead of having the clout that these numbers should warrant, in the current competitive, power-based health care climate, nurses have been scrambling to deal with a system that doesn't value or pay them adequately. In fact, in many circles, the best nurse is a silent nurse – one that doesn't rock the boat or question the growing power structures of medical institutions.

Canada is now short about 20,000 registered nurses. They are dropping out of the profession like flies. There has been a reduction of more than 50 per cent in the annual number of graduates from nursing schools over the past decade. Of those who graduate, three out of ten depart the nursing profession or the country within five years of graduation. Almost 30 per cent of practising nurses under the age of thirty-one are considering quitting the profession within the next year. And it is going to get worse. A new study by statistician Eva Ryten for the Canadian Nurses Association released June 20, 2002, predicts that there could be a shortfall of 113,000 nurses in Canada by the year 2016.

There are many reasons for this development. Registered nurses are poorly paid. They have been sacrificed in cost-cutting exercises, and qualified nurses have been replaced by unqualified caregivers in many provinces. Where home care has been privatized, registered nurses have had to accept lower wages, part-time work, and no benefits in order to stay employed. As a consequence, almost half the registered nurses in Canada are now part-time or casual. Those who still have full-time jobs are overworked, overstressed, and disillusioned. According to the Canadian Nurses Association submission to the Romanow Commission, registered nurses lose more time to illness and injury than members of any other profession in Canada. The entire nursing workforce is aging (the average age is 43.4 years) and approaching burnout.

Nurses report mandatory callbacks, pressure to work overtime hours, and increased anxiety and aggressiveness in the patients waiting in emergency rooms. A 2001 five-country study of 43,000 nurses, as cited by the Ontario Nurses' Association in its brief to Romanow, found that more than 26 per cent of

Canadian nurses reported they didn't have time to teach their patients and their families necessary basic care skills, and almost 50 per cent were left without time to develop or update patient care plans. Perhaps not surprisingly, nurse absenteeism increased 25 per cent between 1986 and 1999.

The Ontario Nurses' Association told the Romanow Commission that the shift from full-time to part-time and casual work has meant that the patient-to-nurse relationship no longer exists, and the continuity of care has been compromised. On any day, said the ONA, a patient may see several nurses, which is both frustrating and potentially dangerous to both patients and nurses. "Nurses were the first to experience the effects of health care cutbacks. Thousands of nurses have been displaced, have lost their jobs, and have experienced a shift of their work status from full-time to part-time and casual – a pattern that continues today."

The Canadian Nurses Association confirmed these patterns in its brief before the Romanow Commission: "Keeping nurses in the system is increasingly difficult due to inadequate support for continuing education and development; insufficient recognition of nursing knowledge and skills; instability of positions (casualization); lack of career opportunities; and workplace policies that often ignore quality of life and the need to balance work and private life."

The Emergency Nurses Association of Ontario echoed the same sentiments in their presentation to Romanow: "Like Wal-Mart, our hospitals have kept us on a need-to-work basis, without benefits and guaranteed full-time hours. Some have maintained full-time hours, but on-call, mostly on weekends, holidays and short notice; this does not provide quality of life for the nurse or her family."

Silenced Voices

There are many in the profession who believe that the denigration of the role of nurses is no accident. They point out that nursing departments and senior positions in nursing were removed with the restructuring of many provincial hospitals and health care systems. The result is that registered nurses now operate more than ever under the direct control of doctors and administrators. The Emergency Nurses Association of Ontario says that nurses have become an "invisible commodity" in our restructured system.

Doris Grinspun, the executive director of the Registered Nurses Association of Ontario, has an explanation. In her Ph.D. dissertation paper, she says the new, denigrated role of registered nurses in the health care system is a reflection of the struggle between a caring paradigm that requires providing appropriate resources to enable care, and a health care system conceptualized as an industry where a concern for cost-cutting dominates. Registered nurses insist on quality care; they don't look to the bottom line. They see the patient as a whole person and have fought the "unbundling" of nursing care into a series of tasks distributed to various untrained and unlicensed "service providers." The new system in many hospitals that operate as a business, says Grinspun, is the "antithesis of patient-centred care."

Lieutenant Colonel (Ret'd.) Shirley Robinson, who served as a nursing officer in the Canadian military for thirty years and was director of nursing at the National Defence Medical Centre, finds this situation ironic. Registered nurses are assumed not to understand the hard realities of the bottom line, she says, even though when they ran hospitals, they were clean, efficient, safe, and inexpensive. Service was the goal. There were inspectors to ensure cleanliness, guard against wasteful practices, and fight infections.

Their main focus was the patient, says Robinson, and they knew what the patient needed. With registered nurses so over-stretched, she asks, who is now defining quality care? "Not the doctors, you can bet on that. And not the CEOs. They never wiped a bum in their lives. Now the personal, physical, emotional, and spiritual lives of patients are neglected." Robinson says that today, physicians, provincial governments, hospital CEOs, and hospital boards have all come to have too much power in the system. The power, she argues, should be in the hands of the public through those who work on the front lines in health care.

Whether by design or accident, the change in the status of nurses has meant the loss of their voices – just as registered nurses, as a group, were becoming more powerful. It is hard to be part of a "caregiver family" when you are running between three jobs. Any solution to Canada's health care problems will require, according to nurses and other front-line health care workers, more respect, better working conditions, and a power-ful voice in the creation of solutions to our health care problems.

Patient Fallout

These conditions, of course, in turn affect the quality of care given to patients. A study by the Institute for Clinical Evalua-tive Sciences published March 22, 2002, in the *Canadian Journal of Nursing Research* shows that nurses make a significant difference in whether patients live or die. In fact, said the study, a shortage of experienced nurses is costing lives. The researchers tracked thirty-day death rates for nearly 47,000 hospitalized patients discharged from acute-care beds in Ontario. When the proportion of registered nurses in hospi-tals was increased by 10 per cent, researchers found there were five fewer patient deaths for every 1,000 discharged patients.

Lower death rates were also associated with each additional year a nurse spent on the same clinical unit.

Lead author Ann Tourangeau, a professor of nursing at the University of Toronto, said that this report provides the necessary evidence to back up what nurses have been saying all along: their care saves lives. "We never really looked at outcomes, such as mortality, because we always thought nursing doesn't make a difference in patients' living and dying. In fact, we found that they do." Tourangeau found that the two most important factors are the number of registered nurses on staff and the years of steady experience on a unit. She added that substituting registered qualified nurses with unlicensed assistant personnel, as many hospitals did in Ontario, was a deadly mistake.

The Saskatchewan Union of Nurses said much the same thing in its presentation to the Romanow Commission. Safe patient care, positive clinical outcomes, and quality service to the public depend on healthy work environments for nurses and other health care providers, they reported. As an example, the union told of how fifteen beds out of a total of twenty-five at the Pediatric, Palliative, and Medical units of the North Battleford Union Hospital have been forced to close because of a severe shortage of nurses in the province. Often there is only one registered nurse caring for very sick children who require constant monitoring. The union said that nurses report that while working alone, they must often take an extremely ill child in a stroller, sometimes attached to an IV, while they do their rounds to attend to other palliative care patients.

Tom O'Brien, who works with the Canadian Federation of Nurses Unions, says that the biggest irony lost on the movers and shakers who have made these decisions is that registered nurses are consistently rated by the public as the most honest and reliable professionals of all – more trustworthy than physicians. In fact, polls show that two-thirds of Canadians would be willing to forgo tax cuts to increase the number of nurses, and nine in ten would cut direct aid and tax breaks to business to increase the number of nurses on the job.

Nurses across the country are unanimous in their demands for better treatment. As the Ontario Nurses' Association told the Romanow Commission, "Nurses have suffered the brunt of government funding cutbacks. Many have decided against returning to nursing in Canada or have left the profession. Concerted efforts by governments and employers must be undertaken to bring nurses back into our public health care system and to keep our nurses nursing. This requires national leadership incentives and recognition of the valuable role nurses perform in delivering health care services in Canada."

Top-Heavy Health Care

As the role of nurses and other front-line health care workers has been downgraded, a whole new bureaucracy has grown in our medical institutions that is costly, highly competitive, and hierarchical. To understand how this happened, we need to remember the compromise that was reached in 1966 when medicare was first introduced. Because of strong opposition to a fully funded program, only visits to doctors and hospitals were insured. All other services, from home care and dental care to eye checkups and drug plans, were left up to individual provinces who put into place a patchwork of public/private services now mostly going private.

In only insuring doctors and hospitals, and not community clinics and home care, Canadians have put most of our energy, expertise, funding, and other resources into the part of the system oriented to doctors, medicine, hospitals, and illness – rather than into a system that might have been more oriented to nurses, wellness, community service, and illness prevention.

This has meant that gradually Canadians have been saddled with unnecessarily high costs for their health care.

In its 2001 annual report the Canadian Institute for Health Information clearly shows that the growth in health care spending from 1998 to 2001 was greater than in any other four-year period in the past twenty-seven years, and that costs are going to continue to climb. (However, it is important to remember that, even with this growth, health care spending in Canada is still lower as a percentage of GDP than it was in 1991.) The study found that hospital costs account for the largest share of expenditures, although they are decreasing over time, as many people are being sent home to be cared for. The major factor in *rising* costs, says the institute, is spiralling drug prices (see Chapter Nine) and wage hikes for health care administrators and physicians.

As the system has become more hospital-, doctor-, and specialist-centred, it is also becoming much more expensive. Patients are forced to go through doctors for help they could find through less expensive registered nurses, nutritionists, social workers, and other salaried caregivers. Some CEOs of hospitals are making $500,000 a year, and administrative costs due to the high salaries paid to professional managers in medical institutions are constantly increasing.

While most doctors are hard-working, honest, and conscientious, the system has allowed some to rake in huge salaries and perks, such as bonuses and houses offered as incentives to relocate. In Ontario, more and more doctors are being exempted from government-imposed caps on how much individual physicians can bill, according to documents obtained by Lisa Priest under the Freedom of Information Act, and reported in the *Globe and Mail* on January 5, 2002. In 1999–2000, 471 Ontario doctors were exempted; several of these billed in the million-dollar range. And uncontrolled drug prices have allowed the big pharmaceutical companies to cream off huge profits as prices rise and rise some more.

The fee-for-service system under which doctors operate is also costing Canadians a lot of money, and reducing their care. In *Revitalizing Medicare,* Michael Rachlis, Robert Evans, Patrick Lewis, and Morris Barer refute the common assumption of a doctor shortage in Canada. They say that Canada now has more doctors than ever before – one doctor to every 550 Canadians compared to one to 950 in the 1960s. The apparent contradiction, these medical experts and practitioners argue, can be explained by the fact that, on average, each doctor is providing less comprehensive services. In general, fee-for-service schedules pay much more for procedural than for cerebral services.

"Put more crudely" they say, "the health care system pays more to cut and prod than listen and think and during the past thirty years, physicians have responded to that by gradually shifting their practices away from those services that take up relatively more of their time per dollar of reimbursement."

Disappearing Family Doctors

In a spring 2002 special series, the *Toronto Star* concurred. Authors Karen Palmer and Vanessa Lee report that family doctors – who are still many Canadians' only link to the system, as well as being necessary for referral to a whole range of specialists – are a dying breed. Many in the cities have stopped doing rounds at hospitals now dominated by specialists. More and more are refusing to deliver babies, and the Institute for Clinical Evaluative Sciences reports that there has been a steady erosion of doctors prepared to make house calls in the last decade.

One by one, family doctors are giving up on patients. As

many as two-thirds say they no longer accept new patients, according to a 2001 survey by the College of Physicians of Canada. While the number of specialists in fields such as ophthalmology, radiology, and dermatology continues to rise, there is a shortage of as many as 3,000 family doctors in Canada – a number expected to soar to 6,000 by 2011. Family doctors, as a group, are growing older, and as they retire, many are not being replaced. And more and more medical students are snubbing family medicine in favour of more lucrative and prestigious specialty areas. As Palmer and Lee report, young doctors, saddled with huge education debts, are "following the money" into walk-in clinics, where they can treat more patients with simple problems, or they choose to provide short-term relief in desperate communities paying premium rates.

All this is happening, of course, as the trend to home care is growing. An increasing number of seniors who are cared for at home rather than in institutions are ever more in need of family doctors and home care services. Patients are also desperate for psychological counselling, the result of a dearth of psychiatrists and a system severely lacking in mental health services.

In Ontario alone, nearly one million residents don't have a family doctor. By 2010, this number is expected to double. As a result, many rural communities and smaller cities are desperate for family practitioners. Municipalities have entered into an expensive bidding war for the dwindling number of family doctors, offering scholarships, free golf memberships, prepaid private school fees for children, interest-free loans, fully equipped offices, free accommodation, and cars.

This shortage of family doctors is part of the same new hierarchy in health care that has downgraded the role of nurses. Family doctors are largely isolated from the rest of the system – outsiders facing a balkanized medical structure, struggling to get timely information on their patients' conditions and get them the care they need. Many are alienated from the very system through which they are supposed to lead their patients. Dr. Jamie Meuser, chief of family medicine with Toronto East General Hospital, is highly critical of the system in which he finds himself. "When we say we have no system, what we really mean is that we have hundreds of systems. Every time people go to another part of the system there's a gap they can fall through."

In *Caring for Profit,* Colleen Fuller asserts that these gaps are not a surprise. Allowing the creation of a mixed public/private health care system in Canada has burdened Canadians with unnecessarily high costs and prevented governments from being innovative. She writes:

> Canada's health financing arrangements do not allow the governments that fund the system to manage services provided by private entities or to prevent private companies from duplicating services delivered in the hospital sector. Governments cannot tell companies to locate in sparsely populated rural communities or to ensure that a full spectrum of population health needs are met, because the mandate of private corporations is to provide a service if the service provides a return on investment – no more and no less.

The restructuring that has taken place in Canada's health care system is making it expensive, cumbersome, impractical, and a bad place to work for many people. For proof, we need to look to the patchwork quilt that is replacing medicare in the provinces.

6

The Provinces Go Private

Years of wrangling over jurisdiction between the provinces and the federal government have not served Canadian citizens well. Right-wing provincial governments have whipped up anti-Ottawa sentiment to cover their own severe social spending cuts and hide their privatization intentions. In turn, federal governments have blamed the provinces for not delivering social and health services at the same time as federal funding was being cut.

As successive federal governments have cut transfer payments to the provinces for health care, provincial governments have responded by chopping their own funding to hospitals, laying off registered nurses, and closing beds. Analyses of health care funding show that, while the federal government's contribution to the total health care budget has steadily diminished over the last two decades, so has that of the provinces and the territories.

This of course goes contrary to the lament of the provinces that they are spending so much more money on burgeoning health care services. A study done by University of Waterloo political science professor Gerard Boychuk for the Romanow Commission and released on July 10, 2002, found that provincial government spending on health care in 2001 comprised

6.2 per cent of the GDP, down one-half percentage point from 1991. The huge increases in spending in the last five years, in fact, were only making up for the massive cuts that took place in the middle part of the decade, and have not kept up with the growth in the economy. And both levels of government have instituted large tax cuts, thereby reducing the funding base for future needs. As Gordon Guyatt of the Medical Reform Group wrote in a July 9, 2002, editorial in the *Globe and Mail,* the provinces have used federal health transfers to fund the tax cuts that have drained provincial revenues by $20 billion for 2001–02. And the federal government has brought in $100 billion in tax cuts in the last five years.

In spite of the completely open nature of many provincial privatization schemes taking place, including user fees and extra-billing, the federal government refuses to act. Perhaps this is because, as the auditor general's office has strongly pointed out in its last three annual reports, the Chrétien government is keeping no record of where privatization is taking place or whether any of these practices are in violation of the Canada Health Act. It may also be because, when the Canada Health Act was passed in 1984, clear criteria for "medically necessary services" were never established. Provinces are now taking advantage of this grey area to privatize.

The downloading of health care and social security to the provinces has also pleased the corporate community, which wants the responsibility for social welfare to reside with lower levels of government. At the time the CHST was created, André Berard, CEO of the National Bank of Canada, noted that lower levels of government do not have Ottawa's ability to set monetary policy, and thus, they have far less budget flexibility. "It is only by decentralizing the state even more that we can obtain more efficient public services and a permanent reduction in deficits," he said. "We should give the power to spend to those who have little power to borrow." In this way, decentralization facilitates the privatization of health care services.

All of Canada's provinces and territories have been forced by the federal cuts to reduce their health care services. But three provinces – Alberta, Ontario, and British Columbia – have used the funding crisis to promote their own ideologically driven privatization agendas.

Alberta

Alberta, of course, has been Canada's Petri dish of privatization. Premier Ralph Klein was the first elected politician to openly promote private health care services. Since 1993, the Klein government has supported massive privatization schemes in "non-core" hospital services. In a major January 2002 report entitled *A Framework for Reform*, the Premier's Advisory Council on Health Care, headed by former deputy prime minister Don Mazankowski, called for an overhaul of the province's health services, including user fees and delisting of formerly covered services. To sell these controversial recommendations, the Klein government is spending $1 million on a public campaign, including a comic book and radio and TV ads.

In a preliminary report published a year earlier, the Premier's Advisory Council called the Canada Health Act an "unregulated monopoly" antithetical to competition and recommended "opening up" the system to an "innovative blend of public and private health services." Referring to the citizens of Alberta as health care "customers," the council advised the government not to let "fear of private medicine" get in the way of making the necessary changes to the delivery of health care.

The council needn't fear. For, as health economists and researchers Kevin Taft and Gillian Steward have documented in their 2000 study for the Parkland Institute, *Private Profit or the*

Public Good: The Economics and Politics of the Privatization of Health Care in Alberta, the government of Ralph Klein is determined to bring in a for-profit system of health care in Alberta regardless of the wishes of the people and the clear evidence that a for-profit system costs more and serves fewer people.

When he came to power in 1993, Klein immediately slashed the health care budget by 22 per cent and the welfare budget by 40 per cent, and laid off 6,000 public service workers. Many hospitals and almost half of the province's hospital beds were closed. More than 3,000 registered nurses were fired and thousands more were shifted from full-time to part-time, casual status. The remaining front-line health care providers were forced to accept wage freezes and rollbacks.

Psychiatric hospital and mental health clinic budgets were slashed as well; thousands of patients were sent into the community with no services to help them adjust. Seniors in public care facilities were being cared for by unsupervised and unqualified staff. The public drug plan was slashed and now covers only a portion of the population. With the tight supply of acute care beds in Alberta, it is now normal for many emergency wards to house patients for twenty-four to seventy-two hours while they wait for a space in the hospital.

Horror Stories

In the wake of the cuts came terrible stories of people dying after having been turned away from closed or crowded emergency wards. Waiting lists for treatment soared. Emergency departments turned away desperate patients. Some lost fingers and toes because of delays in treatment. New mothers were sent home from hospital the day they gave birth; women having radical mastectomies were in and out the same day with no follow-up care. A man dying of cancer was sent home from hospital with no home care – he didn't qualify, he was told, because he had a wife. Another man had to care for his very ill and fragile ninety-year-old mother, including administering enemas, in a city hospital as the nursing staff were so overworked. A daughter slept on the floor in the nursing room after her mother's hip surgery, as the staff couldn't provide even minimal care.

The lone nurse on duty in a pediatric ward was called to an emergency, leaving the maintenance man in charge of the floor. In another, a nurse was forced to put a child with pneumonia into a stroller and roll the child around with her on her rounds. A two-year-old child died while in transit to a distant hospital because her local facility was swamped. At the Sturgeon Hospital near Edmonton, an eleven-year-old boy was admitted with a concussion, a fractured pelvis, and internal injuries after being hit by a car. Because of budget cuts, no pediatric nurse was on duty from 11 p.m. to 7 a.m., so the boy's parents had to stay with him through the night to check on his vital signs, monitor his intravenous drips, and record all information on a chart.

A patient admitted to a hospital was put in a bed that had not been changed since the previous occupant had died; the bed-sheets were still soiled with his body fluids. An elderly pensioner was flown by air ambulance from Medicine Hat to Edmonton for a liver transplant, but he was told to find his own way from the airport to the hospital. Because he was so late arriving, the liver was given to another patient. The man was then told he had to make his own way back to Medicine Hat. He was able to borrow only enough money to get him to Calgary, and had to go without food for the entire trip. His wife had to borrow money so she could drive the 300 kilometres to Calgary to pick him up.

When confronted in the Legislature about these and other terrible stories, Ralph Klein just shrugged and said, "Maybe some will die . . . that would be unfortunate. But that might have happened anyway."

The United Nurses of Alberta asserts that Albertans went from being patients, to customers, to consumers, and then to victims of health care, all in the space of a few years. Needless to say, working conditions for nurses and other front-line health care workers dramatically deteriorated. The UNA documented conditions that are abusive to nurses and patients alike. Many registered nurses were replaced by "generic" workers in homes and hospitals. "Continuing care aides" with only four hours of training were administering medications in seniors' facilities. Cleaning and maintenance staff were bathing, feeding, and shaving patients in understaffed hospitals. In one long-term care residence, the nursing aide had to bathe six bedridden patients from the same bucket of soapy water before the pail could be emptied and refilled with clean water.

Turnaround

The people of Alberta were at their wits' end and open to any innovation that might ease the trauma in their health care system when the Klein government started delisting services and introducing privatized health services. At its 1995 annual convention, the Progressive Conservative party voted to turn some of the closed hospitals over to the private sector. Private eye clinics started competing with the public system; one even asked prospective customers to sign a petition in favour of legislation extending private clinics throughout the province.

Distressingly, the federal government, although bound under the act to uphold universality, gave its blessing to these developments. In 1996, the Chrétien government signed a "Working Understanding" with the Government of Alberta to end a dispute over the province's practice of allowing private eye clinics to charge patients. Among the "Twelve Provincial Principles" included in the "Understanding" endorsed by the federal government were: a strong role for the private sector in health care, both "within and outside" the publicly funded system; the right of consumers to purchase health services outside assessed need; options for private clinics to become completely private or to enter into any of a variety of funding arrangements with the public sector to cover the full costs of insured services; and, the right of physicians to practise in both the private and public systems.

Then, in 1997, in what appeared to be an abrupt turnaround, the Klein government began pouring money back into the system. By 2000, spending levels on health care were back to where they had been a decade before. It is hard not to suspect an agenda. This is an excellent example of the tried and true recipe to soften up a population for privatization of what has been a popular public service. Public services in Alberta were cut to the bone and allowed to become so run-down they no longer served their constituency. Many Albertans lost faith in their health care system as they no longer realized a personal benefit from it, and became willing to shift their support to a private option. Then the tap was turned on again.

The next big move was the passage of Bill 11, which became law in 2000. Dishonestly named the Health Care Protection Act, Bill 11 allows for-profit hospitals to provide surgical services covered under the provincial health plan, a first in Canada. Physicians are now allowed to practise in both the public and for-profit private systems, and several designated hospitals are being converted from non-profit to for-profit status. Under Bill 11, commercial institutions will now have their fees paid partially by provincial health insurance – in other words, they'll receive subsidies from the public purse. People who can top up this public money with their own will go to the front of the line; this totally undermines the principles of universality and accessibility that are the foundation of the Canada Health Act.

Ralph Klein could not have passed Bill 11 without the complicity of the federal government. Robyn Blackadar, a senior Alberta government official with Alberta's Health Policy Division, stated in a memo that was obtained under the Access to Information Act and cited in the Alberta Health Policy Division's *Fact Sheet: Health Resources Group, Incorporated* (March 17, 1997), "Without Health Canada's agreement on the principle that it is acceptable for physicians to work in both the public and private sectors, the existing policy [Bill 11] would have been impossible to implement."

Richard Plain, a University of Alberta economist, told Mark Kennedy of the *Ottawa Citizen* in an interview published on February 18, 2000, that the federal government traded medicare off with this Act: "It's the biggest blunder I've seen in the administration of medicare over 30 years." Then-health minister Diane Marleau, who was replaced by the more accommodating David Dingwall early in 1996, told Kennedy that she was heavily pressured by her own bureaucrats in 1995 to cave in to Alberta's demands, which she refused to do: "My DM (deputy minister) at the time came up to me and said, 'We have this big win. We have an agreement with Alberta, blah, blah, blah.' So she pulls out these principles on the plane, I'll remember this as long as I live, and wants me to sign off on them. This is on a plane to a fed-prov meeting. I looked at them and I said no." The compromise of the "Working Understanding" negotiated between Dingwall and Alberta paved the way for Bill 11 and the other private enterprises now underway in that province.

Accelerated Agenda

Ralph Klein's government is now moving ahead with some of the measures contained in the controversial Mazankowski report, *A Framework for Reform*. In fact, when the report was tabled in January 2002, the premier announced that he would not wait for the Romanow Commission report to be tabled to begin the implementation of parts of the report. To prove it, he immediately endorsed the spirit of the report and announced increases in health premiums that could cost some families another $500 a year. He also set up an "expert panel" on delisting services now covered by medicare, chaired by Bob Westbury, a retired TransAlta executive.

In its analysis, *Real Reform or Road to Ruin?*, January 2002, the Alberta citizens' group Friends of Medicare says that *A Framework for Reform* begins with a major flaw: it is based entirely on the assumption that the current system is fiscally unsustainable and facing imminent collapse. Mazankowski states that by 2008, the Government of Alberta will be spending half its budget on health care. Using new statistics from the Canadian Institute for Health Information and Statistics Canada, Friends of Medicare shows that this is a great exaggeration. In fact, because of its deep budget cuts of the mid-1990s, Alberta's per capita spending on health care fell below the national average and stayed there until 2001. Even now, Alberta spends only about 5 per cent of its provincial GDP on health care, the lowest proportion of any province in Canada.

An even bigger flaw, says the group's expert analysts, is that the Mazankowski report presents privatization as the only solution to existing problems. The report says that medicare is an "unregulated monopoly," and calls for more private-sector involvement, the delisting of many currently listed services, user fees, and more choice, competition, and "accountability" in the system. It recommends increasing health care premiums to cover 20 per cent of Alberta's health care budget, up from the current 11 per cent. (Alberta and British Columbia are the only provinces that charge health care premiums.) The report also calls Albertan citizens "customers" and proposes that an "expert panel" be established that would decide on which currently listed health services should be delisted. It recommends that physicians should be able to work in both the public and private systems.

The most contentious recommendations of the Mazankowski report centres around how to structure patients' payments for treatment: the report calls for further study on "medical savings accounts" (MSAs), a plan by which a set amount of cash would be put into a separate account for each individual Albertan's yearly health costs. Money would be deposited into the account each year, either through the payment of premiums or through a joint payment of premium and government supplement. This money would then be paid out for the individual's health care, with leftover funds being rolled into the next year. If more money is required than is in the account, then the individual would have to pay his or her own costs up to a predetermined maximum, at which point the government might chip in.

The adoption of this proposal would take the government out of the health insurance sector altogether, opening it up to private insurance companies and the governance of the trade agreements. As argued in Chapter Five, because the leftover money is rolled over into the account for the next year, MSAs have the effect of rewarding the healthy and punishing the ill. People could "shop around" for services with the money: healthy people would be able to buy top-of-the-line diagnostic and preventative health care services; those suffering from a chronic illness, or a catastrophic illness early in life, would end up scraping the bottom of the health care barrel. The availability of private health insurance to those healthy and wealthy enough to afford it would add another layer to this inherent inequity. Not surprisingly, this proposal, like much of Mazankowski's report, is a direct challenge to the Canada Health Act.

In *Health Care 'Trojan Horse': The Alberta Mazankowski Report* (January 2002), the Canadian Union of Public Employees said that the Mazankowski report "leaves virtually no stone unturned in the quest to open Canada's public health care system to the private sector." Perhaps that is because some of the members of the Premier's Advisory Council on Health Care have a vested interest in private health care themselves. Don Mazankowski, a director of Alcan and a senior federal government minister in the Mulroney cabinet when free trade was adopted, is also, among other things, a director with the Great-West Life & Annuity Company. And John R. Evans, chairman of the board of Alcan, is also a director with MDS Health Group Ltd., GLYCODesign (a pharmaceutical company), and NPS Pharmaceuticals, Inc.

Premier Klein's intentions are crystal clear, as he stated in the *Calgary Herald* on January 23, 2002: "We will accept, I believe, all of the recommendations of the Mazankowski report, which to me bring about some fairly dramatic changes in the health care system, in the delivery methods, in methods used to raise revenues, of finding ways to create efficiencies and make the system more effective." In a not-very-veiled threat to those who opposed Bill 11, Klein added, "We will use whatever legislative power we require and whatever regulatory power we require to bring about these changes."

The close relationship between Ralph Klein's government and Alberta's corporate sector is becoming as evident in health care as it has been in the oilpatch. Political scientist Laurie Adkin states that Ralph Klein and his cronies have set out to transform the Government of Alberta into "a holding company for an assortment of private health care companies which will be selling services previously provided and managed by the government."

Ontario

Ontario is pursuing privatization more aggressively than any other province except Alberta and British Columbia, and is the province with the greatest private contribution to health care funding: 33 per cent of expenditures. Premier Ernie Eves has said that his government welcomes any "reasonable" proposal from for-profit firms wishing to provide services currently provided by government. "Everything is on the table," he said.

As health experts and professors Pat and Hugh Armstrong describe in *Health Care Limited: The Privatization of Medicare*, in addition to cutting hospital budgets by a massive $800 million in the late 1990s, the previous Mike Harris government amended several provincial laws giving the minister of health new, sweeping powers to "restructure" the hospitals; order hospital shutdowns or amalgamation; allow private medical facilities, such as laboratories, to be established without tendering; impose user fees under the Ontario Drug Benefit Plan; and force thousands of hospital patients waiting for beds in nursing homes to pay a daily charge for room and board.

Like those in Alberta, Ontario's politicians have greatly exaggerated the projected costs of health care as well as their own spending. In April 2001, Health Minister Tony Clement said on April 24, 2001, as quoted in the House Debates, Ontario *Hansard*, "To increase spending well in excess of economic growth is unsustainable. At the current rate of increase, within five years, health care spending would consume 60 per cent of the Ontario government's operating budget – up 44 per cent today and 36 per cent since our government was first elected."

But, despite public pronouncements to the contrary, Paul Leduc Browne and Bill Murnighan of the Canadian Centre for Policy Alternatives reported in two studies (*Public Pain and*

Private Gain: The Privatization of Health Care in Ontario [2000] and *The Ontario Alternative Budget: Selling Ontario's Health Care* [April 2001]), that the Ontario government has in fact reduced spending on health care in real per capita terms over the second half of the 1990s. The Registered Nurses Association of Ontario has an explanation for the apparent contradiction. While it is true that health spending as a percentage of overall government spending in Ontario is rising, says RNAO in their *Speak Out Ontario* action kit, prepared for the Romanow Commission in January 2002, this is only because the cuts to health haven't kept up to the cuts to government spending overall. Government spending is plummeting as a share of GDP, from 18 per cent to 14 per cent since 1995 – a 20 per cent reduction. Health care spending is down 12 per cent in those same years.

As a result of these real per capita losses, Ontario has laid off nearly 25,000 hospital and long-term care workers and had a deficit in health care services estimated at $4.1 billion in 2001. The average long-term care resident in the province now receives less than fifteen minutes of nursing care per day. The Ontario government has also vested itself with the power to override the decisions of local authorities and boards, while downloading responsibility for services to them without their consent. Ontario residents have been obliged to pay more out-of-pocket charges and user fees for health care, and hospitals have moved further down the road to commercialization, contracting out work to the private sector and entering into public-private partnerships.

Shortages of MRIs in the province are sending many patients across the border to the United States for help. Kelly Egan writes in the June 16, 2002, *Ottawa Citizen* that Ontario residents must wait up to a year for an MRI scan. There are only three MRIs in the Ottawa area, which is backlogged by about

6,000 people. In Eastern Ontario, there is only one MRI machine for every 400,000 people.

Bed shortages for women with high-risk pregnancies have led to the practice of sending some women to Buffalo, New York, for treatment. According to Lisa Priest in an article in the February 20, 2002, edition of the *Globe and Mail*, entitled "Pregnancy Cases Show 'Disastrous' State of Care," in one two-week period in February 2002 alone, at least seven pregnant women and three babies from Ontario were sent to the United States for care, putting all at risk. Natalie Mehra of the Ontario Health Coalition says this practice shows that no buffer zone is left in the province's health care system. While no price tag has been made public by the government for these transfers, Priest states in a February 20, 2002, *Globe and Mail* article entitled "Government, Public Await Cost of Care" that the cost of keeping a baby in neonatal intensive care in Toronto is about CAD$5,000; in the U.S., it is about CAD$30,000.

Ontario HMOs?

In 1997, Ontario's Health Services Restructuring Commission published a vision statement recommending the creation of integrated health systems. Pilot projects were launched in 1998 and the Ministry of Health and Long-Term Care has said it intends to bring 80 per cent of all family physicians into its integrated "primary care networks" (PCNs) by 2004. While some in government are promoting this as a primary care system of the kind being recommended by many progressive health groups, Grimsby health researcher Dr. Pamela K. Mulligan begs to differ. In the article "Americanization of Our Health Care" published in the November 1998 edition of *Canadian Family Physicians*, she says that the Ontario PCNs are a forerunner of American-style HMOs in Canada and points out that the chair of the restructuring commission, Duncan Sinclair, said that the networks would provide a "vital and expanded role for the private sector in managing and delivering publicly financed services."

Mulligan explains how this could happen. The new networks are based on two key "reforms": rostering and capitation. Under this system, doctors will be required to join a primary care network consisting of doctors and nurse practitioners offering a predefined range of services. Each patient will be asked to sign a contract (rostering) with a doctor and agree to obtain services only from the network to whom the physician belongs. For each rostered patient, the government will allocate a fixed amount of money periodically, based on a per capita rate (capitation), adjusted for age and sex. Providers will use this prepaid fixed amount to cover all their expenses, including remuneration for doctors and nurse practitioners, operating costs, administration, and all costs related to treating the rostered population.

The problem with this model, says Mulligan, is that because providers assume the financial risk for expenditures, capitation funding gives them an incentive to under-provide services (called "skimping" or "stinting"), and also puts doctors in a conflict of interest that compromises patient care. The transfer of financial risk to providers also creates incentives for biased selection, or "cherry-picking" of healthy "clients." Even if legislation dictates that no one can be denied enrolment in a primary health network on the basis of health status, there are many ways to get around such laws, such as setting up practices in high-income areas or providing poorer services to high-risk patients. Providers could also avoid risk by giving bonuses for limiting expensive services, such as hospitalization.

Rostering and capitation set up a different relationship between patient and doctor, introducing a "contract culture" into caregiving. Physicians are in a lose-lose situation under this system, says Mulligan: "Guided by personal and professional ethics, they want to give the best possible care but find themselves locked into a system where their own financial well-being conflicts with their patients' best interests."

Proponents argue that a system of rostering and capitation in Canada won't go the HMO route of the United States. But Dr. Mulligan effectively argues that competition for desirable patient "clients" could exist under a single-payer scheme. More importantly, although capitation-funded systems in Ontario are supposed to be not-for-profit, contracting publicly financed services to for-profit companies is becoming more common in Canada and is likely to expand as the range of services funded by capitation expands.

Mulligan sums up her opposition with these powerful words: "Capitation is a nasty proposition, which, by design, rewards doctors for withholding services, creates an adversarial relationship between doctors and patients, promises no reduction in costs, and moves us closer to privatization."

Private Opportunities

For-profit private health care is exploding in Ontario. Some private facilities are a mix of public and private funding, providing a direct subsidy to private companies from the public purse. For example, the Ontario government announced in its Spring 2002 budget that it will allow at least twenty private clinics to provide MRI and CT scans that will be covered by the provincial health insurance plan. They will be privately run and for-profit, even though they will receive public funding for "medically necessary" tests, which, by law, must be accessible to all. The world's largest MRI body-scan screening chain will set up shop in Toronto to cater to the "healthy and wealthy" of Europe, the

U.S., and Canada, reported the *Globe and Mail*'s Lisa Priest on June 19, 2002. Valerie McIlroy, CEO of Wellbeing, Inc., told Priest that investors from Canada and the U.S. will be spending $300 million on the chain. "We're looking for you to swipe your Amex card and take preventative, proactive control of your personal health," she added. Syed Haider, the Canadian CEO of Belleville-based Quinte MRI, which owns a $3 million MRI clinic in Ogdensburg, New York, told Mohammed Adam of the *Ottawa Citizen* on June 9, 2002, that he is very excited and will "aggressively bid" for at least ten machines.

"Nurses feel this is the worst thing that could happen to patient care," Barb Wahl, president of the Ontario Nurses' Association, told Graeme Smith of the *Globe and Mail* on June 18, 2002. Doris Grinspun of the Registered Nurses Association of Ontario concurred, warning that profit-driven clinics will "hemorrhage the best people away from the public sector" and will not reduce waiting lists. In an interview published on June 16, 2002, Sandra Conley of the Ontario Hospital Association told April Lindgren of the *Ottawa Citizen* that Ontario's hospitals are already having problems finding technologists to operate their diagnostic machines and worries that private clinics will "cannibalize" existing hospital personnel.

The Ontario government also allows private facilities to receive public financing through the tax system and charge user fees at the same time. One example was uncovered by *Eye* newspaper in Toronto. According to *Eye,* the large private medical laboratories – in particular, Gamma-Dynacare Medical Laboratories Inc. and Medical Data Sciences (MDS) Inc. – are guaranteed an estimated $275 million in public funds every year, no matter how well or poorly they operate.

"How did this happen?" asks *Eye,* then continues, explaining:

Prior to 1998, the Ontario government divided the $145 million it allotted for medical testing among the two dozen labs, which got work based on their quality and service. But the big labs were starting to lose business to smaller labs, so the big ones lobbied the Harris government to pass O.Reg.2/98, which divides the money based on the market share each laboratory had in 1995. For Gamma-Dynacare and MDS, this ensured that they receive 60 per cent of the $415 million (now risen to $458 million), while sharply reducing the shares of the subsidies going to the smaller labs. Incredibly, because the regulation was made retroactive to 1995, the smaller labs were forced to pay back to the larger ones all the revenues they had earned above their 1995 market share.

The subsequent elimination of smaller, not-for-profit labs opened the door to an oligopoly for the big, for-profit outfits.

Toronto is home to the Shouldice Clinic, a private hospital specializing in hernia treatment that was "grandfathered" under the 1973 Private Hospitals Act when Ontario moved to public medicine, thus allowing it to continue to provide private services. The Shouldice Clinic is touted as a model private facility by privatization proponents like Dr. Wilbert Keon, the Ottawa heart surgeon appointed to the Senate by Brian Mulroney in 1991, just in time to vote for the GST. Keon, who told the *Ottawa Citizen*'s Mohammed Adam in an interview published on May 8, 2002, that it is time for Canadians to embrace private health care, thinks that the Shouldice Clinic could be replicated to perform other specialty surgeries, such as orthopedics.

But as Muriel MacDonald asserts in an *Ottawa Citizen* article published on May 12, 2002, Shouldice makes its money by topping up its Ontario patients with out-of-province and out-of-country clients. The clinic charges American clients CAD$3,600 for a full hernia procedure. MacDonald points out that Shouldice does not perform complicated hernia operations requiring other than routine procedures. "This is typical of for-profit health care and 'cream-skimming.' Do routine operations and leave the more complicated and expensive ones for the public sector, a practice decried by the international faculty of public health and medical schools."

Ontario is the first province to ask the private sector to build, own, and maintain a hospital. Up until now, the provinces have put up the lion's share of the operating costs for new facilities; under the plan for the $350 million Osler Centre in Brampton, however, a private company will build the facility and rent it back to the government. It's a great deal for the private company. It will receive loans and other funding to build the hospital, rental fees in perpetuity on a for-profit basis from the Ontario government, and subsidies from both levels of government to operate it.

Under former premier Mike Harris, Ontario allowed the rise of Toronto's King's Medical Centre, which became the largest and most opulent private facility in the country, with "regal rich colours, statues, artwork, plush chairs and warm wood furniture" according to Chris Eby of the *National Post* (March 28, 2001). Opened in 1996 by financier Ron Koval, King's catered to wealthy Canadians and Americans, and was hailed as the future of Canadian medicine by the business community. The business supplied the doctors with everything, including the expensive surroundings, and in turn, took 40 per cent of their gross earnings.

Koval paid himself and his wife, Loren, an annual salary of $1 million, and they drove around in a fleet of vintage cars. They owned a home in Waterdown, Ontario, and a mansion in Hamilton, but lived most of the time at the Toronto Hilton, where they racked up bills of up to $8,000 a month. But the whole empire was built on deceit. In March 2001, the couple was sentenced to seven years in prison by an Ontario Superior Court judge for massive fraud totalling at least $95 million. Said Koval at his trial: "We had a dream to become the standard for private health care providers in this province."

Friends in High Places

Ontario is also the site of the first hospital to hire a CEO (for $500,000 a year) whose role is to lure private business from the United States. According to Lisa Priest in a *Globe and Mail* article from February 8, 2001, responsibilities for the new head of the University Health Network, consisting of the hospitals Toronto General, Toronto Western, and Princess Margaret, include "development, identification, and introduction of new electronic technologies to facilitate the delivery of health care services . . . particularly in the large, resource-rich U.S. market." Dr. Alan Hudson, president of the hospital group, explains that this is the future for Canadian hospitals that want to stay afloat. "What you're looking at in the public sector is the death spiral. The only way to sustain the Canadian health-care system is for private money to go into the public system."

Tony Fell, chairman of the board of the University Health Network, told an April 2002 meeting of the Canadian Club that the Canada Health Act should be reopened to allow for extra-billing and a private insurance scheme similar to that of the U.S. He said the affluent should have the right to buy "exotic" treatment such as hip or knee replacements "to facilitate a better golf game." Fell, who is also chairman of RBC Capital Markets and a well-connected Conservative fundraiser, earns more than $5 million a year. Other board members include prominent Tories Peter Munk, of Barrick Gold, Frederik Eaton, and Tom Long, as well as an assortment of bankers and businessmen.

They can count on the Ontario Conservatives to open the province's health system to profit. As Health Minister Tony Clement told Richard Mackie of the *Globe and Mail* in an interview published on January 22, 2002, "If the private sector can deliver better, cheaper, faster, safer health care, then I would look at it from that pragmatic perspective."

British Columbia

Until the election of Gordon Campbell's Liberals in May 2001, privatization in British Columbia's health care sector had been minimal. The biggest problem was a lack of funding and services for home care and long-term care; the only serious growth in for-profit services took place in these two areas. However, everything changed with the swearing in of the new government. Gordon Campbell has embarked on a massive privatization plan that rivals Alberta and Ontario in scope and speed. The first act of the new government was a whopping tax cut, an indulgence that it would soon come to regret when the extent of provincial debt became apparent.

In early January 2002, not to be bested by Ralph Klein's blueprint for Alberta, Campbell's Liberals announced cuts to government services of 25 per cent over three years – the deepest public service cuts in Canadian history. While the hard facts on what this would mean for health care would not come for several months, the government did consolidate the fifty-two regional health authorities to five (to make it easier, said critics, to implement the coming changes), introduced user fees for eye exams, and subjected seniors to a new means test to determine how much they will now have to pay for prescription drugs. It also admitted that by 2005, the annual B.C. health budget shortfall would be close to $2 million.

Then in late January, the government rammed through legislation that rips up legally negotiated contracts, clearing the way
for hospital closures, service cuts, and health care privatization.
Bill 29 was introduced with no notice and no consultation, and
was passed with only a few hours of debate in the middle of the
night, while most British Columbians were sleeping. Bill 29
allows the government to close hospitals with only sixty days'
notice; eliminate or transfer health services to another community with no consultation; privatize every aspect of the system,
including housekeeping and emergency rooms; and return
community social workers to a low-wage ghetto where their
clients are exposed to instability in their care arrangements.
Amid huge demonstrations, the government of Gordon
Campbell tore up legally binding contracts with his public
sector workers, overriding no-contracting-out clauses in public
service union contracts.

In March 2002, the B.C. Hospital Employees' Union
obtained a copy of secret health ministry documents outlining
the Campbell government's plans to axe nearly 28,000 health
care jobs, increase surgery waiting lists, and shift another $500
million in health care costs onto the shoulders of B.C. families.
Close to $700 million in services are to be privatized, said the
document, and 10,000 fewer surgical procedures are to be
funded every year. At least 420,000 seniors will have to pay
more for drug care under the proposed changes.

The first of these cuts was announced in late April, confirming
the worst fears of the government's critics. Sixty-five hundred
health care jobs are to be cut over three years, although Health
Minister Colin Hansen said at a press conference that other cuts
are possible: "This is a starting process for change." Five hospitals and many acute care beds are to be closed; "specialized
services" such as pediatric neurosurgery and physiotherapy for

cancer patients could now be sold rather than provided under the public system; "business deals" with soft-drink companies and "discretionary room amenities" will generate private funding for hospitals; an undisclosed number of extended care facilities will be shut down; private companies will take over many services such as landscaping, janitorial, security, laundry, food, and building maintenance; and wealthy Americans will be able buy health services in B.C. hospitals.

Racing Ahead

Now open for business, British Columbia is fast becoming a haven for the for-profit health care sector. British Columbia is racing with Ontario to become the first province in Canada to open a private hospital, planned for Abbotsford. The design mirrors a British hospital initiative that has been strongly criticized for providing substandard care while rewarding shareholders with huge profits.

British Columbia is also home to the first private CAT screening clinic – opened in Vancouver in February 2002 by Canada Diagnostic Centres, which also operates private MRI facilities in Vancouver, Calgary, and Hull, Quebec. As reported in the *National Post,* the B.C. CAT screening clinic offers healthy clients a "virtual tour" of their body – their hearts scanned for calcium buildup in their coronary arteries, or their lungs checked for cancerous nodules – to detect clues of future illnesses such as heart disease and cancer. The so-called "yuppie scans" cost $1,200. (Lorne Paperney, president of Canada Diagnostic Centres, is a big Liberal. He was Jean Chrétien's B.C. campaign director in the 1993 election and donated $35,000 to the federal Liberal party.)

As well, a group of specialist doctors is banding together to open a clinic where – for a fee of $350 to $500 – patients can bypass their family doctors to see a specialist without the weeks or months it usually takes to get such appointments. The Specialist Referral Clinic is believed to be the first of its kind in Canada. Its inspiration is Dr. Brian Day – or Dr. Profit, as he was labelled on a magazine cover – a high-profile orthopedic surgeon who is a co-owner of the Cambie Surgery Centre, a private, soon-to-be-expanded Vancouver hospital that caters to people who have third-party insurance coverage for their operations.

Premier Campbell is eager to provide more opportunities for the private sector. He met with Richard Scott, former CEO of Columbia/HCA, the largest hospital corporation in the United States, when they both attended the World Economic Forum in New York in January 2002. The premier invited his new friend to come to Vancouver to advise his government on health care restructuring, saying, according to an article by Jeff Lee in the April 19, 2002, *Vancouver Sun,* that Scott is "an invaluable resource for government leaders like myself who see the need to reform and rebuild health care."

According to Lee, Richard Scott built an empire. At its height, Columbia/HCA was a $20 billion corporation and had acquired 350 hospitals, 570 home care agencies, 150 outpatient surgery centres, doctors' offices and outpatient clinics in 38 states – and employed 285,000 people. Scott liked to say that health care was a business, no different than ball-bearings or munitions. He had big plans to make the company a global player, saying that it would become the Wal-Mart of the health care industry. Scott was forced to resign in 1997, however, after the Federal Bureau of Investigation launched a set of raids on Columbia hospitals that led to one of the largest health care fraud cases in U.S. history. The company has so far paid out almost U.S.$1 billion in criminal and civil penalties.

When the media told Gordon Campbell about the fraud case, he dropped the invitation to Scott, lamenting that the latter had "some very interesting ideas on improving productivity in

health care, and in providing speedier service to patients, which
is what this is all about – improving service to people."

Apparently, government health plans also include bypassing
workers' rights. In May 2002, the B.C. Hospital Employees'
Union released transcripts of phone calls in which representatives of two for-profit companies indicated they wouldn't hire
union members because of wage and benefits expectations. The
two companies, a Canadian branch of French transnational
Sodexho Marriott, and a management consulting firm representing an unnamed Canadian company, hope to win contracts
for health support services by paying $10-per-hour wages
instead of union wages of $17 per hour. Spenser Green, B.C.
regional operations director of Sodexho Marriott, admitted on
one of the calls that these pay rates would leave out most
qualified workers. "We're trying to figure where to get all these
bodies from, but, you can't be hiring people with those kinds of
pays and benefits and think they're going to come and work for,
ah, a third of the cost, you know, and be happy."

Left Behind

Joanne Foote is a recreation aide in a for-profit long-term care
facility in the Fraser Valley and a member of the B.C. Hospital
Employees' Union. Her multinational chain, which she declines
to name to protect her job, owns and manages sixty long-term
care facilities and its Canadian operations earned it $15 million
in profit in 1999. Its goal is an annual profit rate of 25 per cent.

At a Council of Canadians public meeting on March 11, 2002,
on the future of health care in Victoria, Joanne Foote told of the
deterioration of long-term care in B.C. as it becomes more underfunded and privatized. The province has about 25,000 publicly
funded long-term beds, and roughly one-third are owned by
private for-profit companies such as Extendicare and Central

Park Lodge. She pointed out the dangerous combination of neglect of long-term care under former provincial governments and the almost immediate impact of the Campbell government's cuts and restructuring. Already, says Foote, there are more than 7,000 B.C. seniors on waiting lists for long-term care beds.

The plan is to sweep the problem under the carpet, she says, by shifting at least one-third of current beds from publicly funded, licensed nursing homes to unlicensed "assisted living" housing units, a process that has already begun. There, the government will only pay for nursing and personal care, such as bathing, getting dressed, and using medications. People will have to pay out-of-pocket for food, laundry, rent, rehabilitation, private duty nursing, and all other costs. These houses will not be licensed, so there will be no minimum standards, not even staff available at night. Foote asks us to remember that 70 per cent of the people in long-term care have some form of dementia and the majority have complicated health problems.

The private sector is anxious to get its hands on these "hotel services" contracts. And their record is not good, says Foote. When the B.C. Hospital Employees' Union reviewed the inspection reports of Central Park Lodge's twenty U.S. nursing homes, they found that sixteen had been cited for deficiencies in 2001, with problems ranging from inadequate infection control to resident dehydration to medication errors above 5 per cent. In B.C., residents of private homes are now charged $80 for a box of diapers, $7 for each enema and suppository, and up to $30 for monthly recreation fees, even though the majority have dementia and are bedridden. They are also charged for needles, wound dressings, and oxygen therapy.

"How can seniors afford these fees when their median income is less than $16,000 a year?" Foote asks. "First they have to pay at least the minimum $750 monthly fee for staying in the nursing home. Out of the remaining $550, they have to pay for personal items like toothpaste and shampoo, haircuts, phone charges, and other regular necessities." Money for social outings or clothes is almost non-existent, she reports, and when a patient inevitably dies, staff cannot attend the funeral on company time. The bed is filled within hours.

Quebec

While no other province has promoted privatization to the same degree as Alberta, Ontario, and British Columbia, all have suffered from the cuts and most have allowed some private services to develop.

In Quebec, for-profit corporations are setting themselves up in competition with public institutions, especially in areas where the public system can no longer meet the demand. Privatization is growing in long-term residential facilities, home care, convalescence and rehabilitation centres, private physiotherapy and radiology clinics, and medical clinics providing diagnostic services. Indeed, Premier Bernard Landry has stated publicly that he is open to examining a greater role for private clinics in certain types of surgery in order to reduce waiting lists in Quebec.

As economists Pat and Hugh Armstrong document in a 2001 report for the Canadian Centre for Policy Alternatives and the Council of Canadians, entitled *Health Care Limited*, for-profit firms specializing in home care and home-support products and services, such as remote diagnostic and monitoring equipment, technical aids, and nursing services, are rapidly expanding in Quebec as well. And, they report, Quebec hospitals are embracing management practices developed in the private sector, even those evolved among manufacturers of consumer goods. The transfer of the operation of health and social services to the private sector in Quebec is not simply a change in service-delivery methods; it reflects a more general shift in attitude, where a concern for economic efficiencies is gaining ascendency over concern for care, access, or quality.

As a result, Quebec has dramatically cut spending for health and social services. Public spending per person in Quebec is the lowest of all the provinces, and Quebec has gone from the province with the highest percentage of public funding in health care (81.5 per cent in 1980) to one of two provinces with the lowest percentage (69.1 per cent in 1998). Since 1982, every review of insured services has resulted in the removal of services from medicare: physiotherapy, dental care for children aged ten to sixteen, optometrist services, diagnostic tests outside public institutions, and many more. The Government of Quebec has also reduced employer contributions to the Health Services fund, making Quebec employer contributions for health care among the lowest in North America.

Clair Commission

Many Quebecers are most concerned, however, about the recommendations contained in the report of the Quebec Clair Commission, entitled "Emerging Solutions," tabled in early 2001. The commission called into question the fundamental principles of the Canada Health Act, and said they should be replaced by the principles of "fairness" and "solidarity." Critics are concerned that in replacing the notion of equity and universality enshrined in the current act with the notion of "fairness," the commission could be opening the way for a two-tiered system and means testing for public health services in Quebec.

The commission also called for a review of the range of services currently covered by medicare, citing the government's "fiscal vulnerability," and it opened the door to user fees for some hospital stays. The report promoted a policy framework of "partnership" with the private sector and the contracting out of new, long-term care and nursing home facilities. It recommended the creation of a "special health fund" to be financed through a tax on the incomes of all individuals, regardless of the source of income. Under this regressive or "flat" tax, rich and poor would put the same amount of money into the pot. And the commission recommended limits on public spending on health care, even though Quebec's population is growing.

Perhaps most disturbing, the Clair Commission called for Family Medicine Groups, based on an HMO-type capitation system, to replace the popular CLSCs, Quebec's system of public clinics. Finally, the report proposed that all board members of the regional health boards be appointed by the government, thus reducing the democratic space for the public to participate in decision-making processes. As La Coalition Solidarité Santé, Quebec's public health coalition, told the Romanow Commission, even though the Quebec government assured the public that a two-tiered system is not on the table, "our analysis of the Clair Commission's report shows that it will lead us quickly down the road to such a system."

Manitoba and Saskatchewan

Because NDP governments are much more committed to maintaining a public health care system, the provinces of Manitoba and Saskatchewan have not allowed anywhere near the amount of privatization as have Ontario and Alberta, although some private incursions have taken root. Both provinces have shifted much of their treatment out of institutions and into the community. This, in turn, has opened the door to for-profit providers to offer care and support services, such as home care, physiotherapy, and occupational therapy.

Manitoba, under the former Conservative government, had launched a number of privatization experiments, some of which, such as the private Pan-Am clinic, are now being rolled back by the new government. By 1997, 130 private clinics were operating in Manitoba, offering minor surgical procedures. And Manitoba was the site of the first fee-for-service home care experiment. We Care set up shop in Brandon in 1984, and competed with the public system by paying registered nurses substantially less than the province did. The company eventually set up sixty-five franchises across the country before being swallowed by Aetna Health Management, Inc., a subsidiary of Boston-based John Hancock Mutual Life Insurance Co., in 1998.

Manitoba also conducted the first experiment in contracting out some home care services to a private U.S.-based corporation, Olsten Health Services, in 1997. But the contract was not renewed the next year. Olsten, which had recently setttled a massive fraud suit with the U.S. government involving tens of millions of dollars, was a very controversial company in the province. While Olsten insists that it left on account of contract disagreements, the Canadian Union of Public Employees put out a news release announcing, "Home Care Giant Run Out of Manitoba." Under Gary Doer, the Government of Manitoba is committed to expanding home and continuing care services under a public system, and Lorne Calvert's government in Saskatchewan is following the recommendations of its provincial commission under former deputy health minister Kenneth Fyke, who recommended new public monies into primary and specialized care, with built-in performance measures.

Atlantic Canada

In Newfoundland, the shift to per capita funding by the federal government under the Canada Health and Social Transfer has meant great hardship. Newfoundland and Labrador have just over 500,000 people living in some 600 communities, which are distributed over 405,720 kilometres along 17,450 kilometres of coastline. More than half live in communities with populations under 20,000. As the Newfoundland and Labrador Association of Public and Private Employees told the Romanow Commission, per capita funding ignores the reality of geography; it cannot adequately support the provision of health care to a sparse population spread out over a vast majority. The move to per capita funding is the "death knell" for rural communities in the province. As a consequence, individuals are being asked to pay all or part of the cost of some health care services. The Grimes government claims that Newfoundland and Labrador is spending 44 cents out of every budget dollar on health care.

New Brunswick also has a small population and a lot of poverty. In its presentation before the Romanow Commission, the Nurses Association of New Brunswick said that the province faced "insurmountable difficulties in maintaining an acceptable level of services" when federal funding for health care was decreased in 1995. "Without change," Premier Bernard Lord has said, "we will hit the medicare wall." Earlier restructuring of health services in New Brunswick to create Regional Health Authorities based on "accountability" and three-year "business plans" has led to a decline in services and front-line professionals. As the association reports, the workplace situation in recent years has been such that a large number of recent nurse graduates have been unable to find employment, resulting in an "exodus" of newly qualified nurses outside the province.

Premier Bernard Lord has sent mixed messages about the future of health services in his province. On one hand, he has said that further privatization is an option for New Brunswick. But, based on the report of a two-year study by the premier's Health Quality Council, Lord is calling for a community-based network of health centres where people could access primary health card's twenty-four hours a day, seven days a week. He is also calling for a new role for nurse practitioners, an annual report card on the health system, and a patient charter of rights.

Many supporters of public health across Canada are watching the Lord program with high expectations.

In Nova Scotia, deep cuts have left many citizens with greatly reduced services. Areas in the province are without doctors, doors to hospital emergency rooms are closed on weekends, bed closures are rampant, and there is a severe shortage of nurses. The Nova Scotia Nurses' Union says in its Romanow submission that the province is short 600 nurses. After a long and bitter strike by the province's 12,300 nurses and other front-line health care workers in July 2001, the Hamm government agreed to repeal its controversial anti-strike legislation. Cancer care, liver transplants, and other essential services are either reduced or non-existent. As the Nova Scotia Citizens' Health Care Network told the Romanow Commission, there is increasing pressure to privatize and contract out services in such an atmosphere. The Nova Scotia Department of Health was urged recently by an external advisory panel to "consider the role that the private sector could or should play in financing and funding the health system."

And Halifax is home to the first private, for-profit MRI clinic to open in Atlantic Canada. For $725, individuals will be able to go to the Canada Diagnostic Centre Ltd. clinic and abandon waiting lists at the local hospitals. The union representing Nova Scotia health workers is threatening to take the provincial government to court to stop the clinic.

Prince Edward Island, on the other hand, became one of the pioneers in adopting a regional governance model, devolving the planning and delivery of services to the community level. The system is not perfect, of course. P.E.I. has had its share of federal cuts and has had to scramble to fill the holes left in their wake. But as the Prince Edward Island Union of Public Sector Employees told the Romanow Commission, "Overall, we feel that the home care system in place in Prince Edward Island is a definite step forward in meeting the needs of Island seniors and others. The present system has many strengths, as it is easily accessible and offers a wide range of services." Private services are almost non-existent on the island.

Home Care

It is impossible to examine the provincial restructuring of health care without looking closely at the fastest growing sector in the health care field: home care. According to Peter Coyte, with the department of medicine at the University of Toronto, in his book *Homecare in Canada: Passing the Buck,* demand for home care increased in Ontario, for example, by 30 per cent in just one year (1996–97 to 1997–98). Public spending on home care increased at an annual rate of 9 per cent during the 1990s, whereas the total public spending on health care increased by only 2.2 per cent. This is because federal funding cuts have left the provinces scrambling to save costs. Discharging people early from hospital, shifting services from institutions to community clinics, and caring for people in their homes instead of expensive hospitals are all ways to save money, especially in the care of the elderly, who make up nearly two-thirds of home care users.

Hamilton's hospitals, for instance, charge hospitalized seniors $345 a day for refusing to take the first bed offered to them at a long-term care facility. "We have to encourage people to move on," Gord Haugh, spokesperson for Ontario Health Minister Tony Clement, told the Toronto *Star* in an interview published on May 3, 2002. "The system needs the acute-care beds in the hospital. Hospitals don't exist to be long-term care facilities." It is tragic that home care is growing under these conditions, for the sole purpose of saving money. Home and community care also fit into a more humane vision of the future, one in which families, communities, and governments work together to provide more personal care than institutions are capable of giving. Home care could also be an important component of a more holistic approach to health care, one that stresses lifestyle changes, prevention, and general wellness.

There are big problems with the current home care system, however. The shift to home care has not been accompanied by adequate community resources. Peter Coyte says that nationally governments spend only $2.7 billion annually on home care programs, a tiny fraction of the $105 billion in yearly health spending. More and more provinces are sending chronically ill and acute-care patients home without the proper services. There, the burden falls on family members – usually women. According to a study by Status of Women Canada entitled *The Changing Nature of Home Care and Its Impact on Women's Vulnerability to Poverty,* more than 80 per cent of home care is delivered by unpaid family members. If there are no family members or friends who can take up the role of caregiver, patients may have to undergo humiliating means tests to qualify for publicly funded care.

The lack of funding for home care is a direct result of the limits of the Canada Health Act. Home care falls outside the legal definition of insured doctors and hospitals. This is because home care was originally seen as a supplementary service for those who did not require chronic or acute care and, therefore, did not need to be in a hospital or other institution. But now, changes in hospital policies have resulted in home care programs and services being channelled away from the traditional users – and into care for people discharged from hospital earlier than they would have been formerly, or those whose condition used to lead to hospital admittance but no longer does. As hospitals send patients home "quicker and sicker," the fault lines in home health are being exposed.

A recent Health Canada study concluded that Canada's home

care system is not a system at all, but an incoherent mess of pro-grams providing widely varying levels of services and care. Taylor Alexander, CEO of the Canadian Association for Community Care, says the lack of national standards is a big problem. "There are two parallel systems of care in this country: the medical acute-care system with guaranteed insured access under the Canada Health Act, and the patchwork quilt of unin-sured services in home and community care. We need a commit-ment to a new model of care and have been calling for federal leadership to establish a national program."

In a 2001 report, the 400,000-member Canadian Associa-tion of Retired Persons (CARP) graded home care services nationally and in each province, and gave governments failing grades across the board. The group noted that the provinces do not even have a common definition of home care, let alone standards for services and workers or adequate funding and planning.

As Colleen Fuller found in a May 2001 study on home care for the Canadian Federation of Nurses Unions, the lack of national standards and funding for health care delivered outside of the hospital sector is undermining Canadians' access rights across the country. User charges also vary dramatically; resi-dents in Ontario outside the Community Care Access Centres (CCAC) system (set up to implement a competitive home care model for the province) pay an average of $825 a year, while those next door in Manitoba pay no user fees at all.

Another consequence of not being bound by the Canada Health Act is that, unlike hospitals, which are not allowed to turn away patients, home care agencies can pick and choose their clients. Not being bound by the Canada Health Act means that home care is being delivered in a patchwork manner across the country, and many Canadians – especially seniors – are suffering.

Privatized Home Care

While some provinces and municipalities provide home care on
a non-profit basis, more and more are allowing it to become privatized, thereby giving the private sector access to the area of
health care with the most potential for growth, especially as the
"baby boomers" approach retirement. Since home care is not
covered by medicare, individual patients and their families often
have to fork out large amounts of money to pay for basic care.
In its study, Status of Women Canada found that home care
recipients and their families are paying out-of-pocket for many
services, including drugs, equipment, housekeeping, and renovations to homes to accommodate illness and disability. The
same service paid for by individuals in the home care environment would be provided free of charge in a hospital. The
money-making potential in home care is huge, and the private
sector has taken sharp note.

Home care has traditionally been provided by non-profit
agencies such as the Victorian Order of Nurses (VON), or by
religious or other charitable organizations. However, some
provinces have undertaken a tendering process, introducing
market forces into what should be a public service, and allowing
private companies to dip into public health care funds. In doing
so, Fuller points out, Canada is adopting the concept of
"managed competition" that lies at the heart of the American
HMO system. In a situation of managed competition, the provision of a service is put out to tender, and a contract is awarded
to a private provider who then has a monopoly over the service
for the length of the contract.

In the United States, the National Health Service was trans-
formed from being a system of government-financed and provided services to one based on competitive tendering and
contracting. A central aspect of the "reforms" was the movement

of patients out from under the Health Service – where they were provided with free services and where there were higher standards for health care workers – to the care of underfunded local authorities, who had the right to administer means testing and to contract care out to private-sector providers.

Patients felt the difference right away. One U.S. study found that for-profit home care companies offered an average of eighteen visits a year for each client, compared with forty-six for public and non-profit providers. It is through home care that the model of "managed competition" is gaining a foothold in Canada.

Eastern Incubator

Because of small populations and the high cost of institutional care, the Atlantic provinces have embraced home care with a passion. There, much of it is delivered by private, for-profit companies. Comcare, of London, Ontario, is the largest home care corporation in Canada and operates extensively in Atlantic Canada. According to Colleen Fuller, when it set up shop in Newfoundland in 1992, where it was to deliver home care to means-tested seniors, it immediately cut the hourly wages of care providers from $7.00 an hour to $5.25. Fierce public opposition forced the company to pull out of that province four years later.

Comcare also operates in New Brunswick. Fuller regards New Brunswick as the perfect example of what is wrong with health care in Canada today. "New Brunswick's shift to community care underscores the problems being confronted in a part of the health system bereft of federal funding and national standards, and increasingly dominated by for-profit operators such as Comcare."

As a money-saving technique in clear violation of the Canada Health Act, home care recipients in need of chronic care (who are therefore eligible for insured services and would have been hospitalized in a former time) are subjected to a means test to determine how much they will have to pay for services and pre-scription medicine. New Brunswick's home care support workers are the lowest paid in the country, bringing home wages that put them well below the poverty line. Often, they are caring for seniors who also live below the poverty line.

Nova Scotia, where Comcare and other private, for-profit providers also operate, has moved many acute care patients out of institutions and sent them home to fend for themselves. As a result, overall demand for home care in the province, which has an unusually high rate of disability as well as a higher-than-average number of seniors, is skyrocketing. Patients have to buy expensive hospital services themselves or be subjected to user fees and means tests, all of which are banned by the Canada Health Act.

In its presentation to the Romanow Commission, the Nova Scotia Citizens' Health Care Network expressed grave concern over this situation: "We have a serious shortage of home support workers who work for various agencies, which provide varying salaries and benefits. This haphazard approach to home care services does not provide the stability needed." In addition, Nova Scotia will only provide home care to those with "unmet needs" due to lack of family caregivers. Competition has resulted in low wages for home care workers, minimum care for the patients, and a terrible toll on families, who end up having to administer medical care, such as IV therapy and injections, to bedridden loved ones.

The Harris Revolution

Ontario, with the largest unregulated home care workforce and the highest per capita rate of home care clients in Canada, is the province that has taken the most aggressive stance on home care privatization. Mike Harris's Conservative government openly set out in 1996 to fully privatize the system within three years, and under Premier Ernie Eves, the process continues unabated. Discharging thousands of patients from closing hospitals, the province all but eliminated direct public funding of a non-profit, community-based health care system, and diverted health care dollars to the private sector through competitive tendering, in a system similar to that used in the United States.

Ontario has proven to be a bonanza for the private health care sector, particularly the American private health care sector. Since the government amended the Independent Health Facilities Act in 1996, removing the preference for Canadian-owned, non-profit groups in funding and licensing arrangements, American firms can openly compete in Ontario. According to the U.S. State Department "current and foreseeable market conditions in Canada," such as those that exist in Ontario, "offer expansion and/or export business opportunities for many U.S. home care product and service companies."

The Ontario Home Health Care Providers Association is made up of thirty-six for-profit companies, including American transnationals such as Olsten Health Services (the largest private home care corporation in North America, now Bayshore Health Group in Canada), and Canadian chains such as We Care and Comcare. These companies can underbid the non-profit providers because they pay lower wages and offer no benefits or overtime. According to an article by Rita Daly entitled "Home Sweet Profit" published in the March 22, 1998, edition of the *Toronto Star,* until 1997, the VON, a century-old household name, had 90 per cent of the visiting nurses "market" in Ontario. Now, it is struggling to survive, its nurses taking wage cuts in order to compete with low-wage, underqualified, non-unionized workers hired by the for-profit sector.

The Harris government also introduced a series of new regulations and practices that limit services to its citizens and
promote contracting out. Eligibility criteria for access to limited
public funds became more stringent; prescription drug costs
were deregulated and user fees were imposed on seniors and
people on social assistance; and the minimum number of hours
of care in long-term facilities was cut back.

The Ontario government then set up Community Care Access
Centres (CCACs) to act as brokers in forty-three regions around
the province, awarding home care agencies contracts for one to
three years for visiting nurses, therapists, and homemakers. The
centres oversaw the transition to an open market in home care.
According to Colleen Fuller's report for the Canadian Health
Coalition, *Home Care: What We Have, What We Need* (May
2001), non-profit agencies such as the VON had to compete with
other agencies for a proportion of their caseloads, starting with
10 per cent in 1996, and increasing to 100 per cent by 1999. The
CCACs also have the power to determine "eligibility" for their
services, and, when they run out of money, are able to cut off
services to people in need. Ontario spends only 4 per cent of its
total health care budget on home care. In 2002, CCAC budgets
remained frozen for the third year in a row; some CCAC workers
have not had a pay raise in ten years.

Understandably, service to those who need home care has suffered. Ellie Tesher of the *Toronto Star* attended a February 2002
meeting of a coalition of ethnic and religious communities
called Communities for Health Care in Toronto, and reported
on what she heard on February 28. Mary is the caregiver for her
elderly father, whom she can't leave alone. An osteoporosis
patient herself, Mary's doctor ordered her to walk forty-five
minutes daily. She also wanted to visit her mother, who is in a
nursing home. Her CCAC would not provide a worker for even
one hour of respite care. Another woman's husband had a

stroke and couldn't speak or care for himself; she broke her ankle while pushing his wheelchair. The personal care worker who was to relieve her to give him showers, lunch, and washroom assistance was cut from six hours to three, once a week.

Norman, seventy-three, a stroke victim who can't be left alone, has forty-five minutes of home care once a week. The rest is up to his seventy-one-year-old wife. An eighty-eight-year-old woman with heart problems, living alone and legally blind, had her personal care cut in half to one hour twice a week. Reports Tesher, "Family caregivers, especially senior spouses, are exhausted; people trying to live on their own after illness can no longer manage."

In Ottawa, home care and placement programs were merged into the Ottawa-Carleton Community Care Access Centre in 1997. According to an article by Kelly Egan entitiled "Loss of Home Care 'Devastates' Blind Woman," which ran in the May 19, 2002, edition of the *Ottawa Citizen,* within two years the organization had to freeze services in a funding crunch despite the fact that demand is growing at over 12 per cent a year. As of April 2002, almost 500 people in the Ottawa region were on a waiting list for basic services such as bathing, grooming, and feeding. The impact on the community has been devastating.

Gail Blackburn, who worked for the Department of National Defence for thirty years, is now in constant pain, disabled by lupus, fibromyalgia, and depression and in need of basic care, including dressing, grooming, and feeding. Yet, the Ottawa-Carleton CCAC cut her home care service to just three hours a week. Blackburn cannot even change her own bed, but is only allowed home care help to change her bed once a month. In a letter to the editor of the *Ottawa Citizen* on May 25, 2002, she writes: "Would anyone sleep in a bed changed once a month?" she asks, adding that she spends more time in bed than most people. "I live alone and ask nothing more than to be able to live my life with a little respect and dignity."

Joan Crawford-Shanahan echoes this sentiment. In interview with Kelly Egan of the *Ottawa Citizen*, published on May 19, 2002, this single mother tells of losing her job when she became suddenly blind from a rare eye disease called bilateral optical neuropathy in 1992. At first, she had eight hours of publicly funded home care a week. Those hours were reduced to six, then four, then three and then, in May 2002, to none. In a letter explaining the new "services," the Ottawa-Carleton CCAC listed the items no longer coverable. They included shopping, meal preparation, laundry, vacuuming, washing floors, dusting, mending, ironing, or cleaning appliances. Attached to the letter was a list of agencies and companies that offer paid services. Crawford-Shanahan would love to perform these tasks for herself and her daughter, but cannot. She would pay for them if she could, but her monthly pension barely covers housing and food. "I am bloody blind," she says. "What do you have to be to get any help? Dead? This is a crying shame."

7

The External Assault

The assault on Canada's health care system is a domestic manifestation of a global phenomenon. In a global economy, no country or society is immune to what is happening at the international level. While Canada has been struggling with competing forces and ideologies, so too has the rest of the world. Huge financial and trade institutions have grown up in the last several decades that are shaping the social and economic policies of every society in the world.

In many ways, the global economy now has a greater impact on the lives of people around the world than the actions and decisions of their own governments. Or, put another way, these global institutions and financial forces dictate governments' policies by punishing those who dare to disagree with them. To understand what is truly happening to Canada's public health care system, we must look to the global forces that are undermining universal health care everywhere.

The Washington Consensus

Economic globalization – the creation of a single global economy with universal rules set by the private sector – is the dominant economic and social movement in the world today. In its Tenth

Annual Report (July 17, 2000), the British House of Lords Select Committee on European Communities minced no words. Economic globalization, the Lords declared, is about "reducing the power of individual governments in the face of multinational corporations whose annual turnover may exceed the GNP of many WTO member countries." Originally conceived by American business interests, the so-called "Washington Consensus" is a model of development rooted in the belief that liberal market economics constitute the one and only economic choice for the whole world. The term "Washington Consensus" was coined in the early 1990s by John Williamson of the Institute for International Economics, a conservative Washington-based think-tank.

This free-market doctrine has forced successive governments around the world to give up controls on foreign investment, liberalize trade, deregulate their internal economies, privatize state services, and enter into head-to-head competition with one another. The Washington Consensus forms the major philosophical foundation for government downsizing around the world and is behind the privatization of public services in many countries. It is also the foundational ideology of all major global financial institutions, including the World Bank, the Asia Development Bank, and the International Monetary Fund, who in turn use their clout to force it on Third World governments. The Washington Consensus is also at the heart of international trade rules.

Economist Paul Krugman explains that the Washington Consensus now defines "not only the U.S. government, but all those institutions and networks of opinion leaders centred in the world's de facto capital – think-tanks, politically sophisticated investment bankers, and world finance ministers – all those who meet in Washington and collectively define the conventional wisdom of the moment." Of course, Krugman fails to note that

the Washington Consensus exists to protect the powerful –
powerful countries, powerful currencies, powerful corporations
– against the weak. And he fails to note that true competition is
not possible in our world, due to the access to capital of the
Washington Consensus countries and the entrenched power
imbalance between the North and South.

In the new global economy, everything is for sale, even in
those areas once considered sacred; such as air and water, health
and education, heritage and culture, and life itself, in the form
of genetic code. This process could be called "the privatization
of everything." Increasingly, all services and resources are con-
trolled by a handful of transnational corporations operating
outside of any national or international law. According to the
Washington-based Institute for Policy Studies publication, *Field
Guide to the Global Economy*, of the one hundred largest
economies in the world, fifty-three are now transnational corporations. The top 200 global corporations are now so big that
their combined sales surpass the combined economies of 182
countries, and they have almost twice the economic clout of the
poorest four-fifths of humanity.

Under their influence, massive privatization of the world's
resources and services is taking place. Every year, more government services in the areas of education, social security, and health
care are being turned over to the private sector by governments
faced with massive debt-servicing costs – as well as reductions in
tax revenues as a result of wealthy individuals and powerful corporations refusing to pay their share of taxes. This leaves health
especially vulnerable, because it is so intertwined with other
issues such as poverty, hunger, and access to clean water.

Universal Health Care Targeted

The privatization of social and health services was not always an international objective. As described in an earlier chapter, the United Nations Universal Declaration of Human Rights, ratified in 1948, guaranteed a standard of living adequate for the health and well-being of the whole family, and the right to security in the event of sickness, disability, or old age. In several attending covenants, the declaration bound signatory states to accept the legal and moral obligation to protect and promote the rights enshrined in it.

In 1978, virtually all governments adopted the World Health Organization's Health for All by the Year 2000 Declaration. This treaty stated that all people are entitled to basic health rights, and that societies and governments have the responsibility to ensure that their people's health needs are met regardless of gender, race, class, and relative ability or disability. The declaration's centrepiece was "primary health care," a comprehensive strategy based on an equitable approach to the delivery of health services. It called for health ministries and health workers to be accountable to the common people, and included social guarantees to ensure that the basic needs of all people were met by the state.

Unhappily, these commitments were never met. Even as many agencies and some parts of governments tried to move this universal agenda forward, other forces were at work to undermine and sabotage the great dream of health for all. Elsewhere as in Canada, powerful ideological myths about the failure of governments were being promoted by those with a great deal to gain if health care was privatized. The health sectors in most countries were targeted to become subject to the laws of the marketplace and the theory of "managed competition." Rich and poor countries alike were told that the discipline of the market would act to contain costs through competition while more efficiently delivering services according to consumer demands.

Health trends were also following global economic and social trends. International institutions and governments eventually gave up on the goal of universality, and opted for a tiered system instead. The shape of society in almost every country in the world now resembles a pyramid: the few in the top third are getting richer and increasing their power; the middle class is striving to hold on, although it is being squeezed downward by market policies; and the bottom third has become an entrenched underclass. Goals and policy designs for health care in a world that accepts this economic model are different from goals and policy designs for a world seeking equality.

Governments are restructuring health care in order to ensure that those at the top of the pyramid have access to the very best health care – social Darwinism in action. Access to the best is restricted to those who can afford it. A second-tier, public system, obviously funded a little better in rich countries than in poor, is now operating in most parts of the world.

The World Bank and the IMF

This process was promoted by a regime enforced on Third World countries by the World Bank and the International Monetary Fund (IMF). These two powerful financial institutions provide grants or loans to developing countries, supposedly for "development" (usually consisting of megaprojects such as dams) and for stabilizing currency crises. However, they have come under fierce criticism in recent years for a legacy of deep social turmoil and poverty in the South, and for primarily serving the interests of the big corporations and powerful governments of the North.

The Institute for Policy Studies has calculated that nine out of ten energy-related projects financed by the World Bank benefit at least one corporation headquartered in the United States or one of the other six main industrial powers. A top U.S. Treasury Department official bragged to Congress in 1995 that for every dollar the United States contributes to the World Bank, U.S. corporations receive $1.30 in procurement contracts.

During the 1960s and 1970s, transnational banks lent hundreds of billions of dollars to poorer nations at very low interest rates. When interest rates soared in the 1980s, the countries found themselves unable to pay off their debts. The IMF and the World Bank (which has famously described public services as a barrier to the abolition of world poverty) made them an offer they couldn't refuse: agree to implement a set of Structural Adjustment Programs (SAPs), and the terms of their loans would be renegotiated and further aid would be forthcoming. In addition, many countries were given new loans by these institutions, which added to their debt.

About eighty countries were forced to weaken their tools of national sovereignty and adopt the "Washington Consensus" package, including cuts to social subsidies, public education, and health care. The World Bank's health policy explicitly includes support for "diversity and competition" in health services. Public hospitals and health centres have been sold to the private sector, resulting in the pricing of their services out of reach of the poor. Privatization of health services is now a condition of further financial assistance in many countries.

For example, according to David Hall of the Public Services International Research Institute, in Tanzania, the World Bank has a U.S.$22 million "Health Sector Development Program," whose mandate includes the goal "to promote private sector involvement in delivery of health services." The bank's Provincial Health Project in Indonesia has a stated aim of a market-based approach to health care, including decentralization and "alternative," i.e., private, insurance schemes. The bank's health program in Bulgaria calls for "an increased role for the private sector" and "promoting competition among providers." Hospitals are to be re-registered as "trade companies in the light of creating opportunities for subsequent privatization."

In fact, the World Bank actually has a division that invests solely in the private sector. The International Finance Corporation (IFC) has a declared policy of favouring the extension of the private sector in public services, including health care. Its chief executive, Peter Woicke, declared in a May 1999 speech, "IFC is also moving aggressively to invest in sectors where we believe there is substantial scope for more private sector involvement. This ranges from water and transportation investments to healthcare, education and the environment." He added that "a little bit of competition" will have a positive effect on public service providers.

Structural Adjustment

Because of World Bank and IMF policies (incidentally, it is worth remembering that these institutions are funded by public monies), public health services are being denied to millions of people in the Third World. Their structural adjustment policies have led to deep cuts to health care budgets, user fees, and cost-recovery practices. The results for the world's poor – which include increased malnutrition and the resurgence of cholera, tuberculosis, malaria, and plague – have been disastrous. According to *Third World Resurgence,* Costa Rica, the first Central American nation to implement a SAP, experienced a 35 per cent cut in health programs that led to a dramatic increase in infectious disease rates and infant mortality.

Under the dictator Pinochet, Chile followed a SAP agenda

that destroyed its universal health care system, leaving millions without protection. Health care workers and proponents who objected to the destruction of Chile's public system were routinely tortured and killed. Much as in Canada, this agenda included the decentralization of authority, leaving communities without national health protection; "targeting" of services to the poor; and the introduction of private health services. Much as in Canada, the federal government of Chile dropped its shared-cost contribution for health care from 61 per cent in 1974 to 17 per cent of total costs in 1989, reported Trish Elliott in the March 1996 edition of *Briarpatch*, and downloaded its health care responsibilities to levels of government unable to fund them. A two-tier system replaced the universal model and private companies flowed into the country.

Now, wealthy Chileans can buy top health care services and the most sophisticated technology; for others, who cannot afford this expensive system, there are crumbling facilities and long waiting lists, not to mention little access to proper care for serious illness.

In the 1990s, Argentina slashed government subsidies to all non-governmental public health care service providers, as well as funding for government-provided services. The country adopted U.S.-style HMOs, which paid incentives to doctors who ordered less costly treatment. Millions of Argentineans, who had traditionally received quality health care from their union-related co-operatives, were thrown out of work by IMF and World Bank restructuring and lost their health care altogether. In a decade, the national medicare system of Argentina went bankrupt.

Dr. Rene Favaloro was a renowned Argentinian heart surgeon, who performed the first heart bypass operation in Cleveland, Ohio, in 1967 and was a national hero in Argentina. He was a passionate champion of universal health care and ran a state-of-the-art heart institute that catered to everyone from wealthy matrons to street urchins. It became famous throughout South America, conducting groundbreaking research and training specialists for the whole continent.

Rene Favaloro fought the cuts and restructuring with all his might. At first, he refused to turn away patients. But as time passed, he became utterly overwhelmed by the number of people he could not help. According to an article by Anthony Faiola, which ran in the August 25, 2000, edition of the *Washington Post,* Favaloro wrote to a friend: "I am living one of the worst moments of my life, just as the rest of this nation. I have become a servant knocking on doors looking for money to keep the foundation alive. These free-market reforms are better referred to as a neo-feudalism that is bringing this world toward a social disaster." On July 29, 2000, after a light lunch of apples and tea, Rene Favaloro walked into the bathroom of his modest Buenos Aires home and put a .38-calibre bullet through his broken heart.

In the first five years of restructuring, all the progress that had been made in reducing the infant mortality rate in many African countries was totally undone by Structural Adjustment Programs. According to a *Third World Resurgence* special in April 1996, "Bleeding to Death: Health Care in the Marketplace," between 1980 and 1985, the infant mortality rate rose by 54 per cent in seven African countries, including Ethiopia, Somalia, and Uganda. Yellow fever staged a comeback in Ghana. A ten-country UNICEF study found that SAPs had caused a great decline in the nutritional status of African children between 1975 and 1990. Hospital deaths due to malnutrition soared in Zambia. In Kenya, the introduction of user fees at a centre for sexually transmitted diseases caused a sharp decline in attendance and an increase in these diseases in the population.

In fact, as hospitals were privatized all over the Third World, outpatient visits dropped. In Vietnam, the introduction of user fees meant that poor families had to sell their livestock or borrow money to receive even the most basic care. Peter Limqueco, writing in the March 13, 1996, edition of the *Asia Times*, found that as a result, there was a 50 per cent reduction in the number of public health care consultations in the first seven years following IMF-imposed liberalization in 1986.

The massive restructuring of health care in the Third World has caused untold suffering. Jubilee 2000, the international ecumenical movement working for the cancellation of Third World debt, conservatively estimates that 19,000 children die every day as a result of the restructuring proposed and imposed by the World Bank and the IMF. And, of course, when HIV/AIDS hit Asia, Latin America, and, particularly, Africa, the public health infrastructure had already been decimated and the affected countries were unable to cope with this terrible crisis.

The saddest irony is that all this suffering hasn't produced the promised financial security. According to UNICEF, Third World debt has grown by more than 400 per cent since 1980; countries of the South now send more money to the North in debt repayment than they receive in foreign aid and export earnings combined. Foreign aid has been slashed in most developed countries: Canada's aid package has dropped to its lowest level in decades. The World Bank gave less than 4 per cent of its total development finance to basic health, education, water, and sanitation in 2000, representing just 0.1 per cent of total World Bank financing. The global shortfall in annual public spending on basic services has more than doubled to U.S. $90 billion in the last five years.

Private-Sector Champions

There have been winners, however, in the global shift toward privatization. When governments in the Third World abandoned the health care field, they left a huge vacuum. For just as the First World now has an entrenched underclass, the developing world now has its own elite. A health care market was created by the wealthy and new business classes of poorer countries, and it is being filled by private, for-profit health corporations, many of whom are transnationals unconstrained by the domestic laws of any one country.

According to Public Services International, Latin American countries, for example, are experiencing an invasion of U.S. health care corporations and insurance companies, like Aetna International (recently sold to a company in the Netherlands), Cigna, and American International, who report a 20 per cent growth in the region per year and more than five million clients. UnitedHealthcare, a large American HMO, has health schemes in the Philippines and Hong Kong. HealthSouth is a major U.S. operator of outpatient surgery, which has expanded into diagnostic centres and occupational medicine centres in Australia, Puerto Rico, and the U.K. A Singapore-based health corporation, Parkway, owns and operates most of the hospitals and dental clinics in Southeast Asia. South Africa's Afrox Healthcare is operating for-profit clinics in a number of other African countries.

As David Hall of the Public Services International Research Institute has documented in a 2001 report, *Globalization, Privatization and Healthcare*, a number of developing countries, especially in Latin America, started introducing U.S. HMO-style "managed care" schemes in the last decade. In Brazil alone, there are now more than 700, mostly served by a number of private hospitals. Transnational health corporations have invested billions in these private systems. A Texas company, Baylor, has joined Brazilian Groups Care and APPH to form a joint consortium in Brazil called Hospitalium, to buy Brazilian hospitals. Hall also reports on the expansion in clinical diagnostic or therapy services, such as dialysis, blood products and MRI scans. Fresenius of Germany, Scanfert Oy of Finland, and Quest Diagnositcs of the U.S. are all expanding into world markets. Worldcare, a U.S. telemedicine corporation, is also extending its business interests around the world.

According to Hall, the World Bank's International Finance Corporation (IFC) and its Multilateral Investment Guarantee Agency (MIGA), which provides investment guarantees to protect against political risk, are both promoting these corporations in developing countries. In 2001, the IFC invested in a private clinic in Russia run by Finland's Scanfert Oy. It invested U.S.$22 million in four private hospitals for tourists run by the Spanish hospital company Hospiten in the Dominican Republic. In Brazil, the IFC invested U.S.$6.5 million in Innovative Health Services, a joint venture in the delivery of private home care, preventative medicine, and hospital services, with a Brazilian finance company and a Portuguese health company, Jose de Melo Group. In Calcutta, India, the IFC invested U.S.$8 million in a private hospital owned by Singapore's Parkway Holdings.

David Hall exposes another highly questionable scheme involving the World Bank. MIGA joined its World Bank partner, IFC, in financing a big American medical equipment transnational called DVI, in its operations in Brazil. DVI finances the lease of MRI scanners, diagnostic imaging machines, radiation therapy technology and lasers. Because Brazil provides political uncertainty as well as huge potential profits, DVI was grateful for MIGA's involvement.

The IFC formed a joint venture with DVI, called MSF Cayman, in the Cayman Islands, the offshore tax haven favoured by money launderers. MSF Cayman says its role is to provide "cross-border loans and lease financing to private hospitals, clinics and physician groups throughout Latin America, for the purchase of state-of-the-art diagnostic imaging and radiation therapy equipment." MIGA's role was to provide U.S.$75 million of insurance protection against political risks, including the possibility that Brazil would restrict the export of profits. In other words, using public funds, one arm of the World Bank funded a private American health transnational to expand its operation in Brazil, where it stands to make huge profits – while another arm of the World Bank, also using public funds, guaranteed it against political risk. Good deal if you can get it.

Planning Ahead

Transnational health companies are not operating only in the developing world, obviously. There is a great deal of money to be made when governments vacate the field of health care, or at least leave the more lucrative areas to the private sector. Microsoft's Bill Gates is in talks with the government of the U.K. for a multi-billion-dollar contract to supply the National Health Service with online training for more than one million staff. His "corporate university" would be the biggest college of learning in the world, offering electronic courses for all staff from doctors and nurses to cleaners and caterers. Microsoft is already providing an electronic patient record for the NHS, which also signed multi-million-dollar deals with several British corporations to create a single payroll and human resources system for the health service that would "allow effective competition on price and quality between hospitals and other health-care providers," according to a December 10, 2001, report from the *Financial Times* of London.

The service sector is the fastest growing sector in international trade. According to the European Commission, the service sector accounts for two-thirds of Europe's economy and jobs, almost a quarter of Europe's total exports, and half of all foreign investment flowing from Europe to other parts of the world. In the United States, more than a third of economic growth over the past five years has been due to service exports.

Of all services, health care has the potential to be one of the most lucrative. Public Services International (PSI), in its June 1999 report, *The WTO and GATS: What Is At Stake for Public Health?*, cites two sources. The WTO says that the total health expenditure by OECD countries represents CAD$3.5 trillion; the overall size of the world health industry, by direct extrapolation, would be close to CAD$4 trillion. But the UN Conference on Trade and Development (UNCTAD) says that global expenditures are more likely more than CAD$5 trillion a year. If all these services were open to private enterprise, the potential for profit would be staggering. Market saturation for American HMOs has led these health care giants to seek to capture new markets abroad by acquiring lucrative government-run facilities. The industry has received backing for its foreign acquisitions policy from the U.S. government, the World Bank, and the Inter-American Development Bank. Health service corporations target the public funding behind foreign health care systems. The WTO's Secretariat calls the health sector of the OECD countries a "domestic economic giant," according to an article entitled "Rewriting the Regulations: How the World Trade Organization Could Accelerate Privatization in Health-Care Systems," from the December 9, 2000, *Lancet*.

Already, powerful lobby groups have formed in many countries to promote the interests of the service industries. The Coalition of Service Industries in the U.S. is a large group of service corporations with ties to the White House. It includes the major energy, insurance, and financial giants, as well as the major pharmaceutical companies and the newer players in the health care field, including HMOs. "Historically, health care services in many foreign countries have largely been the responsibility of the public sector," says the coalition quoted in an article by D. Price, A. M. Pollock, and J. Shaoul, entitled "How the World Trade Organization Is Shaping Domestic Policies in Health-Care," from the November 27, 1999, *Lancet*. "This public ownership of health care has made it difficult for U.S. private-sector health care providers to market to foreign countries."

The European Services Network and the European Service Leaders Group represent similar networks of European service transnationals. These corporate lobby groups are not just powerful in establishing policies and priorities in their own countries; they are influential players in the international bodies that set global rules on health care. They work intimately with World Bank and IMF officials. The European Services Network has lobbied forcefully to remove exemptions for public services from trade agreements such as the General Agreement on Trade in Services (GATS). (See Chapter Eight for more information.)

The health transnationals also hold an annual trade conference on the global potential for private health care, organized by the Academy for International Health Studies (AIHS), which, David Hall points out, is not an academic institution at all, but a U.S. private health care business association. The annual gathering is attended by big insurance companies like Aetna (U.S. formerly, now Netherlands), Allianz Group (Germany), Aon Healthcare Alliance (U.S.), Cigna (U.S.), UnitedHealthcare (U.S.), and pharmaceutical companies such as AstraZeneca (U.K./Sweden). They hold workshops on the "opportunities and obstacles" to private health-sector investment in the Third World and the "globalization of American managed care." High-ranking World Bank and World Health Organization officials attend as well.

United Nations Collusion

Transnational corporations have become influential in the operations of the United Nations in recent years also, negatively
affecting the UN's ability to provide public health care and
affordable medicines for many millions of the world's poor. In
July 2000, the UN signed a "Global Contract" with fifty powerful CEOs, including several whose companies have poor human
rights and environmental records, such as Royal/Dutch Shell
and Nike. This was the culmination of a process started in 1997
by Secretary General Kofi Annan to chart a formalization of
corporate involvement with the UN and, as he is quoted saying
in *Tangled Up in Blue: Corporate Partnerships at the United
Nations,* by Kenny Bruno and Joshua Karliner, "to forge a close
global partnership to secure greater business input into the
world's economic decision-making and boost the private sector
in the least developed countries."

This new partnership affects health care in a number of ways.
It limits the ability of the UN to affectively criticize the privatizing policies and practices of the World Bank, the IMF, and
the World Trade Organization, as well as the corporations
themselves. The World Health Organization (WHO), a United
Nations agency, has also come increasingly under the influence
of corporations in recent years. For a number of years, the
agency resisted demands by the U.S. government and companies
like Nestlé to abandon its policy favouring breast-feeding over
the use of infant formula in the Third World. The U.S. punished
the WHO, starving it of funds; this left the agency less powerful
than in the past.

Finally it capitulated. According to an article from the July 15,
2000, edition of the *British Medical Journal*, entitled "UNICEF
Accused of Forming Alliance with Baby Food Industry," in 1998,
the WHO Executive Board proposed a resolution promoting

public health over commercial interests. As a result of industry lobbying, the resolution was rejected by the World Health Assembly and returned to the Executive Board. The WHO now says that it wants to enter into more co-operative arrangements with industry in the health sector. Large transnational corporations such as Nestlé already send more delegates to international WHO forums on standards than most governments do. The WHO is also one of a number of UN agencies that form UNAIDS, which is in partnership with five major pharmaceutical companies, some of whom, such as Johnson & Johnson, have been charged by the International Food Action Network with violating the WHO's own infant formula code.

The WHO's Expert Advisory Panel on Drug Policies and Management is promoting the right of the international drug industry to advertise its products throughout Europe, Canada, and Australia, where the practice is still banned. Charles Medawar, a consumer advocate and member of the panel, said in a May 2002 brief to the European Union that the industry – which is booming by all independent analyses – is "in crisis" and has become "unsustainable." Medawar argues that the pharmaceutical companies require "blockbuster drugs" to continue to grow and create new drugs, and they also need to be able to market their products. Advertising of patent drugs is strongly opposed by public health advocates around the world (see Chapter Nine).

Another UN institution is coming under fire for its deference to big business over public health. The Codex Alimentarius Commission is a joint WHO and Food and Agriculture Organization (FAO) food standards commission that harmonizes worldwide food quality standards. However, food giants now dominate the twenty-eight committees of the Codex. The INFACT Canada newsletter from Fall 1996 reported that 81 per cent of non-governmental delegations in committee meetings setting food standards, particularly in infant nutrition, were industry representatives. The fact that Pfizer, a pharmaceutical transnational, has more staff in its marketing department than there are in the whole of the WHO gives an indication of the relative clout of the private-sector players involved.

International Trade Agreements

The jurisdiction in which transnational corporations have come to have the greatest influence, however, is free trade. For service corporations, the biggest barriers to profit are domestic regulations. Rules to protect the environment, health, and food safety are seen as non-tariff barriers to trade. Domestic laws that require some local economic and job enhancement from foreign investment cost them money. Government monopolies on services such as health care and education bar large service corporations from entering nation-state "markets" and making money. Rules designed to nurture local small business, local farmers, or national culture "discriminate" against foreign transnationals.

As legal trade expert Steven Shrybman explains in the 1999 CCPA publication *The World Trade Organization: A Citizen's Guide,* "In the simplest of terms, the essential goal of trade agreements is to deregulate international trade. They set out detailed rules intended to constrain the extent to which governments can regulate international trade or otherwise 'interfere' with the activities of large corporations. Trade agreements provide extensive lists of things governments can no longer do." So it can come as no surprise that the big-business lobby in every country is deeply involved in its government's trade agreements, or that it goes to great lengths, including financial intimidation, to get its way.

It was the Business Council on National Issues (now the Canadian Council of Chief Executives) in Canada and its partners in the United States who first proposed a free trade agreement between the two countries to their respective governments. The close association between the governments of the day and leading corporations on both sides of the border has been thoroughly documented. These corporations openly spent millions of dollars to sell free trade to a wary public.

Meanwhile, as the Council of Canadians discovered in documents obtained through the Access to Information Act, the Department of Foreign Affairs and International Trade (DFAIT) was meeting with the big-business community in Canada over the doomed Multilateral Agreement on Investment (MAI) for three years before it would admit to the Canadian public that such an investment treaty even existed. The original MAI blueprint, which governments of the members of the Organization for Economic Cooperation and Development (OECD) were ready to adopt almost as written before they were forced to back off by a massive public campaign, was drafted by the International Chamber of Commerce in Paris.

In the United States, more than 500 corporations and business representatives have been officially credentialed as security-clear trade advisers to the U.S. government on the World Trade Organization (WTO), according to *Whose Trade Organization?: Corporate Globalization and the Erosion of Democracy*, by Lori Wallach and Michelle Sforza. These include the U.S. Chamber of Commerce, numerous Fortune 500 companies, the Business Roundtable, and a host of industry and service-specific lobby groups.

In Japan, senior members of the Keidanren, the Japan Federation of Economic Organizations, advise the government on trade policy. The Committee on Trade and Investment is chaired by the CEO of Mitsubishi, and the Committee on Environment and Trade is chaired by the CEO of Nissan.

According to the November 27, 1999, *Lancet* article cited above, in Europe, the commissioner of the European Union on WTO Policies and Administration maintains direct links with the European Round Table of Industrialists. The European Community has set up the European Services Network of transnational service industry representatives, led by Andrew Buxton, chairman of Barclays PLC, to "advise" European Union advisers on the key barriers and countries on which they should focus in WTO negotiations.

Transnational corporations now host international trade meetings. The Seattle WTO meetings in 1999 were co-hosted by Bill Gates of Microsoft and Phil Condit of Boeing, who raised U.S.$10 million for the event. At the 1997 APEC Summit in Vancouver and the 2001 Summit of the Americas meeting in Quebec City, corporations could buy their way in to meet with negotiators and senior politicians: the more they paid (payments that might be made in gold, diamonds, or platinum), the more access they were allowed to heads of state.

When the U.S. Congress was debating whether to allow China into the WTO, top business executives issued a warning to federal lawmakers: vote against this deal with China and we will hold it against you when it comes time to write cheques for your campaigns. Phil Condit publicly warned each member of Congress that their "friendliness to business" would be assessed by how they voted on this bill. "We aim our donations at people who support free enterprise and what we see as the free enterprise system," he said in a written statement, which was also signed by several other corporate leaders.

Services and Trade

Before the WTO came into force in 1995, world trade was ruled by the GATT (General Agreement on Tariffs and Trade), a trade agreement whose mandate was to systematically dismantle the world's tariffs (import taxes). Since the creation of the GATT in 1948, there have been eight "rounds" of negotiations, each consisting of a series of meetings, spread out over several years, to negotiate a fixed agenda of issues.

The first six rounds concentrated exclusively on tariff reductions. But the last two rounds, the "Tokyo Round" (1973–1979) and the "Uruguay Round" (1986–1994), began to target "non-tariff barriers": the rules, policies, and practices of governments, other than those pertaining to tariffs, that can have an impact on trade. Governments began to negotiate for rules on "trade-related" items concerning agriculture, genetically modified foods, environmental regulations, and financial and social services.

The changes in these rounds coincided with the growth of the ideology of the Washington Consensus and the creation of global corporations and corporate lobby groups, each intent on adding its sector to the trade talks. This is also when citizens' groups around the world started to sit up and take notice of these until-now obscure meetings.

Nothing was more controversial than services. The Third World, stung by the assault on its services by the World Bank and the IMF, absolutely refused to add services to the negotiations. But the global services industry was gaining momentum and power.

Mega-mergers were taking place in the telecommunications, finance, airline, publishing, insurance, and other service sectors; the new giant transnationals wanted to take down government monopolies in their fields in every country in the world, and they needed free trade to do so. At the same time, global health care, education, food services, maintenance, and security corporations were forming to break into a newly emerging for-profit market in areas that had been exclusively serviced by governments on a non-profit basis. They were not about to give up their goal of a an unregulated global market for their "products" and they knew that international trade rules were essential to their plans.

8

Free Trade's Time Bomb

Free trade is a form of structural adjustment for industrialized countries. Brian Mulroney liked to say that it would bring "the cold shower of competition to the Canadian economy." Unregulated free trade, enforced by a binding set of rules, dramatically limits what governments are allowed to do. Combined with cuts to domestic health budgets, and the restructuring of delivery to allow private companies to provide health services, free trade in its current form will spell the end of public health care in Canada and around the world. It is one of the sad ironies of this story that Canada, home to one of the world's best public health systems, played a crucial role in putting health services on the free trade table.

In the mid-1980s, American service corporations, particularly in the banking and finance sector, decided that they needed some extra clout in order to force a services agenda onto the Uruguay Round talks just getting under way. Services were still very contentious with the majority of the world's developing countries, as well as the countries of the North that had popular universal public programs. So the service companies decided they needed an example of a successful bilateral free trade agreement that would include services to take to the global trade negotiations as a prototype. As they cast around for the perfect partner, their hooks snagged Canada.

Canada First

Canada was ideal. Brian Mulroney's Conservatives had just been elected and the spanking new prime minister's first act had been to announce to a blue-chip audience in New York that his country was "up for sale," and he promised to take down barriers to American goods and investments. The service companies set up the American Coalition for Trade Expansion with Canada, made up of 600 powerful corporations. It was led, not coincidently, by American Express, a financial services company that had long pursued free trade in services at the GATT. For American Express, this was more than a business goal: it was a mission. Harry Freeman, the company's executive vice-president, called free trade "the Lord's work."

As Allan Taylor, then CEO of the Royal Bank, noted in 1986, "A Canada/U.S. agreement which includes services could be the catalyst for multilateral co-operation. Freer trade breeds more free trade – putting pressure on other countries to come into line as the multilateral negotiations proceed." On January 1, 1989, the Canada–U.S. Free Trade Agreement was signed and became the first free trade agreement in the world to include services, albeit with exemptions for public services. (As a reward for its leadership in negotiating the deal, American Express was granted banking status in Canada by the Mulroney government in a secret cabinet meeting on November 21, 1988 – election day.)

A more comprehensive agreement governing trade in services was included in the North American Free Trade Agreement (NAFTA), signed four years later. For the first time, service companies of other NAFTA countries were granted "national treatment" status. This meant that a country or a community could not give any preference to a domestic service provider over a foreign service provider. As well, countries were now required to provide "most-favoured-nation" status to foreign service companies – the companies of all signatory countries had to be treated the same; one couldn't discriminate among them on the basis of, for example, concerns about the ethical behaviour of a company (or the government of its country of origin) in the provision of a service elsewhere in the world. NAFTA granted service companies, especially financial services companies, the right to set up shop in other NAFTA countries and, at the same time, prohibited governments from requiring them to do so in order to create local employment.

In other words, NAFTA spelled out what governments could no longer do to regulate the trade in services. While exemptions were carved out for government contracts and subsidies, as well as for social programs, education, and health care as long as these sectors remained public, a blueprint for international trade in services now existed. If governments wanted to add a new sector, such as health care, it would be subject to all of the conditions specified by the treaty.

Global Services Negotiations

Armed with the Canada–U.S. FTA and then NAFTA, the global services industry became involved in the Uruguay Round talks with renewed vigour. This time, it had more success. When the Round ended with the creation of the WTO in 1995, a new negotiation on services, the General Agreement on Services (GATS) was launched as well. The services corporations have never looked back.

The GATS is one of more than twenty separate agreements administered by the WTO, including the GATT and others in areas such as intellectual property, agriculture, and investment. Like the other agreements, the GATS gains its authority from the WTO, which holds all of the powers and enforcement tools of a global government. Under the WTO's dispute settlement mechanism, member countries can challenge the laws, policies, and programs of other countries. The losing country in a dispute must abide by the decision of the unelected trade tribunals or face severe fines and permanent economic sanctions. In effect, the WTO has the authority to strike down any domestic law, policy, or program judged to be in violation of strict business-friendly trade rules.

The GATS is what is called a "multilateral framework agreement," which means that its broad commission was defined at its inception and then, through ongoing negotiations, new sectors and rules are to be added. Essentially, the GATS is mandated to restrict government actions in regard to services through a set of legally binding constraints backed up by WTO-enforced trade sanctions.

GATS Attack

Through rules on "domestic regulation," which would more appropriately be called "domestic deregulation," the repeated rounds of GATS negotiations are designed to expand the takeover of service delivery by transnational corporations in such critical areas as health care; hospital care; home care; dental care; child care; elder care; education – primary, secondary, and post-secondary; museums; libraries; law; social assistance; architecture; energy; water services; environmental protection services; real estate; insurance; tourism; postal services; transportation; publishing; broadcasting; and many others.

Article VI:4 of the agreement compels governments to demonstrate that their domestic regulations, standards, and laws are "necessary" to achieve a WTO-sanctioned objective, and that no less commercially restrictive alternative is available. It is no wonder, then, that the European Commission states on its Web site that the GATS is "first and foremost an instrument for the benefit of business."

The GATS agreement covers all service sectors and modes of supply as well as most government measures, including laws, practices, regulations, and guidelines – written and unwritten. No government measure that affects trade in services – even to protect the environment or consumers' rights, to ensure that a service is universally available, or to enforce labour standards – is beyond the scope of the GATS.

The GATS' potential for harm to the world's poor has prompted many international organizations and agencies who seldom become involved in political issues to speak out against it. Médicins Sans Frontières (Doctors Without Borders) is one example. Another is Save the Children, an international charity operating in more than seventy countries. In a recent publication, *The Wrong Model: GATS, Trade Liberalization and Children's Right to Health,* by John Hilary, Save the Children warned that opening up health care to private companies in the Third World could have dire consequences.

> The commercial presence of such companies in the health sector threatens to exacerbate existing problems of equity, quality, and capacity. Commercialization of health services has already been shown to exclude whole communities from access to care . . . GATS undermines a country's ability to regulate its health services: restricting domestic regulation in order to remove "unnecessary" trade barriers threatens to drive down regulatory standards rather than raising them to provide the best possible guarantee of public health.

Negotiators in the current talks are pressing to make the rules restricting domestic regulation even more stringent. The United States and Europe want guaranteed, irreversible access to domestic markets, and governments are under greater pressure to list more of their services and exempt fewer. The new talks are aimed at developing new GATS rules to further restrict the use of government subsidies, such as those used to support public works, municipal services, and social programs.

The GATS and Canada

At present, public services provided by government are technically eligible for exemption. Hence, the Canadian government is claiming that our programs will be safe if we choose to exempt them. But under GATS article 1.3C, for a service to be considered to be under government authority, it must be provided "entirely free." That means that the sector in question must be completely financed by government and run entirely on a non-profit basis. This is clearly not the case for the health care sector anywhere in Canada any longer. The WTO itself has been very clear on its interpretation of this article; wherever there is a mixture of public and private funding, such as exists in Canada, the service sector should be opened up to foreign corporations.

Absolutely nothing, including health care, is off the GATS "table." Going into the 1999 WTO ministerial meeting in Seattle, the Canadian government's official, published position on GATS negotiations, as stated in *Canada and the Future of the World Trade Organization: Government Response to the Report of the Standing Committee on Foreign Affairs and International Trade*, October 1999, was that consultations would proceed even in "areas of particular sensitivity, such as health, education and transport." Already, almost 100 countries, including all of Europe, have listed some sectors of health care with the GATS, opening up their health care systems to foreign-based corporate competition.

Canada, astonishingly, listed health insurance for inclusion. This is very significant and dangerous because health insurance is not considered part of the health services sector in trade agreements, where it would be subject to some protection under the health services agreement. Health insurance is categorized along with other forms of insurance as a financial service. In a comprehensive 2001 report on GATS and health care for the Canadian Centre for Policy Alternatives, social policy analyst Matt Sanger documents that by listing health insurance, the very backbone of medicare, the Canadian government has exposed our public system to "national treatment" challenges from foreign private insurance companies, and has allowed a foreign-owned commercial insurer operating in Canada to assert its right to process Canadian health insurance claims and records from outside the country.

Under GATS, hospitals and regional health authorities would be vulnerable to a GATS challenge. Especially at risk are provinces, such as Alberta, that are already permitting public funding of private, for-profit hospitals. Reports Sanger, "A successful trade challenge could give a virtually unlimited number of commercial hospitals beyond our borders a claim on Canada's public funding for health care, exposing Canada to trade retaliation and potentially overwhelming the capacity of provincial and federal governments to contain costs and the quality of care."

Further, listing Canada's health insurance under the GATS regime has exposed Canada to trade threats that will restrict our options for health care reform, such as the inclusion of home care or pharmacare under the Canada Health Act, both of which were promised by the Chrétien Liberals in their 1993 Red Book. A significant expansion of medicare in these areas would allow foreign investors in the private health insurance industry in Canada to seek compensation or other remedies through international trade action.

An American public relations firm with HMOs as clients has referred to Canada's medicare system as one of the largest "unopened oysters" left anywhere. The intention of the United States to use the WTO and GATS to pry our oyster open is a matter of public record. According to the U.S. Trade Representative's Office quoted in the *Lancet* on November 27, 1999:

> The mandate is ambitious: to remove restrictions on trade in services and provide effective market access. Our challenge is to accomplish significant removal of these restrictions across all services sectors, addressing measures currently subject to GATS disciplines and potentially measures not currently subject to GATS disciplines . . . . The United States is of the view that commercial opportunities exist along the entire spectrum of health and social care facilities, including hospitals, outpatient facilities, clinics, nursing homes, assisted living arrangements, and services provided in the home.

NAFTA's Impact on Health

Despite government claims that NAFTA has no impact on health, this trade agreement is being used to erode health and environmental regulations and standards in Canada. NAFTA was the first international trade agreement in the world to allow a private interest, usually a corporation or an industry sector, to bypass its own government and, although it is not a signatory to the agreement, directly challenge the health laws, policies, and practices of the government of another NAFTA country.

Chapter 11 of NAFTA gives American corporations operating

in Canada the right to sue for lost profit if any level of government enacts a new law or regulation that affects its business deleteriously. This right applies even if the government is acting with the full consent of its people and in reaction to new evidence that a particular practice or product is dangerous. Chapter 11 has been used to knock down a number of Canadian health standards.

In April 1997, the Chrétien government legislated a ban on the cross-border sale of MMT, a gasoline additive whose sale has been outlawed in many countries and which many environmentalists believe causes attention deficit disorder in children. When he was in opposition, Jean Chrétien called MMT "a dangerous neurotoxin" and said it could have "truly horrific effects." In introducing the bill, the government declared MMT a public health hazard.

However, the company that manufactures the product is American and, as such, has compensation rights under NAFTA's Chapter 11. Virginia-based Ethyl Corp. launched a CAD$350 million NAFTA challenge against the Canadian government in June of the same year. Rather than pay this much money and risk the embarrassment of losing a NAFTA panel, the Chrétien government agreed a year later to reverse its legislation, pay the company CAD$20 million as compensation for its costs, and write a letter of apology containing a statement – music to Ethyl's ears – to the effect that there is no scientific evidence that MMT poses a threat to human health. Said a spokesman for the company: "It's a very happy day, a significant step for Ethyl Corp. and its business world wide." Meanwhile, MMT is still in our gas and Canadians are still breathing in its by-products, and risking potentially devastating long-term health consequences.

Months later, S. D. Myers, an American PCB waste disposal company, also successfully used a Chapter 11 threat to force Canada to reverse its ban on PCB exports. Canada undertook

this ban to be in compliance with the Basel Convention banning
the transborder movement of hazardous waste. After the ban
was lifted, S. D. Myers successfully sued the Canadian government for CAD$75 million in damages for business it lost when
the short-lived ban was in place.

In December 2001, another NAFTA Chapter 11 challenge was
launched against the Canadian government, this one over a ban
on lindane, a pesticide used on canola. The scientific community
has been studying the effects of lindane for fifty years. In the
past year, wrote Dr. David C. Alexander in the December 11,
2001, edition of the *Globe and Mail*, at least four American
children have suffered lindane-induced seizures, and two different North American reports found that lindane exposure
increases the risk of non-Hodgkin's lymphoma.

Steven Chase reported in the *Globe and Mail* on December 10, 2001, that Connecticut-based Crompton Corp., with
more than U.S.$3 billion in sales in 2000, filed notice in the
spring of 2000 that it is seeking a reversal of the ban as well as
compensation of U.S.$150 million for lost business. Ironically,
one of the catalysts for the Canadian ban was that lindane is
banned for use on canola in the U.S., and Washington had
warned Ottawa that it would start blocking imports of crops
treated with the pesticide from Canada. American canola
growers, meanwhile, consider Canada's use of lindane to be an
unfair competitive advantage.

NAFTA and the Tobacco Lobby

NAFTA was also used to give American tobacco companies the
power to dictate Canadian health policy. When it first came to
power in 1993, the Chrétien government faced criticism over
cigarette smuggling. Canadian cigarette manufacturers were
exporting cigarettes to the U.S., not for U.S. consumption, but

to smugglers who were reimporting them to Canada for sale on the black market. The Chrétien government "resolved" the issue by lowering tobacco taxes to reduce the incentive for cross-border smuggling of Canadian cigarettes. This had the dual corporate advantage of returning profits from the smugglers to the tobacco companies, and reducing the retail price of cigarettes in Canada. The U.S. tobacco giants were very happy.

But the move raised a storm of criticism among children's advocates and health and anti-smoking groups in Canada. And it cost federal and provincial treasuries almost $1 billion in the first year alone. The whole thing could have been avoided with an export tax imposed at the Canadian factory gate; but under NAFTA, such export taxes are illegal.

To offset criticism because of the terrible health effects of lowering taxes on cigarettes, especially on youth, the Commons Health Committee was poised to recommend the plain packaging of all cigarettes to discourage their use. Appearing before the committee on behalf of U.S. tobacco giants that owned Canadian brands was Julius Katz, former chief U.S. NAFTA negotiator. The statement he carried in his accompanying brief was prepared by another former U.S. trade representative, Carla Hills, now working for the tobacco industry as well. Their message was that any such action would violate NAFTA. Roy MacLaren, then Canadian trade minister, objected weakly that health was exempted in NAFTA. Katz replied that the exemption did not apply to intellectual property, including trademarks. The idea was quietly abandoned.

NAFTA was invoked again in March 2002, when tobacco giant Philip Morris International warned the Canadian government that it would be violating trade rules if it proceeds with a proposal to ban the use of the words "light" and "mild" on cigarette labelling in Canada. When he was still health minister, Allan Rock announced he would ban these words from cigarette labels because they deceive smokers into believing such products are safer. His threat of legislation came after an effort to get the tobacco companies to remove the words voluntarily failed.

In a submission to Ottawa about the proposed legislation, Philip Morris warned the government that it considers any ban a form of expropriation under trade rules. "Under NAFTA, Canada must compensate foreign investors when measures expropriate, or are tantamount to expropriation of, investments in Canada." the company asserted. Since she has taken over as health minister, Anne McLellan has been silent on the promise.

NAFTA and the Insurance Transnationals

NAFTA has affected health care directly. It removed a law imposing a 25 per cent ceiling on foreign ownership in the insurance industry, ensuring Canadian control and government regulation of the sector. As Colleen Fuller documents, this led very quickly to the integration of the North American insurance industry. What were once three national markets in Canada, the U.S., and Mexico were merged into a single continental market. This also allowed the profit motive to invade the Canadian health insurance sector in a new way.

The first big takeover in the industry was very controversial. In 1995, Boston-based Liberty Mutual, one of the world's largest insurance transnationals, with assets worth more than all Canadian health insurance companies combined, took over Ontario Blue Cross (OBC), a non-profit insurer wholly owned by Ontario's publicly funded hospitals and managed by the Ontario Hospital Association. OBC had been seeking a private buyer; with more than 2 million clients, its board of directors decided it was time for it to get into the "managed care" business.

According to an article by Tom Walkom from the January 10, 1995, edition of the *Toronto Star,* at the time of the acquisition,

Liberty said that it planned to use Canada "as a base for exporting managed care services world-wide." As Fuller points out,
this sale constituted the loss of a non-profit alternative to the
competitive, for-profit insurance industry, as well as the loss of a
company in which the public had invested. Liberty was soon followed by other U.S. insurance giants such as Aetna, which,
reporter George Anders quoted the company as saying in the
April 17, 1997, *New York Times,* would "redefine the way
health care is provided."

Since then, the foreign private health insurance industry in
Canada has greatly expanded. According to Canadian Life and
Health Insurance Facts, 2001, by the Canadian Life and Health
Insurance Association, of the 140 private health insurance
firms currently active in Canada, thirty-seven are American-
owned and ten are European-owned. Finance Canada, in a
2001 report called *Canada's Life and Health Insurers,* stated
that the market share of life and health insurance sector held by
foreign insurers was just under 30 per cent in 2000. Best estimates suggest that these foreign firms receive as much as
$2.5 billion in private health premiums from Canadians. Any
attempt by any Canadian government to wrest back Canadian
control of this business, or to bring it to the public sector,
would trigger billions of dollars of trade challenges under
NAFTA's Chapter 11 provisions.

The American private insurance industry is no shrinking
violet. It is a powerful player on Capitol Hill and lobbies hard to
maintain a private health system in the U.S. This lobby spent
U.S.$169 million in the 1999–2000 U.S. federal election in
support of its political friends; only the big drug companies
spent more. Aside from wanting to enter into the Canadian
market to invest in current insurance opportunities, private
American insurance companies are hard at work promoting a
private insurance model for Canada. They are the direct

beneficiaries when currently listed health services are removed from medicare coverage.

No Going Back

The worst danger in NAFTA, and its planned successor, the FTAA, lies in the creeping privatization of health services. It is very simple: if a government allows any currently exempt sector, such as public services, to become privatized, or even partially privatized, the sector no longer qualifies for trade exemption status. For-profit companies from other NAFTA countries must now be allowed to enter the sector as competitors.

In a legal opinion released in March 2000, trade expert Steven Shrybman of Sack Goldblatt Mitchell showed that under the current rules of NAFTA, Canada's health care could come in for a challenge in the future. To qualify for an exemption, health care services must be "social services established or maintained for a public purpose." The U.S. is clear, Shrybman asserts, that as soon as any health care service is supplied by a private firm, whether it is on a profit or non-profit basis, it falls under NAFTA's Chapter 11 rules.

Alberta's Bill 11 has opened up the door to privatization for all of Canada, said Shrybman, because once U.S. health corporations gain a legal footing under NAFTA in Alberta's health care system, it will be impossible to stop them from entering other provinces. Under the FTAA's extended services provisions, foreign service corporations will gain competitive rights to the full range of government health services, and will have the right to sue any government that resists for financial compensation.

This is an increasing threat as private health companies move into Canada. As Colleen Fuller argues, North America's health care services, medical devices, supplies, and distribution markets are larger than the automobile, steel, and transportation sectors combined. And they are dominated by corporations based in the United States, which are gaining a powerful foothold in Canada.

According to the Canadian Institute for Health Information Annual Report, 2001, the Canadian health care market is potentially worth at least CAD$95.6 billion to private providers. There are about 250 large corporations, many of them U.S.-based, now operating here. With every privatization, they acquire new rights under NAFTA – either to enter our market and compete with the Canadian non-profit sector for public funding, or to sue for compensation if they are denied access. If a future federal government, for instance, attempted to bring home care under the jurisdiction of the Canada Health Act, it would have to be prepared to pay billions of dollars in compensation to the American corporations already operating in Ontario and other provinces.

The reality is simple: once privatization is established in any public sector, it is almost impossible to reverse. With time, the Canadian government would no longer be able to afford to publicly fund health care, as it would have to be prepared to give equal access to such funding to private contractors from the United States.

The FTAA

The Free Trade Area of the Americas (FTAA), the planned successor to NAFTA, will make matters substantially worse. With a hemispheric population of 800 million and a combined GDP of U.S.$11 trillion, the FTAA would take jurisdiction over the largest free trade zone in the world. But it will do more than expand the free trade agreement to the rest of the western hemisphere; as proposed, the FTAA significantly expands coverage of the service industries, thereby putting the health care systems of every country at risk.

The services proposals of the FTAA are very broad, calling for "universal coverage of all service sectors," including the "rules, procedures, decisions, administrative provisions, or practices" of every level of government. Proposals to exempt certain vital public services such as health, education, and social services are qualified by the criterion that to be exempt, a sector must be entirely free of competition: a criterion met by almost no public service in any FTAA country. In any case, no country has yet proposed a clear exemption for any public service, including health care.

As well, the FTAA contains new constraints on domestic regulation of service corporations, and protective measures for domestic providers. Combined with the services proposal, these measures are a deadly recipe for health care in the Americas. Foreign, for-profit health service corporations from anywhere in the hemisphere could gain the right to establish a "commercial presence" anywhere in North, Central, or South America.

Foreign corporations could have the right to compete for public dollars with public institutions such as hospitals, nursing homes, and health clinics. Standards for health care professionals would be subject to FTAA rules, and would be reviewed to ensure they are not an impediment to trade. Foreign-based telemedicine services would become legal. And no country would be able to stop transborder competition from low-cost health care professionals.

The governments of the western hemisphere appear poised to extend the "investor-state" provisions of NAFTA into the new agreement. If these are included, then if any government at any level – federal, provincial, or municipal – attempted to resist these developments and maintain services under domestic control, every service corporation of the hemisphere would have the legal right under the investment provisions to sue for financial compensation for lost revenues.

That the real goal of this services/investment juggernaut is to reduce or destroy the ability of the governments to provide publicly funded services (because these are considered "monopolies" in the world of international trade) is demonstrated clearly by the words of Organization of American States (OAS) deputy trade director Sherry M. Stephenson in a report entitled *The State of the FTAA Negotiations at the Turn of the Millennium*: "Since services do not face trade barriers in the form of border tariffs or taxes, market access is restricted through national regulations. Thus the liberalization of trade in services implies modifications of national laws and regulations, which make these negotiations more difficult and more sensitive for governments."

9

Structurally Adjusted Canada

As intended, Canada is restructuring its economy and its
social policies to conform to the rules of economic globalization and free trade. Piece by piece, Canada's social security net is being dismantled and the private sector is moving
into the resulting vacuum. Health care is not necessarily
singled out – just the victim of the logic of a society dominated
by the market ethic.

It is important, however, not to see Canada as a victim of the
trade deals. The Canadian government under Jean Chrétien has
taken a leadership position in promoting the values of the
Washington Consensus. Canada was an ardent supporter of the
MAI, an early proponent of the WTO, and plays a prominent roll
at the GATS. Sergio Marchi, Canada's trade ambassador to the
WTO and a former trade minister, was, until recently, the chair
of the new "round" of GATS negotiations. Upon taking office in
1993, Jean Chrétien merged the old Department of External
Affairs with the Department of Trade, creating the Department
of Foreign Affairs and International Trade (DFAIT) and giving
the trade secretariat increased powers relative to both foreign
affairs and most other departments.

While the funds of other departments were cut in the 1995
budget, funds for trade development in DFAIT almost doubled.

DFAIT launched the Team Canada trade missions, which enlist senior politicians to shill for Canadian business around the world. As one department official explains, "We used to go with lists of political prisoners we wanted released. Now we go in with lists of companies that want contracts."

DFAIT also acts as a watchdog over other departments, both federal and provincial, to ensure that any and all policy proposals they are considering do not violate trade rules. It has a chilling effect on those areas of government that are responsible for the protection of the cultural, environmental, or health rights of Canadians.

Abandoning the Precautionary Principle

The "Precautionary Principle" allows countries to control or ban substances that they have concerns about, but about which they do not yet have full, treaty-proof evidence of harm. As long as a country's regulatory measures are in keeping with its own health and environmental standards, it would not have to get approval from a trade panel. This principle is particularly crucial to controlling the introduction of new drugs and chemicals to a country, to allow for testing to that country's standards.

It is widely believed in environmental and health circles that Canada is actually opposed to the inclusion of the Precautionary Principle in domestic health and environmental legislation, because of a concern about finding itself in contravention of trade agreements such as the WTO and Chapter 11 of NAFTA. Rumours circulating on Parliament Hill that Trade Minister Pierre Pettigrew had dictated an anti-Precautionary Principle policy in a confidential cabinet memo led Liberal MP Clifford Lincoln, in an October 2000 exchange at a parliamentary environment committee meeting, to ask trade department officials if it were true. Nigel

Bankes, a senior official in the DFAIT, admitted, "On that specific question, 'Has the department been arguing against simple references to the Precautionary Principle?,' I think you are correct. I'm aware of at least one instance of that."

Intellectual Property

Another "structural adjustment" Canada has undergone is bringing its drug patent and intellectual property laws into global conformity. Both NAFTA and the WTO contain provisions to protect "intellectual property" that are being used by transnational drug companies to deny affordable medicines to millions of people around the world.

"Intellectual property" refers to types of intangible property, such as patents, which generally grant holders an exclusive right to the use of something such as a design, trademark, or formula. Trade rules on intellectual property extend this exclusive right, often held by corporations, to the other signatory countries to the agreement. Intellectual property rules in trade agreements set enforceable global rules on patents, copyrights, and trademarks that have gone far beyond their initial scope of protecting original inventions or cultural products; they now permit the patenting of genetic lines of plants and animals, promoting the property rights of corporations over the genetic heritage and traditional medicines of local communities.

The impetus for an international system of intellectual property protection was the rise of the "knowledge economy." Wealthy countries such as the United States and the countries of Europe wanted to maximize their returns on knowledge through licences on their patents across the globe. According to Madelaine Bunting in an article entitled "Intellectual Property Rights: The New Colonialism," which ran in the February 13, 2001, edition of the *Guardian* of London, 70 per cent of U.S.

export earnings are now linked to intellectual property; intellectual property provisions of the WTO protect the spread of American economic and cultural hegemony.

The stakes are so high in the knowledge economy, Bunting reports, that applications for patents in the U.S. have skyrocketed from 150,000 a year in the late 1980s to 275,000 today. In October 2000 alone, there were patent applications for 126,672 human gene sequences. The figure for February 2001 was 175,624. Needless to say, very few patents are held in the countries of the South, even though they are often the original source of the knowledge being patented.

TRIPS

As of January 1, 2000, all member countries became subject to the rules of the WTO Agreement on Trade-Related Aspects of Intellectual Property Rights (TRIPS). By 2006, each of them must have legislation in place providing twenty-year protection for pharmaceuticals. This will grant the drug companies exclusive monopoly rights to market their drugs and medications in all WTO member countries for a twenty-year period. The TRIPS Agreement has become a powerful weapon for the pharmaceutical industry and its government allies to use in prying open profitable markets for their products around the world, especially in developing countries.

As reported by Sarah Boseley in the February 12, 2001, *Guardian*, more than 2.5 million people die every year from AIDS-related illnesses. There are more than 32 million men, women, and children infected by HIV/AIDS in developing countries. AZT and 3TC, the basic antiretroviral drugs in the West, would keep them alive and well, but the price tag is U.S.$10,000 to U.S.$15,000 per patient per year – well above the annual income of most people in the Third World. There are alternatives:

cheap copies of life-saving medicines called "generics," made mainly in Brazil, India, and Thailand, whose national laws allow them to ignore drug patents in cases of dire human need.

Tina Rosenberg in the January 28, 2001, edition of the *New York Times* writes that Thailand says it could supply South Africans with HIV/AIDS generics that cost U.S. $200 per person a year, and that the South African government wants to import these drugs now. But forty-two pharmaceutical companies, including giant GlaxoSmithKline, retained virtually every patent lawyer in South Africa to block these imports, and the U.S. government imposed trade sanctions to convince the South African government to withdraw a legislative proposal allowing compulsory licensing and parallel importing. These threats were only withdrawn after a massive global campaign by non-governmental groups who put the international spotlight on this travesty. The government of South Africa, however, has been persuaded by the United States and the large drug companies to postpone its promised "Medicines and Related Substances Control Amendment Act" for two years. With each victory, the people of South Africa face new hurdles, and thousands more die from government inaction and corporate greed.

And the United States hasn't given up. It had already stopped Thailand from moving ahead with its patent laws in the early 1990s, and has recently launched a WTO/TRIPS challenge against Brazil for its manufacture and use of generic antiretroviral drugs. A similar case is pending against India. Quite simply, trade-enforced patent laws are killing millions of people.

At the Fourth Ministerial Meeting of the WTO in Qatar in November 2001, a "deal" of sorts was reached whereby developing countries appear to be given a little more flexibility to use generics in times of medical emergencies. This development was hailed by some as a breakthrough for poor countries. But the wording of this "side agreement" renders it purely political; it has no legal standing. It only confirms what is already in the original TRIPS agreement, namely, that countries have the right in a national emergency to use their own generic drugs instead of those of the brand-name companies. As the U.S. and Canada have not honoured this clause in the past, there is little reason to think that the Doha declaration will have any real long-term effect.

In any case, most poor countries cannot take advantage of this so-called exemption. If they do not have the financial and technological capacity to produce their own generic reproductions of the brand-name drugs, they are not allowed under WTO rules to import them from another country. The TRIPS agreement states that a country can only produce generic drugs for emergency use in its own domestic market. Only three countries are producing affordable drugs for AIDS: Brazil, India, and Thailand. The WTO now prevents these countries from exporting their AIDS generics to the desperate millions in Africa.

The Drug Pushers

The United States' (and Canada's) support of a strong TRIPS regime in the WTO and elsewhere is directly related to the global strength of the major transnational drug companies and their reach into the power circles in Washington and Geneva.

A handful of companies dominate the pharmaceutical industry – Merck, Pfizer, GlaxoSmithKline, Eli Lilly, Bristol-Myers Squibb, and Johnson & Johnson – and they wield enormous clout. There was a time not long ago when these and other corporate giants were merely the size of nations. Now, after a frenzied three-year period of pharmaceutical mega-mergers, they are behemoths that outweigh entire continents. According to Julian Borger in a special report entitled "George Bush's America: The Industry that Stalks the U.S. Corridors of Power," which ran in the *Guardian* on February 13, 2001, the combined worth of the world's top five drug companies is twice the combined GDPs of all of the countries of sub-Saharan Africa.

In a May 2002 release, Ralph Nader's Public Citizen's Congress Watch reports U.S. industry profits have soared in recent years to a rate of return on investment that is more than twice the U.S. average. The drug industry is far and away the most profitable major industry in the U.S. In 2001, the pharmaceutical industry in the U.S. topped all three of Fortune 500's measures of profitability, making this the third record-breaking decade for the industry. While overall profits of Fortune 500 companies fell by 53 per cent in 2001, the top ten drug makers increased profits by 32 per cent. Together, the ten drug companies had the greatest return on revenues, reporting a profit eight times higher than the median for all Fortune 500 industries.

Says Frank Clemente, director of Public Citizen's Congress Watch:

> During a year in which there was much talk of sacrifice in the national interest, drug companies increased their astounding profits by hiking prescription prices, advertising some medicines more than Nike shoes, and successfully lobbying for lucrative monopoly patent extensions. Sometimes what's best for shareholders and chief executive officers isn't what's best for all Americans, particularly senior citizens who lack insurance cover for prescription drugs.

The drug companies operate like a cartel, seeking to exercise monopoly control. They have been enormously influential in putting intellectual property on the global free trade agenda and provide perhaps the best evidence that free trade is anything but. For they do not seek a competitive, open international drug market, but a closed and protected monopoly for their products.

The companies defend their size and profits by arguing that they put a great deal of money into research to produce their designer drugs. But much of this research money comes from government subsidies and is publicly funded. In fact, says Public Citizen, taxpayer-funded research has substantially helped launch the most medically important drugs in recent years, including all of the top five sellers. Further, less than one-quarter of the new drugs brought to market in the last two decades were innovative drugs representing important therapeutic gains over existing drugs. Most were replications and variations of existing successful drugs.

In any case, the profits of these companies dwarf their investment in research. Médecins Sans Frontières reports that Glaxo Wellcome made U.S.$589 million on one AIDS drug in 1999 alone, recouping more than twice its research and development costs in just this one year.

Consumer Advertising

Research costs are also dwarfed by the cost of marketing the drugs. Marketing is where the companies really spend money, and this is why they are seeking long-term monopoly protection. In an article entitled "The Pill Preachers," which ran in the January 26, 2002, *Ottawa Citizen*, Shelley Page reported that the Boston University School of Public Health found that brand-name drug makers employ 81 per cent more employees in marketing than in research, and that staff employed in marketing jumped by 59 per cent between 1995 and 2000, while research staff declined by 2 per cent. A report published in July 2001 by Families USA, a non-profit group for affordable and high-quality drugs, found that drug companies spend more than twice as much on marketing, advertising, and administration than they do on research and development.

More and more, this marketing is directed into peoples' homes. Of industrialized countries, only the United States and New Zealand permit direct advertising of prescription medicines to consumers. While some restricted advertising had been allowed in the U.S. for several years, the U.S. Food and Drug Administration relaxed the law in this regard in 1997 and Americans have been bombarded with drug ads on radio, television, and in magazines ever since. As Helen Branswell reported in the *Globe and Mail* on February 14, 2002, the Harvard School of Public Health stated that spending on direct-to-consumer drug advertising more than tripled over the next three years, rising by 35 per cent in 2000 alone.

Drug makers spent U.S.$2.5 billion that year to promote their drugs to U.S. consumers. Merck spent U.S.$161 million to promote its arthritis drug, Vioxx, in 1999; this is more than PepsiCo spent to advertise Pepsi or Budweiser spent to advertise beer. As a result, sales of Vioxx in the U.S. alone quadrupled in one year. Pfizer spent U.S.$58 million to promote its cholesterol-lowering drug Lipitor in 2000, prompting a 39 per cent increase in sales over the previous year.

Studies show that the advertising works. A team of researchers from the Harvard School of Public Health published their findings in the February 2002 *New England Journal of Medicine*. They reported that drug advertising is having a significant impact on the practice of medicine, corroborating an earlier study that reported that 71 per cent of family physicians said they believe direct-to-consumer drug ads pressure doctors into prescribing drugs they would not ordinarily prescribe. Another study found that 91 per cent of Americans had seen or heard a prescription drug ad – and 80 per cent of patients who asked their doctors for a drug – had seen it on television.

According to an article by Shelley Page, entitled "Drug Ads: Saving Lives, or Selling Snake Oil?," which ran in the January 28,

2002, edition of the *Ottawa Citizen,* a number of studies show that patients are unaware of the side effects of the drugs they are demanding, even ignoring the mandated warnings in the ads. A study in the *Journal of Family Practice* found that women are 2.6 times more likely to be targeted in these ads than men. It also found that the ads do not provide information necessary for informed decision-making, nor do they describe other helpful activities that could be tried for peoples' ailments, such as changes in diet and exercise.

Barbara Mintzes, a Vancouver-based epidemiologist who works for the Centre for Health Services and Policy Research at the University of British Columbia, is highly critical of this practice. She argues that Americans are doing a lot of self-diagnosis, and that many doctors are unquestioningly compliant. Mintzes described several examples of what she considers to be dangerous advertising. Eli Lilly's Sarafem, dubbed "Prozac in pink" because it is the popular anti-depressant repackaged for women, was pulled by the FDA because it appeared to be aimed at all women suffering from premenstrual syndrome, and not the small number of women who suffer from a severe related condition called premenstrual dysphoric disorder. An ad by another drug manufacturer encourages healthy women over thirty-five to use Nolvadex (tamoxifen) to prevent breast cancer; but Mintzes reports that the drug has been linked to cancer of the uterus and fatal blood clots.

Page reports that some advertised drugs have been pulled off the market, but not before they caused damage. Rezulin, a drug for Type 2 diabetes, was advertised in the U.S. for two years after Great Britain withdrew it for safety reasons. By the time it was withdrawn from the American market in 2000, it was suspected in nearly 400 deaths.

Targeting Doctors

The drug companies also aggressively court prescribing doctors. As Shelley Page documents, perks for drug company-friendly physicians include vacations, flowers, wine, tennis camps, spa packages, and more. In the U.S., there is one drug company representative for every eleven practising doctors. Page reports that the National Institute of Health Care Management says that American drug companies spend about U.S.$16 billion on promotion every year – the bulk on free samples of drugs to doctors and visits from drug company reps bearing perks. In 2000, reports the institute, American drug companies hosted 314,000 so-called "education meetings" with physicians. In Canada, an estimated CAD$1.35 billion a year – more than $20,000 per physician – is spent marketing drugs to doctors.

McGill researcher Dr. Ashley Wazana conducted a study of the literature on this practice that was published by the *Journal of the American Medical Association* in 2000. He found that doctors learn about new drugs almost exclusively from drug reps, who visit an average of four times a month. Doctors are more likely to prescribe a drug after such a visit and to request that drug be added to the hospital list. Wazana also reports that the practice starts in medical school, where students receive an average of six gifts a year, such as meals and calculators, from drug companies.

Three physicians from Mount Sinai Hospital in Toronto found strong financial links between pharmaceutical companies and doctors who draw up guidelines for treating medical disorders. The study, published in the February 2002 edition of the *Journal of the American Medical Association,* found that 87 per cent of surveyed doctors who set clinical practice guidelines had some connection with the drug industry, including 58 per cent who received research funding and 38 per cent who had actually

worked for a drug company. Nearly 60 per cent had relation-
ships with companies whose drugs were part of the treatment
guidelines they helped draw up. Study authors Niteesh Choudhry,
Henry Stelfox, and Allan Detsky stated that their findings highlight the need for complete disclosure of financial conflicts of
interest by guideline doctors.

Washington Insiders

Obviously, the drug giants have a great deal of clout with governments. George W. Bush was elected in no small part due to
the American drug companies and their lobbies, such as the
Pharmaceutical Research and Manufacturers Association. As
reported in an article entitled "A Muscular Lobby Rolls Up Its
Sleeves: Drug Makers Gain Remarkable Access in Washington,"
which ran in the November 4, 2001, edition of the *New York
Times,* the PRMA also spent an unprecedented U.S.$197
million to elect Republicans friendly to free trade to Congress in
the 2000 U.S. election, making it the biggest and costliest corporate campaign in U.S. political history. This powerful drug
lobby, which employs 625 high-paid lobbyists (more than the
535 members of Congress), targeted twenty-six House races;
only four of the industry-backed candidates lost.

Not surprisingly, reports Glen McGregor in the April 6,
2002, *Ottawa Citizen,* drug prices in the U.S. are soaring – up
17 per cent in the last year. In fact, drug prices have risen so
high in the U.S. that politicians in thirty-seven states are considering laws to set limits on them. Even some of the largest
American corporations, including General Motors and Wal-
Mart, have joined the call to change the patent laws, as
the cost of their employee health plans have ballooned. The
coalition Business for Affordable Medicine, which also has
support from several unions and state governors, is highly

critical of the American patent laws that keep generic drugs off the market.

According to Theresa Agovino, writing in the May 1, 2002, *New York Times*, the coalition says that seventeen major drugs are set to lose their patents by 2004. Fortune 500 companies spent nearly U.S.$2 billion in 2001 on those drugs and could save almost half of that if the patents are not extended through loopholes. GM, for example, spends U.S.$1 million a week covering employees' prescriptions for the ulcer drug Prilosec. In 1998, Prilosec manufacturer AstraZeneca PLC invoked the law to challenge generic makers' efforts to bring their version of the drug to market. The companies are serious: "We have to bring some attention to the current practices of some drug companies contributing to the high cost of drugs," says the director of human resources for Motorola.

The Drug Pushers in Canada

As in the U.S. and Europe, the major transnational drug companies are present and powerful in Canada. According to a March 1997 report for Industry Canada entitled *Canadian International Business Strategies*, eight of the top ten companies in Canada with more than $100 million in annual sales are foreign-owned brand-name corporations. They account for almost 90 per cent of drug sales revenue, and spend well over CAD$1 billion every year to promote their products. As in the U.S., the drug companies target doctors in Canada with free drug samples and gifts, spending more than CAD$20,000 on marketing per physician every year. As in the U.S., they have formed powerful ties with the government of the day. And, as in the U.S., they have used the intellectual property regime of the trade agreements to gain monopoly rights and patent protection for their products, allowing them to maintain artificially high prices. To do this, they had to kill a Canadian law that had kept drug prices low for decades.

In 1968, as part of its commitment to its newly passed medicare bill and to keep drug prices affordable for all Canadians, the Trudeau government passed "compulsory licensing" legislation that created a thriving generic drug industry in Canada. The law forced brand-name pharmaceutical companies to allow the production of knock-off drugs in exchange for a 4 per cent royalty. But the foreign drug companies were very unhappy with this situation; when Brian Mulroney was elected, they moved in to have the law changed. They found a friend in both the Mulroney Tories and NAFTA, which contained intellectual property rights provisions for drug patents.

In 1993, knowing that NAFTA's passage was imminent, the Mulroney government passed Bill C-91, repealing the compulsory licensing system and extending monopoly protection for corporate drug patents from seventeen to twenty years. They had already extended patent exclusivity for the drug companies, most of which were American transnationals, up to ten years with the passage of Bill C-22 in 1987. Regulations under the new law also gave the brand-name drug companies a unique legal privilege by granting an automatic twenty-four-month injunction preventing Health Canada from approving a generic equivalent in response to an *allegation,* rather than *proof,* of patent infringement. This differs from patent dispute resolution in any other industry. With the passage of Bill C-91, Canada became the only other country, besides the United States, to give this special protection to the big drug corporations.

As a result of abandoning the compulsory licensing system for a regime that protects the monopoly rights of giant drug transnationals, Canadian drug prices soared. According to the Canadian Health Coalition's brief to Romanow, between 1987 and 2002, spending on prescription drugs increased 342 per cent. In a June 20, 2002, press statement, the Patented Medicine Prices Review Board reported that in 2001, total annual sales by manufacturers of pharmeceuticals in Canada increased by 15 per cent to $11.5 billion. It noted that the brand-name patent drugs did especially well; sales of these drugs increased by just under 19 per cent. Patented drugs now account for 65 per cent of total sales, up from 43.9 per cent in 1995. According to an April 2002 report by the Canadian Institute for Health Information, each Canadian spends an average of $500 on drugs annually. The share of prescribed drugs in the total cost of the public health system has more than doubled since the mid-1980s, the report confirmed. Prescription drugs are now the fastest growing component of health care costs. In its submission to Romanow, Green Shield Canada calculates that the cost of new prescription drugs is rising by about 21 per cent a year. Canada now spends more on drugs than on physician care.

Coverage for those who cannot afford the high cost of prescription drugs varies from province to province. But what is certain is that many Canadians cannot afford the drugs they need. Several provincial drug plans have recently had to announce increases in deductibles for seniors, Nova Scotia to $350 a year from $215, and Quebec to $325 from $175. In December 2001, British Columbia announced that it will increase user fees and deductibles for its drug plan. More than three million Canadians now lack any drug insurance at all; another six million have inadequate coverage. According to Health Canada, in Ontario alone, almost two million people have absolutely no drug coverage whatsoever, and another 700,000 have inadequate coverage.

Corporate-Friendly Liberals

While in opposition, the Liberals took a strong position against monopoly patents for the drug giants. During the 1993 election campaign, they made repeal of Bill C-91 an issue. In an article entitled "Take Two Patents . . . And Call Me Next Year," which ran in the January 20, 2002, edition of the *Ottawa Citizen*, Glen McGregor reports that Brian Tobin called the Conservative government "back-room muggers" and said they were stealing money from the poor, the sick, and the elderly. Bill C-91, he declared, would "rape them daily in the cost of their drugs." Opposition Leader Jean Chrétien actually stopped for a campaign photo-op at the North York headquarters of Apotex, a leading Canadian generic company, and said that his government would accept the moral obligation to keep drug costs down. He promised a five-year review of Bill C-91, should his party come to power.

At the 1997 review, an all-party parliamentary committee was presented with the hard evidence of just how dramatically Bill C-91 had affected drug prices in Canada, punishing poorer citizens, especially seniors, just as the Chrétien Liberals had predicted when they were in opposition. By this time, however, the Chrétien government had become a best friend to the big pharmaceutical companies and a promoter of unregulated free trade; Health Minister David Dingwall made it clear that the whole review exercise had been a sham. Because of NAFTA, he said, the government could never consider tampering with the drug patents. Prime Minster Chrétien pleaded for understanding. Canada was bound by trade agreements "unless an epidemic broke out or something like that," he said.

Then in 2001, the Chrétien Liberals passed another law giving even more rights to the drug companies. The only concessions Canada had kept from its former drug patenting regime were to allow Canadian firms to produce and stockpile generic equivalents of patented medicines for future commercial sale before the patent period has expired, and a grandfathering of seventeen-year patents for pharmaceuticals approved prior to 1989.

Through the WTO/TRIPS regime, the European Union challenged the "stockpiling" practice and the U.S. challenged the grandfather clause; the WTO ruled against Canada in both cases, and, in spring 2001, Canada passed Bill S-17, bringing Canada into compliance with the new rulings. The patents for roughly thirty commercially significant drugs had come under the grandfather clause; these were granted three more years of grace before the generic firms could sell cheaper versions of the medicines, producing a windfall of $200 million for the big pharmaceutical companies.

As Glen McGregor reports in his January 20, 2002, *Ottawa Citizen* article, during hearings for Bill S-17, then-industry minister Brian Tobin was reminded of his former position on drug patents by Senator John Lynch-Staunton. The senator remembered that Tobin predicted that Bill C-91 would cause "festering wounds . . . inflicted on the exposed ankles of Canada's poorest citizens." Why the change? Lynch-Staunton asked. "Senator," replied a smiling Tobin, "you obviously have not heard that there was a very effective ankle cream developed as a result of the drug regime in this country. The ankles of this country are in very good shape."

For a while, it seemed that Canadians concerned about rising drug prices had a friend in former health minister Allan Rock. It is widely rumoured that as health minister, Rock clashed with John Manley when he was industry minister over Manley's strong support of trade patent rules. Certainly, on many occasions, Rock openly chastised brand-name drug companies for being greedy and complained about the consequences of rising drug costs.

But upon becoming industry minister in the January 2002 cabinet shuffle, Allan Rock defended the patent system. "I believe firmly in the law. I want to protect the law on patent rights," he told Jack Aubrey in the May 8, 2002, *Ottawa Citizen*, adding, "The patent law is there to protect and encourage innovation and to reward those who have new ideas. That's how civilized societies do that, by granting a period of market protection, so people who have innovated can be rewarded." In a May 7, 2002, appearance before the House of Commons' Industry, Science and Technology committee, the minister defended current drug prices and patent protections, saying that the use of expensive pharmaceuticals sometimes eliminates the need for surgery.

Committee member and Liberal backbencher Dan McTeague, who has long fought to have the patent law repealed, was not amused. According to Glen McGregor, in an article that ran in the June 24, 2002, *Ottawa Citizen*, McTeague called the minister's arguments "weak" and his body language "telling." McTeague told a reporter that he thought Rock knew right from wrong on this issue, which is why the minister failed to look him in the eye while answering his questions.

A Clear Agenda

It is fortunate indeed that the transnational drug companies operating in Canada have friends in Ottawa, for they have very specific goals. They are worried about a proposal to require better cost-benefit analyses of new drugs before they are approved by Health Canada. Currently, drugs must be shown to be safe and effective, but not necessarily good value for the price they command. Clearly, new regulations would pose a problem for the expensive patent-protected drugs over their less expensive generic competitors.

The companies also want to be allowed to advertise drugs directly to consumers, as they do in the U.S. This would mean that Canadians, like Americans, would be faced with a barrage of hard-hitting ads on television every night promoting the miracle of a wide variety of drugs. Already, Canadians can see ads for drugs such as Viagra and Zyban, the smoking-cessation treatment, on television and billboards, leading critics to charge that Health Canada is not enforcing its own rules. But a new coalition of the brand-name drug companies and the advertising industry called the Alliance for Access to Medical Information is turning up the heat. It wants the government to allow direct-to-consumer ads and has organized a well-financed lobby of politicians. Health Canada is examining changes in the Health Protection Act in the near future and appears to be open to the demands of the drug industry.

The big pharmaceuticals want to continue to block the export of Canadian generic drugs to the Third World. Currently, Canadian law does not allow generic drug manufacturers to export medicines that are under patents in Canada to countries where there is no patent protection, or where the patents have expired earlier. Canada asserts that the TRIPS provisions prevent all countries from allowing their domestic generic industry to compete with the transnational drug companies internationally. Thus, badly needed generic drugs made in Canada are not reaching millions of sufferers around the world.

The drug companies also want to protect their privileged position at the Health Protection Branch of Health Canada, the agency whose mandate is to ensure that our food and drugs are safe for use. The branch is under new marching orders from Industry Canada to run more as a commercial enterprise, and has been told to "make Canada the preferred place of business from a regulatory point of view." According to the Canadian Health Coalition, with its funding slashed to the bone, the branch now depends on fees paid by the transnational drug companies to provide at least 70 per cent of its budget for drug approvals, making the companies "clients" of the branch.

Maintaining Privilege

Another high priority of the brand-name drug companies is to preserve the regulations governing patents. And they are lobbying to protect their privileged status under the 1993 patent regime, which allows them to stop Health Canada approval of a generic drug dead in its tracks simply by alleging patent infringement.

For example, as thoroughly described by Glen McGregor of the *Ottawa Citizen* on January 20, 2002, Anglo-Swedish pharmaceutical giant AstraZeneca has enjoyed a Canadian patent on Losec, a drug used to treat ulcers and heartburn, giving it the exclusive right to market the drug in Canada. Losec is a money-maker for the company; its global sales in 2000 were well over U.S.$6 billion. Two years ago, AstraZeneca's patent expired and the Canadian generic Apotex announced that it was ready to go to market with a much cheaper version of Losec.

This should have been a win-win situation. AstraZeneca has made huge profits on the drug, repaying its original investment many times over. Canadians would now have access to a much cheaper version of the drug and provincial governments would save money. Losec sales in Canada account for approximately 3 per cent of Canada's annual $11.4 prescription drug bill. In Ontario alone, the generic Losec would save the government $38 million each year.

But AstraZeneca has taken advantage of Bill C-91, the drug

patent legislation that says that a government cannot approve a generic drug if there are disputes over its patent status in the courts. As McGregor explains, a brand-name company can keep a generic product off the market for at least two years simply by alleging a patent infringement. In a process called "evergreening," AstraZeneca has filed successive challenges to Apotex that could keep its product off the shelf for years. The giant drug company got approval from Health Canada to sell its product as a tablet, instead of a capsule, and acquired twenty-year patent protection on the drug in its new form. It also filed new patents on minor modifications of the drug, such as the coating of the pill, changes in the amount of drug contained in each pill, and changes affecting the drug's interaction with antibiotics.

Each new patent has given AstraZeneca another way to impede Apotex, and other generic drug makers in Canada, by invoking successive two-year injunctions against their products. This process is time-consuming and expensive for AstraZeneca. But it is well worth it; the company figures that it will earn more than $1 million in sales in Canada every day the generic version is kept off the shelves.

What is much harder to understand is why the Canadian government, seeking new sources of funding for medicare, will not revise legislation that permits this kind of tactical manoeuvring that is costing ordinary Canadians so much money. MP Dan McTeague successfully persuaded the House of Commons Industry committee in June 2002 to examine these regulations that allow the drug companies to block their generic competitors from the market, calling the automatic injunctions "the most draconian part of the [patent] leglislation and one that merits universal contempt." But given the close bond that now exists between the ruling Liberals and the big drug companies, McTeague has his work cut out for him.

One Happy Family

The Elections Canada Web site attests to the fact that several of these companies contributed handsomely to the Liberal party during the 2000 federal election: AstraZeneca Canada Inc. gave more than $13,000; Merck Frosst Canada Ltd., more than $17,000; Glaxo Wellcome Inc., more than $39,000; and BioChem Pharma Inc., almost $65,000.

The drug companies in Canada have also formed close ties to the governing Liberals through their powerful lobby machine, Canada's Research-Based Pharmaceutical Companies (Rx&D) – formerly the Pharmaceutical Manufacturers of Canada. Its president is Murray Elston, a former Ontario Liberal cabinet minister whose ties with the federal Liberals are so deep that he chaired their annual fundraising event, the Maple Leaf Dinner, in November 2001. Jacques Lefebvre is now the director of public affairs for Rx&D. He went there straight from Sheila Copps's office, and still works on her leadership campaign.

The *Ottawa Citizen*, in an article by Glen McGregor on October 14, 2001, has documented the intimate relationship between the industry and the government, including the hiring of senior Liberal backroom strategists and former aides to cabinet ministers by Rx&D members to lobby the government. GlaxoSmithKline Canada has retained Warren Kinsella, former aide to Jean Chrétien; Michael Robinson, who has close ties to Finance Minister Paul Martin; and Jeff Smith, former aide to Heritage Minister Sheila Copps.

Merck Frosst hired Gary Anstey, a close friend and former executive assistant to former industry minister Brian Tobin. Derek Kent worked as press secretary to former health minister Allan Rock until he joined Veritas in 2000. Veritas is a communications consulting company specializing in health-related issues. Among its clients are Bristol-Myers Squibb, Glaxo,

Upjohn, Schering Canada, and Merck Frosst. Chris White is a former executive assistant to former international development minister Maria Minna, who represented Canada at an international symposium that discussed AIDS drugs for developing countries in 2000. In the summer of 2001, White joined Glaxo as a full-time lobbyist and initially registered to lobby his former minister – a violation of the government's conflict-of-interest code.

"For every lobbyist we can hire, they've got seven," says Jim Keon, president of the generic pharmaceuticals group, the Canadian Drug Manufacturers Association. "In our industry, you live and die by patent rules. Knowing the system, knowing the politicians, knowing the staffers, has proved to be very valuable to these companies."

Just how much clout these global drug giants have in Ottawa became clear in October 2001, when the Ministry of Health bought the anti-anthrax drug Cipro from the generic firm Apotex instead of from Bayer, which holds the patent. When Bayer threatened to sue, then-health minister Allan Rock immediately worked out a deal with the two companies in which Bayer agreed to supply the drug at a lower price and got the contract, while the Canadian taxpayer remained on the hook to honour the government's deal with Apotex as well. (Apotex later agreed to release the government from its contract if its version of ciprofloxacin was not used.) Now, as Industry minister, it is Allan Rock's job to deny countries like South Africa and Brazil the same rights in a much worse crisis.

Privatized Genes

It is not only brand-name drug companies that have gained patent rights affecting the health of Canadians. Private patents on genes are limiting the public's access to medical research.

For instance, as Julie White of the Canadian Cancer Society explains in the April 12, 2002, edition of the *Globe and Mail*, an American company, Myriad Genetics, has been awarded a series of patents that give it extensive control over the genes that have been identified with breast cancer, as well as the test the company has developed for identifying their presence. According to White, women with mutations in the breast-cancer genes known as BRCA1 and BRCA2 have as much as an 80 per cent chance of developing breast cancer. This year, as many as 2,000 Canadian women will be diagnosed with breast cancer linked to these mutations. The genes also increase the risk of ovarian cancer.

Myriad has claimed a twenty-year patent monopoly on both the whole BRCA1 and BRCA2 genes, any information relating to or derived from them, and all methods developed to diagnose and treat hereditary breast and ovarian cancer. As White says, the company is exercising those excessive rights to the full. In 2001, Myriad sent letters to provincial governments demanding that they use only the company's test for the breast-cancer genes, even though the test, at $4,000, costs far more than other, equally valid tests. However, if government researchers use any other test with these genes, they would be infringing on Myriad's patent, which is illegal under the patent laws.

In response, British Columbia suspended its breast cancer gene-testing program, leaving women there to pick up the cost of Myriad's test themselves – or forgo testing altogether. Some other provinces, including Ontario, chose to continue testing and risk legal action. Says Julie White:

> If Myriad's patent stands, access to the test is not the only price Canadians pay. We lose because science loses. The company claims the right to store all new information about the breast-cancer genes in its own facility, giving it a

monopoly on knowledge about these genes. If only Myriad is allowed to collect DNA samples from high-risk individuals, it will be able to construct the world's largest data bank on breast-cancer and ovarian-cancer genes. It will soon have total control over vital genetic information about these diseases.

Every discovery is based on the collective knowledge base and research of many players. Yet a company that comes along and "discovers" the final key to unlock a medical secret can now take out a protected patent monopoly and deny access to its "discovery" to academic and government-sponsored researchers. Many other companies have patents on other key genes. If these patents are allowed to stand, says the Canadian Cancer Society, genetic research will become the preserve of a few large corporations. The effect on public health and science will be disastrous.

Canada Inc.

The patenting of genes and life-saving drugs is one component of the privatization of health care. The Canadian government is aggressively promoting another component: the export of Canadian health care expertise to the world. Canada is actively, if quietly, seeking global markets for its health care industry. For instance, as the Canadian Life and Health Insurance Association reports, the international operations of Canada-controlled health insurance companies has grown dramatically in recent years. In 2000, foreign operations accounted for 55 per cent of total premium income of Canadian insurers, up from 37 per cent in 1990. The twist is, of course, that we cannot ask other governments to open their health services sectors unless we are prepared to reciprocate.

In *Reckless Abandon: Canada, the GATS and the Future of Health Care*, Matt Sanger documents how Industry Canada and the Department of Foreign Affairs and International Trade are working together to expand global markets for Canadian health services exports. The approach adopted by the federal government, working closely with commercial health corporations, is to identify the "barriers to market access" that exist in other countries and that block Canadian health industry exports. These foreign barriers are often exactly the kind of domestic protections that have been put in place in Canada to keep health care accessible, public, and non-profit.

(Health Canada is not the only department selling its wares internationally. As the *Globe and Mail* reported on January 17, 2002, Canada Post is negotiating to operate the postal service of Bulgaria on a for-profit basis. Bulgaria must sell off its state assets in order to qualify for a U.S.$300 million loan from the International Monetary Fund. Under the rules of international trade, Canada might be required to open its postal service to competitive bids as a right of reciprocity.)

DFAIT's "Trade Team Canada" committees commissioned a series of studies that define the Government of Canada's export promotion priorities. The Canadian International Business Strategy (CIBS) reports, which guide interdepartmental committees in their work, have singled out health care, especially telehealth and home care, as a high-priority area for export growth. Citing a claim that the potential global market for direct patient telehealth services is now estimated to be worth at least U.S.$800 billion, the CIBS targets the domestic regulations and standards in other countries that would prevent Canadian, for-profit telehealth companies from entering those markets.

Sanger points out that the measures Canada has targeted for elimination are of crucial importance to the viability of any country's health system: maintaining professional standards and qualifications, guarding against malpractice and fraud, containing costs, and ensuring patient privacy and confidentiality. "To identify them as 'barriers to market access' for Canadian telehealth exports is to target in other countries, the counterparts to the regulatory regimes which support the Canadian health system."

Shockingly, Industry Canada recognizes that the commercialization of Canadian health care is a necessary condition for the promotion of Canada's health exports abroad. In a 1998 report on sector competitiveness, *Industry Canada, Sector Competitiveness Framework Series: Telehealth Industry*, the department praises health "reform" practices such as reduced public funding, increased revenue generation, and increases in privately funded services. The CIBS claims that Canada has the potential to capture 10 per cent of key world telehealth markets by the year 2005, "provided domestic barriers to growth are addressed."

In another report, *Trade Team Canada, Health Industries Canadian International Business Strategy: Introduction*, on future markets for Canada's health services, the department says that the small size and domestic orientation of Canada's health industry renders it uncompetitive and calls for the consolidation of Canadian providers with "foreign" companies to make them competitive. While Industry Canada recognizes that profiting from "market potential" is primarily the responsibility of private companies, "governments have an important role to play in setting the business climate at home, in managing the Canadian regulatory regime, and in supporting international business development."

Tony Clarke and Darren Puscas, in *Waiting in the Wings*, give another example. Export Development Canada (EDC), the country's export credit agency, has backed Interhealth, a 100 per cent health services export company specializing in hospitals and hospital services in its for-profit overseas business. EDC featured the company in a recent issue of *Export Wise*, the agency's official magazine, where the agency declared that, "Interhealth is at the forefront of a growing trend which some experts believe is Canada's next gold mine exporting services."

Small wonder that the Canadian International Development Agency (CIDA) does not advance public health care as a model when it distributes almost $80 million on health promotion oversees every year, nor does it set conditions that the funding be used by recipient governments to provide access to health care as an obligation. (See, for example, the North-South Institute's *Canadian Development Report*.)

Business in the Lead

Not surprisingly, big business is sitting at the head of the table as these studies are being designed and decisions are being made. The chair of the Sectoral Advisory Group on International Trade on Medical and Health Care Products and Services (SAGIT), which advises DFAIT on trade in this sector, is none other than Brian Harling, vice-president of corporate affairs for MDS Inc., a company that led the commercialization of diagnostic health services in Canada and has become what Colleen Fuller calls "Canada's largest and most aggressive health and life-sciences corporation." MDS Inc. and other health care corporations have direct access to International Trade Minister Pierre Pettigrew and all of the trade negotiators. Tony Clarke and Darren Puscas of the Polaris Institute report that in the 2000 federal election, MDS contributed $12,537 to the Liberal party and $11,950 to the Canadian Alliance party.

In a March 2000 letter to the minister, Harling made it clear that Canada has to be prepared to open up its own barriers to trade in health care. "The SAGIT is supportive of any opportunities for Canadians to increase their ability to offer their services internationally. Members cautioned that there would be a price to pay, i.e. granting similar opportunities to foreigners."

It is a wonder, then, that Pettigrew could look Canadians in the eye and assure them that new services negotiations do not pose a threat to medicare while, at the same time, his negotiators were listing health insurance as a tradeable commodity under the GATS. And it is a wonder that former industry minister John Manley can aspire to become prime minister of this great country even though he presided over a department openly undermining the principles of the Canada Health Act. Or that Health Minister Anne McLellan can claim to speak as the national voice of medicare when she herself has publicly supported opening the Canada Health Act to allow for private hospitals, and when her own department has forged a partnership with DFAIT and Industry Canada to promote a thriving domestic, for-profit health care industry in Canada for export.

Ed Aiston, director general of the International Affairs Directorate of Health Canada, had said, in a presentation to the International Health Business Opportunities Conference in Calgary in October 1997, that his department has come to the realization that "investment in health is beneficial to the Canadian economy and part of the understanding in our Department that Health Canada is not only a regulatory body but also needs to be an ally of the Canadian business community." Aiston argues that Health Canada's goals include efforts to harmonize the regulatory framework governing Canada's health sector with global rules – efforts that will "make us key partners in the Canadian export of medical and pharmaceutical products and in the promotion of foreign investment in Canada." He adds that these initiatives are "carried out in full recognition of the lead of Foreign Affairs and International Trade Canada and Industry Canada."

What can one say of such hypocrisy? It is becoming blatantly clear that the Chrétien Liberals have abandoned medicare, which they view as an anachronism. While they mouth the words about defending Canada's most cherished social program, they have cut funding, shifted responsibility to the provinces, allowed foreign transnationals into the sector, looked the other way when provinces broke the Canada Health Act, and done nothing to curb the skyrocketing costs of drugs.

The Chrétien Liberals were elected in no small measure on their promise to protect medicare, our most cherished social program. The vast majority of Canadians support medicare and want it strengthened, not weakened. But the Liberals, like the Mulroney Conservatives before them, have aligned themselves, politically and ideologically, with the big-business community. In doing so, they have adopted all the soul-destroying values of the global economy. These values cannot coexist with the values of public health care – values such as equity, justice, and democracy. These politicians, along with many of their provincial counterparts, have betrayed the Canadian people.

10

It's Not Too Late

How will ordinary Canadians save medicare? Well, we can start by getting involved, really involved. Canada's health care system is at a crossroad; every Canadian must take part in this vital dialogue about our future. At the beginning of this new millennium, we have a unique vantage point. We can go back into our history and choose to recommit to the aspects of the original system we want to retain, while building a system that will work for Canada now and in the future. For example, while Canadians continue to cherish the public delivery of health care, we also want more personal control as well as more local choices so that we are seen as knowledgeable partners in our own care.

Right now, health care is at the top of the country's political agenda. Polls show that Canadians want their governments to tackle medicare's problems and they don't want to wait. Provincial governments, faced with rising health care costs and an increasingly anxious public, are moving to take matters into their own hands, in some cases, by breaking the conditions of the Canada Health Act. Without substantive new federal funds, they are saying, we have no choice but to opt for user fees, medical savings accounts, and private hospitals. The Chrétien Liberals, meanwhile, preoccupied with their bitter leadership battle, are in a weakened position and not likely to take major action on this or any other policy initiative without strong public pressure.

Commissions, Commissions

Thankfully, the country is awash in commissions on health care that have kept the issue front and centre. Two high-profile federal inquiries – the Commission on the Future of Health Care in Canada, led by former Saskatchewan premier Roy Romanow, and the five-volume report of the Senate Committee for Social Affairs, Science and Technology led by Liberal Senator Michael Kirby – contain very different prescriptions for medicare's future.

The Kirby report foresees a major role for the private sector. Its very language is commercial, including such terms as "consumers" for the "health care industry," and providing "customer services" in health care. The Canadian Labour Congress says that the preliminary Kirby Committee papers on issues and options could be called "Let us count the ways we can entrench for-profit health care into the public system." This might not be a surprise, considering that Senator Kirby has been a director of Extendicare, a for-profit, long-term care corporation, since 1985. As well, the Senate Committee process was selective, with groups and individuals appearing before the senators on invitation.

Roy Romanow and his commission, on the other hand, travelled across the country listening to literally thousands of Canadians from all walks of life. He also heard from Canadians via an unprecedented review of Canadian public opinion on health care from 1985 to the present. Headed up by Queen's University professor Matthew Mendelsohn, researchers identified more than 1,000 survey questions in more than 100 polls.

Through this process, the Romanow Commission found that medicare is still Canada's most cherished social program; that 88 per cent of Canadians want to keep a strong, national, publicly funded system; and that while they want more personal control over their health care services, Canadians are still deeply committed to the collective provision of health care.

"Canadians strongly believe that the government should pay for the health care of all citizens and believe that the health care system is a public good," said the Mendelsohn report. "They have reached a mature, settled public judgment, based on decades of experience, that the Canadian health care model is a good one."

The Romanow Commission, unlike the Kirby Committee, sees an expanded role for publicly funded health care, wants the federal government back in the game, believes that Canadians are willing to pay for improved health services, and rejects a large role for the private sector. In fact, at the end of his cross-country hearings, Romanow challenged medicare's opponents to come up with proof that the private sector can save the system money, saying that in all his deliberations, he never came across any convincing evidence that it can.

As mentioned in Chapter Six, there are also a number of recent provincial reports circulating, including that of the Clair Commission in Quebec, which called for the adoption of a policy framework of partnership with the private sector; the Fyke Commission on Medicare in Saskatchewan, which rejected user fees and called for primary care health centres with multi-disciplinary, health service teams and the provision of prescription drugs as part of the public health system; and the recent Mazankowski report in Alberta, which recommends a radically privatized future for health care.

It is very important that Canadians become involved in the political processes that these commissions and studies have engendered. It is a sad fact that governments often commission public hearings that are then ignored, especially if they call for more commitment from cost-cutting governments. This is what happened to the recommendations of the 1997 report of the National Forum on Health Care, which called for a strengthened universal health care system. After receiving it with much fanfare, the federal government put it on a shelf to gather dust. This must not be allowed to happen to the Romanow Commission report.

Nor is this the time to be reactively defensive of medicare. There are serious problems with the system in most parts of the country, and medicare's supporters will do this social program no good to pretend otherwise. In fact, now is the time for those who believe in the Canada Health Act to come forward with a bold new vision for medicare's future. Such a vision should be rooted in a set of principles that can be defended by citizens across the country.

PRINCIPLES FOR A NEW NATIONAL HEALTH PROGRAM

1) The Profit Motive Must Be Rejected

The profit motive does not belong in Canada's health care system. When health care is treated as a public service, it can be delivered very well at low cost. When it is a business, it must realize a profit. The more the system is run as a business, the more it will be squeezed for profit all the way down the line. Studies in other countries show that market forces in health care cause costs to rise and efficiencies to fall.

As Roman Catholic Bishop Fred Henry of Calgary told the Romanow Commission, "Most Canadians believe health care is not just another commodity to be sold for profit, like a loaf of bread or a new pair of shoes. Most of us are also convinced health care is a fundamental human right; that medicine and nursing must not be diverted from their primary tasks – the relief of suffering, the prevention and treatment of illness, and the promotion of health – and that potential financial incentives that reward over-care or under-care, weakening doctor-patient and nurse-patient bonds, should be prohibited."

It is essential that Canadians not allow this debate to become one of rich versus poor. A healthy society is good for all. One of the reasons that many countries originally adopted a public health system was to stem the spread of communicable diseases such as typhus, polio, tuberculosis, and sexually transmitted diseases. Being wealthy did not guarantee personal safety then. It will not guarantee it now. A society divided by the ability to pay for basic health would be the worst possible outcome for our country.

The Canadian people must insist that the profit motive be removed from our health care system at all levels of govern-ment; that the federal government strictly enforce the Canada Health Act in order to ensure universal access to services and immediately move to halt the practice of extra-billing, user fees, and private hospitals, by whatever name they are called; and that a moratorium be placed on public/private partnerships.

2) The Federal Government Must Recommit to Medicare

Years of underfunding medicare and restructuring to give the provinces more power over health spending has all but robbed the federal government of a meaningful role in Canada's health care system. Provinces are openly defying the principles of the Canada Health Act because the federal government has little clout to enforce them. As well, there are no clear, agreed-upon definitions of what constitutes a "medically necessary service." Without a strong federal presence, Canada's health care system is fast deteriorating into a patchwork quilt of services with no cohesive framework and few national standards. This must change. It is time for the federal government to reinsert itself into the process.

This does not mean that the provinces would no longer have jurisdiction to deliver health services. Provincial authority in this area is entrenched in the Constitution. In any case, in a country with an increasingly diverse population, a "one-size-fits-all" model is less and less attractive or realistic. The reality is that the provinces, more than ever, take on the majority of organizing and providing health care for their citizens. It is unlikely that, after being handed so much authority by federal governments intent on minimizing the national presence in health care, the provinces will be willing to hand it back easily.

There are a number of calls for a renewed federal/provincial mechanism to overcome the tensions that now exist. In their book *First Do No Harm,* Terrence Sullivan and Patricia Baranek call for new federal transfer conditions imposed on the provinces to extend a base of flexible public coverage to home care, long-term care, and pharmaceuticals, but which would allow each province to design its own standards to qualify for federal transfers. Tom Kent, fellow of the Institute for Research on Public Policy and former right-hand man to Lester B. Pearson, has been described as one of the "fathers of medicare." As he wrote in *What Should Be Done About Medicare?* published by the Caledon Institute, Kent wants a federal-provincial Canada Health Agency to consult on health policies, collaborate in defining the content of agreed medicare programs, and facilitate co-operation in improving the delivery of services. In her submission to Romanow, former health minister Monique

Begin suggests a "Council of Provincial Health Ministers" that would work with its federal counterpart in a co-operative model. All agree, however, that without renewed federal funding, any such arrangements would be doomed.

The Canadian people must insist that federal funding for health care be returned to at least 25 per cent of total spending immediately, with a view to increasing the federal share to 50 per cent over time; that this funding be directly tied to spending on health care and accompany clear guidelines on what services are "medically necessary"; and that the federal government initiate negotiations with the provinces to create a common definition of "core services" that should be publicly insured by all provinces; and that the federal government cooperate in the delivery of provincial programs adhering to the principles of the Canada Health Act.

3) The Canada Health Act Must Be Extended

Medicare's original compromise of insuring only doctors and hospitals has meant that the most expensive parts of the health care system have ballooned at the expense of other, less expensive and more efficient models. Many services delivered by health care professionals other than doctors are not covered under the Canada Health Act, nor are services delivered outside of hospitals. These include home care, long-term care, rehabilitation services, primary health care, dental care, and pharmaceuticals, when provided outside of hospitals. These omissions were not intentional; the covering of doctors and hospitals was merely seen as the first step in a more complete process. But it is clearly inadequate today, as more and more care is shifting outside of institutions and the cost of drugs is rising.

Funding health care through an insurance mechanism is

failing to protect and maintain Canada's non-profit system of delivery, and is obstructing the development of more afford-able non-institutional alternatives such as community clinics and home care. It is time for Canadians to start thinking about a completely public health care system – in both funding and delivery. The kind of health care system Cana-dians want will not materialize unless and until we bring services, as well as payment, into the public sector. Some rec-ommend reopening the Canada Health Act to include its prin-ciples to community services; others, such as the Registered Nurses Association of Ontario, are calling for a Community Care Act as companion legislation to the Canada Health Act that would serve the same function.

Funding new services such as community clinics would mean ending the fee-for-service as the exclusive method of paying doctors – a proposal that is less contentious than many would think. Doctors in private practice have high overhead costs and few benefits. As well, doctors who believe in service find them-selves at a disadvantage compared to those who view their pro-fessions as a business. A 1999 Canadian Medical Association physician questionnaire found that only 33 per cent of doctors favour the fee-for-service arrangement. An expanded system would also mean equalizing the power base between doctors and other health care workers, especially registered nurses, who have been systematically disenfranchised in the system.

The Canadian people must insist that the federal government move, over time, to a fully funded and serviced health care system; that home care, long-term care, and pharmaceuticals be included in the plan and be adequately funded; and that regis-tered nurses and other front-line health care practitioners be guaranteed a role in all decision-making about the future of health care.

4) Trade Agreements Must Not Be Allowed to Dictate Health Policy

The federal government has exposed medicare and the principles of the Canada Health Act to marketplace disciplines of international free trade agreements. The values embodied in free trade are anathema to the values that underlie universal, public health care. Canada's international trade policy objectives for the biotechnology, pharmaceutical, food, and health services industries are incompatible with its stated goal to protect Canada's health care system from the rules of international trade.

Under the rules of international trade, particularly the services agreements of the WTO and the FTAA, Canada is obliged to reciprocate when other countries open their markets to Canadian pharmaceutical, biotechnology, medical device, home care, health information technology, and health industries. The Canadian government must move to exempt health care from trade agreements and establish food, environmental, and health standards that cannot be superseded by trade challenges. Chapter 11 of NAFTA must be revoked.

Canada's eager embrace of free trade and economic globalization has meant a new and different role for Canada on the international stage. In its support for global trade in services, Canada is now undermining international efforts to develop universal health care. Instead, Canada should join leading health experts in their efforts to build international mechanisms for addressing health as a "global public good." This would mean ensuring that international collaboration to advance health is not obstructed by trade rules, and strengthening the World Health Organization as a body to promote and oversee a public, universal future for health care.

The Canadian people must insist that the government of Canada negotiate an airtight general exemption in all trade agreements for health care systems, including services, invest-ment, and insurance; that Canada negotiate the inclusion of the Precautionary Principle into all international trade agreements; and that Canada renew its heritage of enlightened internation-alism by working to establish health as a global public good and supporting international efforts to bring universal health care rights to all people.

5) The Patent Monopoly of the Drug Companies Must Be Broken

The Canadian government's acquiescence to the TRIPS regime of the WTO and NAFTA have given the pharmaceutical transna-tionals monopoly rights that must be broken. Twenty-year patent rights for the brand-name companies combined with their right to quash lower priced generic competitors in court challenges have driven drug prices up exponentially, resulting in punishing costs for Canadians. The Patented Medicines (Notice of Compliance) Regulations allow brand-name pharmaceuticals to preserve their exclusive markets by filing lawsuits against generic manufacturers even after the twenty-year patent term on the drug has expired. Green Shield Canada, the company that runs Ontario's drug benefits program, is calling for an end to this expensive favouritism.

Dr. Andreas Laupacis of the Ontario Ministry of Health's Institute for Clinical Evaluative Sciences says, in an *Ottawa Citizen* article by Shelley Page from January 26, 2002, that drug companies should have to justify the prices they charge. "In an ideal world, the drug company would charge a price that reflected the costs of developing a drug, the need for funds for future research to develop new drugs and a reasonable profit margin. I have never seen a submission that explicitly justified the price for a drug."

As well, big drug companies spend an estimated $1.35 billion a year marketing their products to doctors and other medical practitioners, directly affecting the type and quantity of drugs that are prescribed to patients. This practice is unethical and dangerous. Further, many doctors who draw up guidelines for treating medical problems are financially linked to the drug companies whose drugs they approve and promote. Many in the medical profession are calling for regulations that would require complete disclosure of financial conflicts of interest by doctors. It is also imperative that the drug companies not be allowed to advertise their products directly to the public as they do in the United States – and as they wish to do in Canada.

The Canadian people must insist that the Canadian government repeal Bills C-91 and S-17, thus breaking the monopoly of the big drug companies in Canada, while negotiating changes to the intellectual property rights provisions of international trade agreements to break the same monopoly in other countries; that Canada continue to ban direct advertising by drug companies while implementing stringent new regulations in regard to the marketing of drugs to doctors; and that the Canadian government enact legislation requiring drug companies to justify their prices before approval by Health Canada.

6) Canada Must Move Toward a Community-Based Primary Health Care System

In keeping with the above principles and recommendations, it is time for Canada to adopt a policy of primary health care. For decades, universally accessible, primary health care services have been recognized around the world as critical for any really

effective health care system. Primary health care is a comprehensive approach, taking all factors that influence health into
account. It is delivered in community clinics by an interdisciplinary team of doctors, nurse practitioners, social workers, and
others, on a salaried basis, twenty-four hours a day. Although
there are many fine examples of primary health clinics in
Canada, they are underfunded, politically vulnerable, and
always fighting for survival.

There are many rewards of a primary care health system, not
the least of which is a substantial reduction of costs. Shifting
resources to less expensive community clinics – where staff are
on salary and where doctors aren't called upon to treat every
ailment – would save the system millions.

Similarly, many seniors would prefer to be in their homes if
the services were better. Home care, even well-serviced home
care, is infinitely cheaper that institutionalized care. If the profit
motive were removed from elder care, more support could be
given to home alternatives. Further, as the National Children's
Alliance told the Romanow Commission, there is a desperate
need for community care for children with special needs.

A community-based, primary health care system is the
answer to Canada's health care problems. (Please see the next
section for details.) This system would mean that we could
reject a private health care model while keeping costs under
control. However, for such a system to really work, it is crucial
that both the federal and provincial governments make a commitment. Without federal funds and federal support, community clinics will continue to be vulnerable. The system must
also be properly funded – otherwise, community clinics and
home care will be second-rate programs shunned by a distrust-
ful public.

The Canadian people must insist that governments and deci-sion-makers in the health system equalize the power base between the hospital sector and other health sectors such as elder care, home care, and community care; that a true, com-munity-based primary health care model with care available twenty-four hours a day, seven days a week, and delivered by interdisciplinary teams of health care professionals, be adopted; and that the federal government introduce legislation stipulating conditions for federal funding of these programs, including home care, long-term care, and pharmacare, on a fifty-fifty basis.

Primary Health Care

What is primary health care and how does it work? In places where it is operating, primary care is usually the first point of contact that people have with the health care system. It sup-ports individuals and families to make the best decisions for their health and includes advice on health promotion and disease prevention, individual health assessments, diagnosis and treatment of chronic conditions, and supportive and reha-bilitative care. Services are coordinated, accessible to all members of the community, and provided by a team of health care providers who have the right blend of skills to meet the needs of the community.

The Canadian Health Coalition described primary care in the following manner in their brief to the Romanow Commission:

> Broad definitions of primary care reform encompass every-thing from a physician in solo practice to a health care centre where teams of providers are concerned with social development and governed by an elected community

board. The definitions suggest a common commitment to serving whole persons, close to their homes where everyone knows their names and circumstances. They suggest as well an emphasis on keeping people healthy and, when this fails, on providing a smooth and comforting transition to appropriate treatments.

The Canadian Healthcare Association added to this definition in their presentation to Romanow:

Primary health care is much more than a reorganization of the existing system. It embraces a holistic approach, recognizing that health depends on many complex and interrelated factors. It empowers people to make decisions about their own health needs and how best to meet these needs. It is based on multidisciplinary teams of health and other human services providers who collaborate to address the needs of individuals, families, and communities. Primary health care is funded and structured in a way that encourages and permits a system-wide balance of treatment, rehabilitation, health promotion, and disease prevention.

Colleen Fuller's program, as laid out in her book *Caring for Profit,* would be comprehensive:

Such a system would be based on federal criteria, with community input and control, providing a broad spectrum of primary health, social, and related services available in one location in each community. Community-based clinics would feature teams to deliver a full spectrum of care, from family counselling and physiotherapy to inoculations and eye examinations; an emphasis on prevention, health promotion, education services, and community development;

and salaried remuneration of physicians and other health care professionals.

Adds the Canadian Labour Congress in its submission to Romanow: "The goals of primary care are broad, including diagnosis and treatment, providing care in the community setting, health promotion and prevention, and directing patients to other forms of care as needed. In part, the terms 'family doctor' and 'community health centre' suggest a relationship marked by security and trust."

Primary health care is not to be confused with primary medical care, which is currently covered under the Canada Health Act and is delivered by physicians focusing on illness-oriented care at the expense of health promotion and illness prevention. Primary medical care underuses the knowledge, skills, and expertise of other health professionals, such as registered nurses, and it misses important opportunities to create health in the population.

Primary health care, on the other hand, includes concepts such as health promotion, illness prevention, rehabilitation, and preventive care along with curative care. The other key dimension to primary health care is the strong community component, both in terms of decision-making and in terms of the importance of a community development, healthy community emphasis. Through delisting and other privatization practices, as well as the fact that home care and long-term care are not currently deemed to be covered by the Canada Health Act, the current delivery of primary health and preventative care is disorganized, underfunded, and threatened by a growing for-profit industry wanting to get its hands on this market.

In *Towards a Sustainable, Universally Accessible Health-Care System,* a discussion paper for the October 2000 National Nursing Forum, five nurses' unions lay out a blueprint for an exciting health care vision. The nurses identify five key elements to a comprehensive primary health care system: universal access to a defined range of primary health care services in which there would be no preconditions for care and no one could be dropped; services that are accessible twenty-four hours a day, seven days a week; Primary Health Care Groups (PCGs) – multidisciplinary primary health teams made up of physicians, nurse practitioners, registered nurses, therapists, social workers, midwives, and other providers – to facilitate the provision of primary health care; the provision of services based on the needs of the community rather than the availability of the provider; and funding for the system based on the needs of the population served.

It is clear that, for a primary health care system to be effective, the community would have to be a full partner with health providers. On its Web site, Health Canada affirms that community empowerment and participation are critically important to health and provide the rationale for a community development approach to health promotion. To empower themselves, says Health Canada, people seek to recognize and value the health experience and knowledge that exists in the community and use it for everyone's advantage: "Community development means building genuine partnerships with the people whose health is at stake, working with them as equals on their issues in a relationship of trust and respect. It means taking time to tap into community views on problems and solutions and then truly respecting these, even if they don't fit with existing plans and agendas."

Community Health Care

Community health centres (CHCs) are the embodiment of primary health care. They are non-profit, community-governed organizations that provide primary health care, health promotion, and community development services using the multidisciplinary teams referred to above. As the Association of Ontario Health Centres points out in *Community Health Centres: A Cost-Effective Solution to Primary Health Care Reform*, there are currently more than 300 CHCs in Canada struggling to survive. Many serve communities that do not have local hospitals and that depend on them on a daily basis.

CHCs also serve a more sophisticated and knowledgeable citizenry. Canadians have much more of a feeling of ownership over their own health care today than they did in the "father knows best" decades of the 1950s and 1960s. Information on health, lifestyle, and drugs is all around us, especially accessible in the age of the Internet. No one health care provider can retain all the information health-savvy Canadians want; a variety of providers, each with a unique area of expertise and method of practice, is a bonus that community health centres offer. As a result, the Association told the Romanow Commission, community health centres have been able to reshape the practice of health care to meet community needs in a way single practitioners cannot.

Ontario has fifty-six CHCs in operation. The City of Ottawa was a pioneer in setting up a network of about ten centres that are considered a model for the province. Patty Deline, a founder of the Centretown Community Health Centre, has also been a patient there for thirty years. In a May 2002 letter to the *Ottawa Citizen,* she extols its triage system, which determines the level of expertise necessary in each case. If a physician is needed, a physician is available. But often, a nurse or other front-line health care worker is more appropriate to the situation. Together, she says, the team at Centretown provide first-rate health care to a very large number of patients, and at a very low cost compared to doctors working alone on a fee-for-service basis.

The West Elgin CHC in West Lorne, Ontario, offers more than thirty-five programs and initiatives, including Healthy Beginnings, Arthritis Self-Management, Health Smart Eating, Farm Safety, Flu Clinic, Breakfast Program, Conflict Resolution for Youth, Parent Drop-in, Nutrition Education, Counselling, and Seniors Outreach. The twenty-two family physicians, thirty-six specialty consultants, and eighty-five support staff of the Albany Clinic in east Toronto process 1,000 patients every day. So dedicated is this team that patients come from all over Toronto for the high quality of treatment they receive.

Roy Romanow reacted very positively to Quebec's 146 community health centres, called "centres locaux de services communautaires," or CLSCs, when he visited Quebec during his commission's hearings. Open nights and weekends, CLSCs integrate family health services with mental health, home care, public health, and a provincial telephone health advice line. They co-operate with police and social services to address social issues, and in rural communities where there are no CLSCs, they work with local hospitals and long-term care facilities. "I have been very impressed with what Quebec has done with the CLSCs," Romanow told a news conference in Quebec City on March 24, 2002. "Canadians outside of Quebec could learn much, involving not only health, but social services – the determinants of health."

New Brunswick premier Bernard Lord is so impressed with the community health model, he announced in January 2002 that his province was going to restructure its health care system entirely around it, promising a community-based network of health centres where people can access primary health care twenty-four hours a day.

This excitement about the system is repeated in communities across the country where CHCs have been founded. In Winnipeg, the Nor'West Co-op Community Clinic has expanded its

role beyond primary health care to provide a wide range of services and programs to address the broader determinants of
health, including pre-school support for children, family violence and substance abuse, poverty, food security, and active
living. The Prince Albert Health Co-operative operates from the
premise that good health includes the social and emotional well-
being of people and offers a variety of programs aimed at caring
for the "whole person."

The Calgary CHC was able to improve access and quality of
care to its community by expanding the role of nurse practitioners. In Edmonton, the Multicultural Health Brokers Co-operative brings together women from Chinese, Vietnamese, South
Asian, Filipino, Arabic-speaking, and Spanish-speaking back-
grounds to assess the health care needs of their communities and
match them up with services. In Surrey, B.C., the Rainbow
Community Health Co-operative operates from the offices of a
local immigrant service centre and meets the health needs of
immigrant and visible-minority populations of the region.

Community health centres are very important to First Peoples
as well. As the National Aboriginal Health Organization told
the Romanow Commission, CHCs embrace a vision of health
that is much more integrated with the whole person and the
community – in keeping with their tradition: "In general,
Aboriginal belief systems define health as a life lived in balance
with other systems of which an individual is a part. These
include such systems as environment, community, and family. A
health care system therefore, according to this definition of
health, must be holistic, flexible, and responsive, not just to the
disease or condition, but to the individual and their role in
restoring the balance necessary for health."

It is crucial that the Canada Health Act be extended to home
care as well as community care. As described in earlier chapters,
home care is growing at an exponential rate, but without nearly

the resources needed to make it truly work. As Paul Cartwright with the New Brunswick River Valley Health Network explains, governments are now using home care to "dump" their health responsibilities on families. An investment in home care would have untold benefits. Many seniors and chronic care patients want to stay in their homes, but do not want to burden their families. Being able to stay in their homes and communities instead of expensive and far-away institutions would be good for both seniors and the system.

Community health can begin to address other determinants of health, such as poverty, violence, racism, and pollution. However, governments across Canada must move to address these systemic causes of poor health in a much more proactive way. As the Canadian Union of Public Employees told the Romanow Commission, "When Health Minister Anne McLellan feels it's important to tell Canadians that being fat is bad for their health (and the future of medicare), we have noted that she has not told Canadians that being poor, or a single mom, disabled, aboriginal, or living near the Cape Breton tar ponds is also bad for their health. It is critical that this Commission recognize the social and economic determinants of health and develop recommendations that reflect this."

Dr. Dorothy Goldin Rosenberg is a Toronto expert on environmental health. In her submission to Romanow, she sounded alarms on the need to reduce environmentally related disease, and the need for Canada to ban toxic chemical dumping and ratify the Kyoto Accord on climate change. "Both First Nations and Nobel Award scientists have stated what most of us know: we can't have a healthy life on a sick planet. We do not need more studies to tell us that pollution is bad for our health."

Paying for Medicare

The question remains: how will we pay for an expanded Canada
Health Act? Over time, it will pay for itself. Diverting funds
from expensive hospitals, specialists, and institutions to community centres will save a great deal of money and free up space
when those services are really needed. For example, in its first
year of operation, the Sault Ste. Marie Community Health
Centre reduced hospital occupancy in that city by 30 per cent, as
cited by Seniors on Guard for Medicare in their submission to
Romanow. Primary health care also provides a significant relief
for emergency services, which also saves money.

As well, most hospitals have patients in acute care beds who
would be better served, for less cost, in good long-term care
facilities or at home with adequate home care. All hospital emergency rooms are filled with patients who shouldn't be there but
who have no alternatives.

Resources put into home care would be returned to the taxpayer many times over. A July 2001 study prepared by the
Ontario Community Support Association, the voice for 360
non-profit home care services in Ontario, showed that institutional care for seniors is ten times more expensive than home
care. In a study of services for New Brunswick seniors in
1995, Paul Cartwright found that it cost $500 a day for an
intensive care bed, while good home care cost $75 a day. He
points out that the beds are more expensive today than they
were in 1995, but that the cost of home care has not risen
much. A Saskatchewan study found much the same thing; it
concluded that it costs $850 a day more to care for recovering
patients in hospital than it does to discharge them and care for
them at home.

As well, there are huge savings to be found in breaking the
drug patent monopoly and making prescription drugs affordable

again. As described in earlier chapters, Canadians are now spending more on drugs than on doctors. Dr. Joel Lexchin, in his March 2001 study for the Canadian Centre for Policy Alternatives, *A National Pharmacare Plan: Combining Efficiency and Equality*, estimates that a national pharmacare program would decrease drug costs for individuals by 10 per cent, or $650 million. If cost savings to government were added to the equation, the amount would likely be in the billions. In just one case, that of Losec, a drug used to treat ulcers and heartburn, the generic counterpart, which is ready for market, would save Ontario alone $38 million a year. According to the Australia Productivity Commission, as reported by Andrew Duffy in the *Ottawa Citizen* on January 19, 2002, Australia, which did not abandon its compulsory licensing laws, has a national drug plan that has enabled it to keep its drug costs 30 per cent lower than the OECD average, while Canada's are almost 30 per cent higher. Australia takes a national approach to listing the drugs eligible for insurance coverage and uses a system called "reference-based pricing," which sets limits on the amount that can be reimbursed to the patient by the government within a given family of drugs. If patients want a more expensive, brand-name drug, they must pay the difference.

However, this will all take time. If the federal government does recommit to medicare and increase its share of funding to at least 25 per cent of the total, new money will have to be found, especially to help fund a national system of community centres. This would mean that the federal government would have to find an additional $6–$8 billion every year to put toward health care. This is well short of the estimated $10 billion surplus the federal government is expected to enjoy this fiscal year, and about the same amount of money as it gave to nine foundations and trust funds since 1997 that are unaccountable to Parliament, and that Auditor General Sheila Fraser says were set up simply to shrink embarrassing budget surpluses.

The federal government could also start collecting taxes owed by big corporations and the wealthy. In an internal Canada Customs and Revenue Agency analysis obtained for Southam News by access-to-information researcher Ken Rubin, government officials privately admitted that a lot of businesses, including some very large corporations, pay no taxes – and many small and large firms pay little tax.

From 1995 to 1998, says the memo, corporations in total were assessed annual income tax ranging from $17 billion to $24 billion a year. However, 96 per cent of the small firms with gross annual revenues of less than $15 million were assessed zero tax and as many as forty-one large corporations with revenues of more than $259,000 paid no taxes at all. And of those large corporations and their subsidiaries that did pay taxes, almost 80 per cent paid less than $25,000 on average in these years. The memo noted that it is becoming "increasingly difficult" to collect taxes on electronic commercial transactions that the auditors estimate will total more than $200 billion by 2003.

In a summer 2002 report called *Where's the Money Coming From?*, Ed Finn of the Canadian Centre for Policy Alternatives outlines the many ways in which the Canadian government gives financial breaks to corporations that would never be given to ordinary citizens. There are "grants" and "loans" that are often given to large, profitable corporations, such as those by Human Resources Development Canada (HRDC) and Industry Canada. In a recent two-year period, forty-nine grants went to companies that reported profits of at least $70 million. Big oil companies, whose combined revenues stand at about $70 billion, receive about three-quarters of a billion dollars in government handouts most years.

Much of this money is not repaid to the Canadians taxpayer.

Heather Scoffield of the *Globe and Mail* reported in May 2002 that corporations in Canada paid back only 1.25 per cent of the $1.6 billion given to them as "repayable investments" by Industry Canada's Technology Partnerships program between 1996 and 2001. This falls scandalously short of the agreed-upon schedule of repayment for funds that went to such companies as Bombardier, Pratt & Whitney Canada, Allied Signal Aerospace, and CAE Inc.

Ed Finn also points to the use of tax havens by corporations to avoid paying taxes. *The Economist* reports that more than 30 per cent of the profits of transnational corporations, including a number of Canadian companies, sit in sixty-seven tax havens around the world. This comes to U.S.$8 trillion! Another form of tax evasion is the practice of transfer pricing, whereby parent companies inflate the costs of imports and maximize the costs of exports to their foreign subsidiaries in order to avoid paying taxes. Billions of dollars of taxes have been lost in North America through this practice, according to researchers at the Florida International University.

Another loophole in the law is the practice of tax expenditures and deferrals, which Finn rightly describes as "forgone tax revenues" – potential tax revenue that the government knows about but chooses not to collect. In 2001, the government opted not to collect at least $22 billion from corporations, a practice former Liberal MP George Baker called "legal tax evasion." As well, tax cuts to corporations since 1984 amount to $250 billion – 64 per cent of it going to the highest income earners. The capital gains tax exemption alone (announced in Paul Martin's 1995 budget, which slashed $7.4 billion from health care, education, and social assistance), gave about $12 billion extra to the stock traders, real-estate flippers, and commodity speculators in the following five years.

While no single dollar figure has been calculated for these practices, it is clear that Canadians have lost, and continue to lose, many billions of dollars in revenue to corporations taking advantage of overly generous grants, loans, tax loops, and tax cuts. While waiting lists grow and emergency wards are shut down, the Chrétien government, and many provincial governments as well, turn a blind eye to this injustice. Given the power that large corporations such as the brand-name drug companies have in Ottawa, and the support they give to friendly politicians, it is little surprise that this favouritism toward big business continues. As Canadians fight for an improved national health care system, we must not be intimidated by the charge that we can't afford it. There is all the money we need for health care in this country; we simply have to start looking in the right places.

A Call to Action

Medicare, Canada's most precious social program, will not survive the current assault unless Canadians from all parts of the country, all walks of life, all ages, and all cultures come together to save it. Our universal system was won by ordinary people with an extraordinary dream; we must not allow it to be taken from us by those with a private or political agenda.

Medicare is threatened from within by those who would profit from the knowledge garnered by generations of dedicated health care professionals who believed in a public system, and from without by international trade agreements designed to force governments to relinquish their public services to the private sector. Waiting in the wings are powerful transnational health care and drug corporations who seek to gain control of health care services around the world for their profit. They are very determined.

If Canadians do not move quickly to save medicare, it will be lost, and it will be very difficult to retrieve it later. We must do more than speak out, however, against the forces who would destroy public health care, and we must do more than defend the status quo. We must launch a proactive campaign for a national health program based on the completion of the original plan for medicare.

A community-based primary health care system is the answer to the question, "How will we save medicare?" We must embrace a clear, alternative health care system based on a workable, affordable, and improved model. Canadians can have top-quality, publicly funded health care that is fair and economically sound by embracing the best from the past together with the urgent changes that are needed for the future.

There are so many other innovative ideas and recommendations to examine. In recent years, those who work on the front lines of health care have provided us with innovative and practical ways to save and improve medicare. The National Nursing Forum has called for a national health advisory council, which would bring together federal and provincial health officials as well as practitioners and the public, to raise the level of collaboration among the various sectors of the system. This advisory council would be charged with establishing better co-operation among the different levels and sectors, monitoring programs, doing away with duplication, identifying "best practices" guidelines, and performing an accountability service.

But none of this can be realized if we continue on down the for-profit health care path we are currently on. Medicare is threatened as never before. Never has there been a more urgent time for Canadians to stand up and be counted. Write to your members of Parliament and your MLAs. Write to your local newspapers. Talk to your neighbours. Support registered nurses and let them know that you appreciate their vision. Join the campaigns to save medicare and come out to meetings. Support your local coalitions as well. However you choose to do it, stand up and be heard.

Our parents and grandparents did not wait for experts, professionals, or specialists to give them permission to fight for their rights. Ordinary Canadians from one end of the country to the other fought hard for our right to medicare. Unless we put up a similar fight now, and put in motion a counterweight to the corporate juggernaut on the other side, we will surely lose universal health care in Canada. Now is the time for Canadians to speak out loudly and firmly: medicare is not a privilege; it is our birthright, and we will not allow it to be taken from us a piece at a time.

You are not alone. There are a number of national, provincial, and local organizations working to save medicare who are happy to share materials, fact sheets, and briefs with other Canadians. The Council of Canadians has launched a major health care campaign and its more than seventy local chapters are hard at work with others to save and expand medicare. The Canadian Health Coalition (CHC) is an umbrella organization with many members. In its excellent submission to the Romanow Commission, *Standing Together for Medicare: A Call to Care* (which is reprinted right after this chapter), the CHC presented a detailed set of recommendations on protecting health care from commercial exploitation and trade agreements, federal financing of health care, needed extensions to the Canada Health Act to include home care and pharmacare, and a whole host of other areas.

A number of unions, including the Canadian Labour Congress (CLC) and the Canadian Union of Public Employees (CUPE), work closely with citizens' groups such as the Council of Canadians and have also presented detailed briefs to the Romanow Commission. Nurses are taking leadership in this fight. The Canadian Federation of Nurses Unions, the largest federation of nurses' unions in Canada, representing 120,000 registered nurses, has been at the forefront of the fight not only to protect universal health care, but also to create better working conditions for front-line health care workers. Also involved are the Canadian Nurses Association and provincial nursing registration bodies. And every province has local groups and coalitions fighting for medicare. Contact information for these national and provincial groups is given at the end of this book.

Last Words

If ever we Canadians took our public system for granted, now is the time to stop. As senior John Milne of Vancouver says, "It's good to remind this generation who grew up on medicare that the bad old days aren't any further away than the Beatles." Debra McPherson, president of the British Columbia Nurses' Union, summed up the view of so many Canadians in her submission to the Romanow Commission: "Universal health care, in my opinion, is the only system worth having. It defines us as a caring, compassionate people. We need to fight all attempts by anyone to 'profitize' this system, while making the changes needed to make its delivery more efficient."

Arthur Schafer is the director of the Centre for Professional and Applied Ethics at the University of Manitoba. In a recent Southam editorial, he beautifully argued the ethical case against private medicine. The danger of applying the market metaphor to medicine, he says, is that it obscures the fundamental truth that physicians are pledged to behave as professionals, committed to their patients' well-being. Trust between patient and doctor is the very soul of medicine, and privatizing it would force doctors and other health caregivers to see themselves as beleaguered businesses and their patients as consumers. "When we are sick and vulnerable," argues Schafer, "we need to be able to count on health care professionals and institutions to serve unequivocally as our impartial advisers and advocates. Hence, the highest principle of the physicians' code of ethics pledges: 'The life and health of my patient will be my first consideration.'"

Perhaps Kathleen Connors of the Canadian Federation of Nurses Unions put the case for medicare most poignantly in her submission to the Romanow Commission:

I, myself, have just recently experienced the system from the patient's side of the bed. I was treated for uterine and bowel cancer for eighteen months. From 1999 through the year 2000 and into the first few months of this year, I received care in hospital, in my home, and as an outpatient. The quality of care I received was great – though it's plain to see that the system is under great strain. But please be aware that, if I get another catastrophic illness, I will get great care again. Unlike our neighbours to the south, I will receive no call from some silver-tongued insurance agent saying, "Ms. Connors, hearty congratulations on your recovery and it's been really great to have you as a customer, but unfortunately, you are no longer insurable with our company."

We can all rest assured that we won't get that call. At least . . . for now. That's not exactly a comforting thought, is it?

Standing Together for Medicare:
A Call to Care

The following statement was issued following the Conference on the Future of Health Care, sponsored by the Canadian Health Coalition and the Canadian Labour Congress, October 12, 2001, Ottawa:

> The peoples of Canada believe that health care is a fundamental right of every human being without distinction of race, gender, age, religion, sexual orientation, political belief, economic or social condition. Organizations representing millions of Canadians will mobilize to defend this right and to ensure that the following principles shape the future direction of the health care system.
>
> 1. The recognition of the highest attainment of health as a fundamental right throughout life and the necessity of preserving public health through active measures of promotion, prevention, and protection including such determinants as housing, food safety, income, education, environment, employment and peace.
> 2. The recognition of health care as a public good in which the few must not profit at the expense of the many. We affirm the need for a system of public health care, which is organized on the basis of public administration, public

insurance, and the delivery of services on a public, not-for-profit basis.

3. Opposition to any commercialization and privatization of health. Therefore the federal government must negotiate a general exclusion of health services and health insurance from all trade agreements.

4. The need for the federal government to fully assume its responsibilities in respect to health, particularly by restoring and increasing federal transfers to levels sufficient to secure the integrity and enforcement of the Canada Health Act, 1984.

5. The reaffirmation of the original vision of a truly comprehensive public health care system for Canadians providing a continuum of services. The next steps are the expansion of the public system to include a universal system of home care and long-term care services and pharmacare.

6. The need to move away from a fee-for-service model towards a community-based, multidisciplinary approach to the management, organization and delivery of services and care. Levels of services must be sufficient so that the burden of care does not fall on families, mainly women.

7. A health care system that is accountable through democratic participation and governance at all levels.

8. The recognition that health care workers are critical to the effective operation of the health care system and that decent wages, working conditions and training opportunities are essential to high quality care and the retention of health care workers.

Regardless of where we live, it is now imperative to reaffirm the social values we all share. These values must guide our collective choices for future social and public health care. They are incompatible with the commercialization of all public services sought by the international trade agenda.

We believe all governments in Canada must adhere to these values, even though jurisdiction is largely a provincial or territorial matter. Therefore, the principles of the Canada Health Act should be enshrined in the laws of each province and territory.

We come together to commit to direct political action to ensure that governments throughout Canada protect and expand health care based on the foundation of the Canada Health Act, 1984.

What stands between Medicare and its destruction are the peoples of Canada.

Future generations are depending on our vigilance.

Get Involved! Contacts for Action

National Groups

Council of Canadians
Tel: 1-800-387-7177
613-233-2773
Fax: 613-233-6776
www.canadians.org

Canadian Health Coalition
Tel: 613-521-3400 (Ext. 311)
Fax: 613-521-9638
www.healthcoalition.ca

Canadian Union of Public Employees
Tel: 613-237-1590
Fax: 613-237-5508
www.cupe.ca

Canadian Federation of Nurses Unions
Tel: 1-800-321-9821
613-526-4661
Fax: 613-526-1023
www.nursesunion.ca

Canadian Centre for Policy Alternatives
Tel: 613-563-1341
Fax: 613-233-1458
www.policyalternatives.ca

Medical Reform Group
Tel: 416-787-5246
Fax: 416-782-9054
www.hwcn.org/link/mrg/index.html

Parkland Institute
Tel: 780-492-8558
Fax: 780-492-8738
www.ualberta.ca/parkland

National Union of Public and General Employees
Tel: 613-228-9800
Fax: 613-228-9801
www.nupge.ca
www.savemedicare.com

Tommy Douglas Research Institute
Tel: 604-685-7277
Fax: 604-689-4118
www.tommydouglas.ca

Regional Health Coalitions

The Health Coalition of Newfoundland and Labrador
Tel: 709-726-8745
Fax: 709-754-1220

Prince Edward Island Health Coalition
Tel: 902-892-9074
Fax: 902-892-3878

The Nova Scotia Citizens' Health Care Network
Tel: 902-455-9164
Fax: 902-455-0400

New Brunswick Health Coalition
Tel: 506-488-2407
Fax: 506-488-2980

Cape Breton Health Coalition
Tel: 902-567-7878
Fax: 902-567-7829

Coalition Solidarité Santé
Tel: 514-527-4577
Fax: 514-527-4578

Ontario Health Coalition
Tel: 416-441-2502
Fax: 416-441-4073

Toronto Health Coalition
Tel: 416-929-1545
Fax: 416-929-8521

Manitoba Medicare Alert Coalition
Tel: 204-944-9408
Fax: 204-957-1508

Saskatchewan Health Coalition
Tel: 306-652-0300
Fax: 306-664-4120

Alberta Friends of Medicare
Tel: 780-986-0463
Fax: 780-986-7676

British Columbia Health Coalition
Tel: 604-734-3431
Fax: 604-739-1526

Sources and Further Reading

Alberta Association of Registered Nurses, Canadian Nurses Association, Ontario Nurses' Association, Registered Nurses Association of Ontario, and United Nurses of Alberta. *Towards a Sustainable, Universally Accessible Health-Care System.* Discussion Paper prepared for the National Nursing Forum. October 2000.

Anderson, Sarah and John Cavanagh. *Field Guide to the Global Economy.* New York: Institute for Policy Studies and The New Press, 2000.

Armstrong, Pat, Hugh Armstrong and Colleen Fuller. *Health Care, Limited: The Privatization of Medicare.* Prepared for the Council of Canadians by the Canadian Centre for Policy Alternatives. Ottawa: February 2001.

Association of Ontario Health Centres. *Community Health Centres – A Cost-Effective Solution to Primary Health Care Reform.* Toronto: April 2000

Atkinson Charitable Foundation. *Is There a Cost Crisis in Health Care?* and *Health Care Reform, Lost Opportunity.* Occasional Letters. Toronto: November 1996 and October 2000.

Badgley, Robin F. and Samuel Wolfe. *Canadian Health Care and the State: A Century of Evolution,* edited by David Naylor.

Kingston and Montreal: McGill-Queen's University Press, 1992.

Barlow, Maude and Bruce Campbell. *Straight Through the Heart: How the Liberals Abandoned the Just Society.* Toronto: HarperCollins, 1995.

British Columbia Nurses' Union. Presentation to the Commission on the Future of Health Care in Canada. March 15, 2002.

Browne, Paul Leduc. *Public Pain, Private Gain: The Privatization of Health Care in Ontario.* Ottawa: Canadian Centre for Policy Alternatives, 2000.

Canadian Co-operative Association and Le Conseil Canadien de la Cooperation. *Maintaining and Strengthening Our Canadian Health Care System.* Brief presented to the Commission on the Future of Health Care in Canada. Ottawa: November 2001.

Canadian Health Coalition. *Standing Together for Medicare: A Call to Care.* Submission to the Commission on the Future of Health Care in Canada. Ottawa: November 2001.

Canadian Institute for Health Information and Statistics Canada Annual Report. Ottawa: December 2001.

Canadian Labour Congress. *Health Spending in Canada.* Research Paper. Ottawa: October 2001.

Canadian Medical Association. *Prescription for Sustainability.* Ottawa: June 2002.

Canadian Public Health Association. *A Fine Balance: A Public Health Perspective on Health System Reform.* Presentation to the Commission on the Future of Health Care in Canada. Ottawa: April 4, 2002.

Canadian Union of Public Employees. *A Health Care "Trojan Horse:" The Alberta Mazankowski Report.* Ottawa: January 2002.

Canadian Union of Public Employees, Saskatchewan. *Strengthening Medicare, Embracing Equality.* Submission to the Commission of the Future of Health Care in Canada. Regina: March 4, 2002.

Connors, Kathleen. *The Future of Health Care.* Presentation of the Canadian Federation of Nurses Unions to the Commission on the Future of Health Care in Canada. Ottawa: November 2001.

Council of Canadians. *Power Game: Five Problems with the Current Social Union Talks.* Ottawa: January 1999.

Coyte, Peter. *Homecare in Canada: Passing the Buck.* Evaluation and Research Centre, University of Toronto. Toronto: May 2000.

Devereaux, Dr. P. J., et al. *A Systematic Review and Meta-Analysis of Studies Comparing Mortality between Private For-Profit and Private Not-For-Profit Hospitals.* Hamilton: Faculty of Health Sciences, Clinical Epidemiology and Biostatistics, McMaster University, May 2002.

Evans, Robert. *Health Care Reform: Who's Selling the Market, and Why?* Oxford University Press, 1997.

Finn, Ed. *Where's the Money Coming From?* Canadian Centre for Policy Alternatives. Ottawa: July 2002.

Friends of Medicare. *Real Reform or Road to Ruin? Analysis of the Premier's Health Advisory Council Report.* Edmonton: January 2002.

Fuller, Colleen. *Caring for Profit: How Corporations Are Taking Over Canada's Health Care System.* Vancouver and Ottawa: New Star Books and the Canadian Centre for Policy Alternatives, 1998.

———. *Home Care: What We Have and What We Need.* Prepared for the Canadian Health Coalition. Ottawa: May 2001.

Grinspun, Doris. *Realities and Fallouts of a Flexible Workforce: Implications for Nursing.* Dissertation Paper. Toronto: York University, September 2001.

Heeney, Helen. *Life Before Medicare.* Toronto: The Stories Project, Ontario Coalition of Senior Citizen's Organizations, 1995.

Hilary, John. *The Wrong Model: GATS, Trade Liberalisation and Children's Right to Health.* London, United Kingdom: Save the Children, 2001.

Kent, Tom. *What Should Be Done About Medicare?* The Caledon Institute of Social Policy occasional paper. Ottawa: August 2000.

Khor, Martin, Walden Bello, Vandana Shiva, Dot Keet, Sara Larrain and Oronto Douglas. *Views From the South: The Effects of Globalization and the WTO on Third World Countries.* San Francisco: International Forum on Globalization, 2000.

Ludmerer, Kenneth M. *Time to Heal: American Medical Education from the Turn of the Century to the Era of Managed Care.* Oxford University Press, 1999.

Manitoba Nurses' Union. *Report on Long Term Care.* Winnipeg: 2001.

McGregor, Glen, Shelley Page and Andrew Duffy. *Drug Habits, Behind Canada's Giant RX Bill.* Ottawa: *Ottawa Citizen*, January 19–29, 2002.

National Union of Public and General Employees. *The Last Prescription.* Submission to the Commission on the Future of Health Care in Canada. Ottawa: Fall 2001.

Newfoundland and Labrador Association of Public and Private Employees. Submission to the Commission on the Future of Health Care in Canada. St. John's: April 15, 2002.

Nurses Association of New Brunswick. Submission to the Commission on the Future of Health Care in Canada. Fredericton: April 19, 2002.

Prince Edward Island Union of Public Sector Employees. *Proper Elder Care = Proper Home Care + Proper Institutional Care.* Presentation to the Commission on the Future of Health Care in Canada. Charlottetown: April 18, 2002.

Public Services International. *The WTP and the GATS: What Is at Stake for Public Health?* France: 1999.

Public Services International Research Unit. *Globalisation, Privatisation and Healthcare – A Preliminary Report,* edited by David Hall. London, England: January 2001.

Puscas, Darren and Tony Clarke. *Waiting in the Wings! How for-profit health corporations are planning to cash in on the privatization of medicare in Canada.* Ottawa: The Polaris Institute, July 2002.

Rachlis, Michael, Robert Evans, Patrick Lewis, and Morris Barer. *Revitalizing Medicare: Shared Problems, Public Solutions.* Vancouver: Tommy Douglas Research Institute, January 2001.

Registered Nurses Association of Ontario. *Ontario Registered Nurses Speak Out for Medicare.* Submission to the Commission on the Future of Health Care in Canada. Ottawa: November 2001.

Relman, Dr. Arnold. *For Profit Health Care: Expensive, Inefficient, and Inequitable.* Presentation to the Standing Senate Committee on Social Affairs, Science and Technology. Ottawa: February 21, 2002.

Romanow, Roy, Q.C. *The Shape and Future of Health Care.* Interim Report. Ottawa: February 2002.

Sanger, Matt. *Reckless Abandon: Canada, the GATS and the Future of Health Care.* Ottawa: Canadian Centre for Policy Alternatives, 2001.

Saskatchewan Federation of Labour. Presentation to the Commission on the Future of Health Care in Canada. Regina: March 4, 2002.

Saskatchewan Government and General Employees' Union. Submission to the Commission on the Future of Health Care in Canada. Regina: March 4, 2002.

Saskatchewan Union of Nurses. Submission to the Fyke Standing Committee on Health Care. Regina: July 17, 2002.

Service Employees International Union Canada. Submission to the Commission on the Future of Health Care in Canada. Ottawa: October 2001.

Shrybman, Steven. *The World Trade Organization: A Citizen's Guide.* Ottawa: Canadian Centre for Policy Alternatives, 1999.

————. *A Legal Opinion Concerning* NAFTA *Investment and Services Disciplines and Bill 11: Proposals by Alberta to Privatize the Delivery of Certain Insured Health Care Services.* Ottawa: Canadian Union of Public Employees, 1999.

Sinclair, Scott. GATS: *How the World Trade Organization's New "Services" Negotiations Threaten Democracy.* Ottawa: Canadian Centre for Policy Alternatives, 2000.

Sullivan, Terrence and Patricia Baranek. *First Do No Harm: Making Sense of Canadian Health Reform.* Toronto: Malcolm Lester & Associates, 2002.

Taft, Kevin and Gillian Steward. *Private Profit or the Public Good: The Economics and Politics of the Privatization of Health Care in Alberta.* Edmonton: The Parkland Institute, University of Alberta, 2000.

Third World Resurgence. *Bleeding to Death: Health Care in the Marketplace.* Penang Malaysia: Third World Network, #68, April 1996.

Acknowledgements

I am deeply grateful to many people for their help in the writing of this book. The staff at the Council of Canadians has given me courage and support beyond measure. Patricia Perdue, my assistant, has, as always, been unflaggingly supportive and gone beyond the call of duty to help me. Anil Naidoo, our health care campaigner, is a steady, knowledgeable presence in my life. Brant Thompson's never-ending passion for this issue was an inspiration for the launch of the council's medicare campaign early in 2002. Bill Moore-Kilgannon oversaw much of this process in his quiet way. Suzanne Purkis came up with the great title and I thank her for letting me use it. I also wish to thank Christy Ferguson for her excellent research and Physicians for a Smoke-Free Canada for sharing her with me.

There is a whole community in Canada working to save medicare. I cannot name them all, but want to pay special tribute to Colleen Fuller for her outstanding commitment and the quality of her work. Our movement would be greatly diminished without her. Similarly, we all owe a great debt of gratitude to Pat and Hugh Armstrong, who have tirelessly worked to maintain and improve public health in Canada, and Robert Evans, Michael Rachlis, Gordon Guyatt, and Joel Lexchin. Then there are the wonderful nurses across this country who never give up.

In particular, I want to thank Kathleen Connors of the Canadian Federation of Nurses Unions, Heather Smith and Trudy Richardson of the United Nurses of Alberta, Doris Grinspun of the Registered Nurses of Ontario, and Debra McPherson of the British Columbia Nurses' Union. You are the best.

Mike McBane and his team at the Canadian Health Coalition are the glue that keep us all together. I thank them. Judy Darcy and the wonderful people at the Canadian Union of Public Employees are a joy to work with and tireless fighters for their members and all Canadians. Bruce Campbell and all the dedicated team at the Canadian Centre for Policy Alternatives provide state-of-the-art research for which I am deeply grateful. The local health coalitions and chapters of the Council of Canadians are the grassroots that keep our work alive.

I thank Jennifer Warren and Steve Beatty for their tough edit of this book. I especially thank Don Bastian, formerly of Stoddart, who first had faith in this book and guided it through its early stages. Not being allowed to see it through to completion was hard for us both. I am equally grateful to Jonathan Webb of McClelland & Stewart for picking it up and walking it and me through a very difficult time.

Finally, I would like to thank Roy Romanow and his team for their incredibly hard work and their openness to all who came before them. Canadians across the country put their faith in you. Such dreams come true.

Index